the BEST
of everything

the BEST
of everything

Edited by William Davis

ST. MARTIN'S PRESS
NEW YORK

CONTENTS

INTRODUCTION

———◆———

'Best' is a concept which, inevitably, means different things to different people.

For some it's a matter of size: in their eyes, biggest is also best. By that reckoning, the blue whale is the world's finest animal, the *Panorama of Mississippi* – all 1·3 acres of it – the best painting, and the Sears Tower in Chicago the greatest architectural marvel of all time.

For others, best means the most expensive. It makes Liberace the world's foremost pianist, the Gutenberg Bible the best book, and the Celestial suite at the Astroworld Hotel in Houston the most sublime accommodation money can buy. Neiman Marcus, the Texas store long famous for its outlandish and expensive gifts, publishes an annual Christmas catalogue which aspires to offer the very best. It usually means the most vulgar. What else can you say of midget submarines, his-and-her windmills, and life-size portable replicas of customers or their loved ones 'programmed to laugh as long as you like at your jokes'?

You probably feel, as I do, that both these definitions – biggest and most expensive – are too absurd to merit serious consideration. Best is . . . well, what? People have argued about it ever since Adam and Eve had that debate about apples in paradise. (Personally, I have never cared much for the conventional picture of paradise. Endless sunshine and snakes don't add up to *my* idea of perfection. The same goes for heaven: imagine having to spend an eternity listening to harps.) Popular notions of 'best' have changed with each generation. A painting which looked flawless to Victorians may seem quite hideous to collectors today. And who in his right mind would now go into raptures over the best form of travel in the Middle Ages – a gold coach without springs?

When William Randolph Hearst built his pleasure dome, Hearst Castle, he combined what he considered to be the best in Spanish, Moorish, Roman, Gothic, Romanesque, and Californian roadside architecture. He obviously liked the result, but if you have seen it you may well agree with me that the whole thing is a gaudy mess.

Whichever way one looks at it, 'best' is a subjective judgment. It can hardly be anything else. The fastest runner is not necessarily the best; a lot of people insist that style (which, for the British, includes the ability to lose with a smile) is no less important. A 'best-selling' novel is not necessarily a masterpiece; indeed the chances are that it is not. The novel with the highest sales of all time is Jacqueline Susann's *Valley of the Dolls* and no-one would call *that* a masterpiece.

Patriotic pride frequently produces the claim that this or that is 'the best in the world'. Every nation likes to feel that it is ahead of others. Sometimes it is, but all such claims are still a matter of opinion, not of fact.

Critics are paid to express their views, but even they are not infallible. Critics thought Van Gogh's work was worthless, and that Picasso had no future as an artist! They are, however, concerned with the pursuit of excellence and this is what *The Best of Everything* is all about. Ideas may differ and standards may change, but there will always be people who take pleasure in the chase. This book is for them.

When I first approached some of our distinguished contributors, several assured me that we had set ourselves an impossible task. 'Even in half a million words,' said one, 'no satisfactory answers could be arrived at.' But they agreed to try. Each section has been contributed by an author who knows his or her field well, but we do not pretend that their verdicts are the last word on the subject. Far from it. We fully expect you to disagree with some of the judgments.

Our aim has been to provide a lively, stimulating guide which is both useful and entertaining. *The Guinness Book of Records* was launched to settle arguments: *The Best of Everything* is bound to start them. Have fun.

WILLIAM DAVIS

ANIMALS

Gerald Durrell

BEST ZOOLOGIST *Charles Robert Darwin*
Charles Darwin was born in 1809 and died in the year 1882. He was not only responsible for the Theory of Evolution, which completely revolutionized biological and religious thought, but left a prodigious amount of work behind him; not only *The Voyage of the Beagle* but works on earthworms, coral reefs, fertilization of flowers and numerous other studies. Unlike the blinkered, one-subject scientists that we are so happy to produce today, Darwin had a wide-spectrum mind and nothing escaped his eye or his interest, whether it was an earthworm, a bird, a fossil or the observation that in a tropical storm in the Andes his red flannel waistcoat glowed with luminescence. He probably did more than any one person in changing biological thought and yet his innate modesty made him write in his autobiography, 'As for myself, I believe I have acted rightly in steadily following and devoting my life to science. I feel no remorse from having committed any great sin, but I have often and often regretted that I have not done more direct good to my fellow creatures.'

BEST SEXY ANIMAL *The female giraffe*
For gracefulness of movement, size and lustre of eyes, length and thickness of eyelashes, the female giraffe is incomparable. True, when she chews the cud, the ball of food rather startlingly travels up her neck like a lift and she does have to spread her legs very wide in order to drink, but if there is reincarnation, no-one should have any complaints if they come back as a male giraffe.

Best Domestic Animal *The Camel*

For taking you into difficult terrain, the camel is unique. The nostrils can be closed in case of sandstorms; the feet are large and well padded so they do not sink in the sand. It can live on the most meagre fare of desert plants and it can go for lengthy periods without water in excessive heat. Not only is it useful as a beast of burden but its milk can be drunk and, in places, its blood too. It can be eaten, its fur and wool can be utilized and, finally, its dung can be used as fertilizer or, when dried, as fuel. There is apparently no foundation in fact for the rumour that a camel is a horse designed by a committee.

Best Curious Sea Animal *The narwhal*

This large aquatic mammal with a twisted horn on its nose is one of the most curious of sea inhabitants. The horns, in medieval times, were sold as genuine unicorn horns and a drinking cup carved out of one would ensure that you never got poisoned. So it is not surprising to learn that the tusks were literally worth their weight in gold. Only the male has the tusk and its use is not yet fully understood, though it may be a defensive weapon used in mating battles.

Best Large Animal *The blue whale*

Perfectly designed for its aquatic life, the blue whale averages a length of between 24 and 33 metres. It weighs as much as 25 elephants, 150 cattle or 1,600 men – a mere 130 tons. The largest of the prehistoric dinosaurs, the Brontosaurus, weighed only a quarter of this. Although still threatened with extinction, there is hope that the blue whale may be saved. It would be a criminal act to exterminate this, the largest mammal that has ever lived.

Best Unlikely Animal *The duck-billed platypus*

It was no small wonder that when a specimen of the duck-billed platypus was first sent back from Australia, scientists refused to believe that such an animal existed, and insisted that it must have been put together from bits and pieces of other creatures. Looking like Donald Duck with a fur coat, the duck-billed platypus has small, twinkly eyes, fur like a mole, a bill like a duck, webbed feet like a duck and a flattened tail somewhat resembling that of a beaver; in addition, it has poison spurs on its hind feet which are almost as venomous as a poisonous snake. Added to all these anomalies, it lays eggs and yet produces milk for its young like a mammal. It is found in Australia which has aptly been described as 'the attic of the world' since it contains so many curious animals left over from past ages.

Best Reptile *The so-called flying snake*

These arboreal snakes are found in the Far East. When disturbed in the trees, they launch themselves like arrows and glide off to another part of the forest. This is made possible by the reptile pulling its stomach in so that it resembles

'*You know the rules – no helping the dogs.*'

a piece of guttering and this, combined with a stiffening of the body, enables the air to carry its weight on a long, downward glide.

BEST ANIMAL DEFENCE *The pancake tortoise*
This strange small tortoise is found in the southern part of Africa and has a curiously flattened shell unlike a normal domed tortoise shell. The shell itself is as soft as damp cardboard and at first you cannot see how this could possibly act as a defence mechanism until you see the tortoise slide into a crack in the rocks and then inflate himself like a balloon so that he is firmly wedged in the fissure and it is impossible to get him out without the aid of dynamite.

BEST MEDICAL ANIMAL *The armadillo*
This curious little mammal has been around for a number of years and apart from being eaten by the odd Indian or gaucho and its shell used to create mini-guitars, nobody thought it was of any use. It has now been discovered, however, that because of its curious metabolism the armadillo can be used to create cultures of leprosy and will thus aid not only in the cure of this unpleasant disease but might also be of great help in cancer research. Thus it goes to show once again that it is very important not to indiscriminately exterminate animals or plants since we never know when they will turn out to be of benefit to man.

BEST PARENT ANIMAL *The surinam or pipa toad*
This very curious aquatic amphibian toad will certainly not take any prizes in a beauty contest, since it looks like a toad that the week before had been run over by a steam-roller and has been decomposing ever since. It has, however, a charming and original way of dealing with its offspring. In the breeding season, the female's back becomes spongy and pitted with holes. When ready to mate, the male mounts on the female's back and she meanwhile has protruded a long ovipositor like a small hosepipe; this the male, with wriggling motions, proceeds to wrap over her back and as the eggs are produced he fertilizes them and each one is then pressed into a pocket in the female's skin. One half of the egg protrudes above the surface and soon hardens so that it looks like the top of a bubble-car. In these pockets, the eggs turn into tadpoles and eventually when the tadpoles have grown their legs and lost their tails they push off the lids of their pockets and emerge into the water. It is probably one of the most unusual methods of caring for your young in the whole amphibian family, which has many curious examples of this sort of thing.

BEST ANIMAL SONG *The Gnu*
Written by that incomparable couple, Flanders and Swann, who also gave us such charming animal songs as *The Hippopotamus Song* and *The Ostrich*.

BEST ANIMAL PHOTOGRAPHER *Wolf Suschitzky*
Over the years, he has produced some marvellous and sensitive animal pictures.

BEST ANIMAL DISH *Smoked reindeer*
A beautiful and exotic meat, but it is best not to serve it at Christmas time to children of a sensitive nature.

BEST WORST ANIMAL DISH *Hippopotamus meat*
Whatever you do to it, even if you marinate it in curry, it still tastes like an old boot which has been soaking in cod-liver oil.

BEST ANIMAL NOVEL *Tarka the Otter by Henry Williamson*
This is, without doubt, the best book that has ever been written about an animal. It is difficult for an author to get inside the skin of an animal, as it were, without being anthropomorphic. This Henry Williamson does brilliantly and, apart from his minute and detailed observation of the otter's behaviour, his observations and descriptions of the English countryside are incomparable.

BEST ANIMAL SHORT STORY *Tobermorey by Saki*
This story, by that most urbane and witty of writers, who was unfortunately killed in the First World War, is about a cat that learns to talk and the havoc this causes at a rather stuffy house party. Saki had a wicked wit and like all his short stories this is uproariously funny.

BEST SMALL ZOO *The Jersey Zoological Park*

Headquarters of the Jersey Wildlife Preservation Trust, Channel Islands. This zoo concentrates, to the exclusion of all other things, on keeping and breeding colonies of animals in danger of extinction – a work that should be done by all zoos but unfortunately is sadly neglected by the majority. It also studies these animals in great detail, and personnel and zoo staff go out on rescue expeditions to obtain these threatened animals and to do work in the field to try to promote their protection in their natural habitat. The Trust also runs a training scheme so that foreign students can come from all over the world to learn the techniques of this form of conservation breeding and then return to their countries where, hopefully, they will promote captive breeding to save their native fauna.

Once large enough stocks of the different species have been built up in captivity (under ideal conditions with adequate food supplies and freedom from predators), then the ultimate plan is to take specimens back to strengthen the minute populations left in the wild or else to create new groups in suitable habitat elsewhere. The Trust has a membership of 10,000 and members receive newsletters and an illustrated annual report and free admission to the Trust's animal collection.

BEST BIG ZOO *San Diego, USA*

In this enormous zoo, the accent has always been on the breeding of rare animals and San Diego is probably foremost of the world's zoos in its 'firsts'. It has recently built a huge park which contains great herds of cloven-hoofed animals – rhino, hippopotamus and other such creatures, living under almost natural conditions. With the future for so many animals in the wild looking so bleak, it is quite possible that our only chance of seeing many of these species will be in zoological gardens like San Diego.

BEST ANIMAL COLLECTOR *Carl Hagenbeck*

Operating in the late 1800s, Hagenbeck was a remarkable animal dealer who employed a great staff of people to scour the world for specimens for him. He was, however, not just simply a dealer. He created the zoo in Hamburg, which was constructed on unique lines for that day and age. Hagenbeck showed his animals in great moated enclosures with artificial rock-work as a background and it was he who insisted that tropical animals, provided they were acclimatized carefully and had access to warm, dry quarters, were far healthier and lived longer if they were allowed access to sunshine and fresh air. In those days, when all tropical animals were kept in germ-ridden steamy heat and died very rapidly as a result, this was a controversial novelty, but today all zoos of the world have adopted Hagenbeck's principles and in consequence we now have animals breeding in captivity which before could scarcely live long enough to reproduce and we now have creatures setting up longevity records in captivity which outstrip their age records in the wild.

'*It took some time but finally we got him house-trained.*'

Best Sanctuary *Kaziranga in Assam*

Although not a large sanctuary, it is an excellent one for seeing the Indian fauna, and to go out on elephant back and move slowly through dozens of grazing Indian rhinos, various deer, Indian tiger, wild pigs, wild buffalo and herds of wild elephants is an unforgettable experience. Although other game reserves (such as Serengeti) have greater concentrations of animals, Kaziranga is, without doubt, the best small reserve.

Best Animal Painter *Louis Agassiz Fuertes*

Without doubt, Fuertes was the finest bird and animal painter that has ever lived. His studies of North American birds and mammals and his beautiful bird and mammal paintings done in the field during an expedition to Abyssinia have never been surpassed and it was tragic that, at the height of his career, he should have been killed in a train accident.

Best Aquarium *Vancouver Aquarium, Canada*

This mainly marine aquarium is a splendid one with spotless tanks containing a fascinating array of fish and crustaceans and growing seaweeds. Impressive, too, are the great outside tanks that contain the beluga or white whale and the killer whales. Without doubt, the big boardroom of the Vancouver Aquarium is the most spectacular in the world – when the curtains are drawn back you see that the whole of one wall is composed of thick glass against which a pair of killer whales bump their noses amicably. The Board tries to make decisions while doubtless looking nervously over its shoulder.

BEST SURPRISE ANIMAL *The mudskipper*
This curious little brown fish, with a head exactly like a hippopotamus, is always a surprising sight because it spends almost as much time on land as it does in water. To watch mudskippers with their protuberant eyes scrambling over the rocks or else by vigorous wiggling of their tails propelling themselves over the mud in mangrove swamps with the skill and fluidity of stones on ice is a constant source of amusement and indeed you cannot help imagining that you are watching our very earliest fish ancestors emerging onto the land for the first time, aeons ago.

BEST POISONOUS ANIMAL *The poison arrow frog*
These diminutive tree-frogs, of several different species, are found in the rain forests of the Amazon basin. Their colours almost defy description, since they are spotted and striped with scarlet and green and blue and yellow and a host of other subtle tints according to their species. The Amerindian tribes put these frogs on a leaf, which they then put over a warm fire. As soon as the frogs get too hot, they exude a highly poisonous slime from their skins; this the Indians scrape off onto their arrow-tips and use them in hunting for birds and small mammals which the poison rapidly affects so that they fall to the ground. The area penetrated by the arrow is then carefully cut out and the rest of the creature goes into the cooking pot. Poison arrow frogs are not much bigger than the last joint of a man's little finger and for their size are remarkably potent and remarkably colourful.

BEST COLOURFUL ANIMAL *The tragopan*
This beautiful pheasant, found up in the Himalayan regions of India and China, is a most spectacular bird. The thatch of feathers on the male's head is black with a bright orange stripe down the middle. He has bare, bright sky-blue skin under his chin and throat and two little bright blue horns hanging down like pigtails at the back of his head. The body is a marvellous combination of burnished bronze and orange and various shades of russet-red. Just seeing the male bird ordinarily is breathtaking, but his courtship display almost beggars description. First, he parts his feathers on his head and then wiggles his two little blue horns about to attract the female's attention. As soon as he feels that he has done this, he suddenly unrolls from under his chin a great flap of skin which hangs down like a curtain over his breast. This skin is all wrinkled and pleated and is scarlet, bright sky-blue and orange; it looks like an oriental rug or tapestry. He keeps rolling this up and then unfurling it again in order to

dazzle the female with its beauty. Like all hen pheasants, she is very drab and has a perpetual air of bewilderment, appearing to ignore totally all the male's overtures – so indifferent is she, indeed, that you wonder how they ever get around to the egg-laying process.

BEST BESTIARY *The Book of Beasts*

Being a translation from a Latin bestiary of the twelfth century, edited by T.H. White. Not only are some of the medieval bestiaries very beautiful as books, but they are very amusing as to their ideas of natural history. This one is no exception, for here both real and mythological animals rub shoulders, and their private lives, as portrayed by the medieval writers, are extremely amusing; but what makes this bestiary different from all the others is T.H. White's remarkably long and terribly funny footnotes which display an extraordinary wealth of wit and erudition. One could almost wish that White had lived in medieval times, as a bestiary written by him would, one feels, have surpassed all others. This is, however, the next best thing to it.

BEST PREHISTORIC ANIMAL *The coelacanth*

This fish was supposed to have become extinct with the dinosaurs but has come down hardly changed over sixty million years. Since scientists and ichthyologists thought it could be safely classified as an extinct 'prehistoric' creature, it was somewhat confusing when a live one turned up in a fisherman's net off the coast of South Africa in 1938. It was sent to Miss Courtenay-Latimer, curator of the East London Museum, and she decided that it was so curious that she preserved it and sent drawings of it to Professor J.L.B. Smith, the world-famous ichthyologist, who was astonished and greatly excited at this discovery. In spite of an enormous amount of publicity on the part of Smith and the distribution of pamphlets all over the south and east coasts of Africa, no other specimen was apparently caught until 1952 when one was captured in the Comoros and Professor Smith had a perfectly preserved specimen at last. Since then, over three dozen have been caught. It is an extremely important find of enormous value as a 'living fossil'. The study of this fish can give us tremendous insight on the evolution of all vertebrates, including man. It is interesting to note that, sensational though the discovery of the coelacanth was to ichthyologists and biologists, it had long been known to local native populations and as a rather undesirable fish it had been sold cheaply in the market places dried and salted. Its very rough scales had been used as a sort of sandpaper and it had been found that they were excellent for scraping inner tubes before patching them. There seems to be a moral in this story but one is not quite sure what.

ART

Bevis Hillier

Best Painting *Rembrandt's Bathsheba* (*Louvre, Paris*)

Best painting does not mean best-known painting. Probably the best-*known* painting in the world is Leonardo da Vinci's *Mona Lisa*. It is also a great painting (though some would argue that *Girl with an Ermine* by the same artist, in the Czartoryski Collection, Cracow, Poland, is greater). But tourists who seek out the *Mona Lisa* as the one absolute 'must' on their visit mostly go for the mawkish satisfaction of seeing 'how her eyes follow you round the room'. The *Mona Lisa* has become an almost kitsch icon, and it was for that reason that Marcel Duchamp, the Dadaist, chose her image to desecrate with a superimposed moustache.

The best painting must be an oil painting: the greatest water-colour never achieves the profundity of a great work in oils. And among artists in oils, we must look for one who (in the best sense) 'exploits' the medium to greatest effect. The German art historian Heinrich Wölfflin minted the word '*malerisch*', painterly, to describe this quality, this capturing of the quintessence of the medium. The quintessence of oil-paint (as opposed to water-colour in which the white paper shows luminously through washes of colour) is that it can be applied in thick, porridgy *impasti*, in which the tergiversations of the brush are registered and petrified like animal spoors in clay – so that, centuries later, we can almost reconstruct the very motions of the artist's virtuosity, the orbits in which his brush moved. Jan Vermeer of Delft (1632–75) was a great *artist*, but was he, with his bland, enamelled surfaces, a great *painter*? The craftsmanship is flawless, but the essence of oil-paint is not fully exploited. The supreme master in oils is Vermeer's near contemporary and compatriot, Rembrandt van Rijn (1606–69), who deployed his rich pigments in swathes and furrows and wave-crests that mark the route of his genius. Those who have seen that master-piece, the Charles Laughton film of Rembrandt's life (imperfect historically but still a wonderfully sympathetic portrayal), will have some idea of the force of emotion that passed like an electric charge from Rembrandt's brush to his canvas – and this ability to make inward feeling physical, and communicate it to the viewer, is something else we must demand of a great painter.

Which of Rembrandt's works to choose? It is tempting to plump for one of the self-portraits: no artist ever explored his own physiognomy with more unflinching truth than Rembrandt, and the sequence of self-portraits from un-wrinkled youth to blotchy old age form an autobiography as revealing as Jean-Jacques Rousseau's. Or one might choose one of his grand set-pieces, such as *The Night Watch* in the Rijksmuseum, Amsterdam, or *Belshazzar's Feast* in the National Gallery, London. The National Gallery also has a painting which shows Rembrandt at his most dashingly informal – the *Woman Bathing*, in which a tender and erotic subject is rendered with an almost brutal technique of jabbing, Impressionistic brush-strokes. Or one might settle for one of the miraculous portraits of Mrs Tripp (both in the National Gallery, London): the portraitist John Singer Sargent said he understood how most portraits were painted, but the sublime technique of the Mrs Tripp portraits defeated him.

But finally the palm must go to his *Bathsheba* in the Louvre, Paris. The woman it represents is by no means an idealized vision of womanhood, which is something one might claim for the *Rokeby Venus* (National Gallery, London) by that other supreme master of quintessential oil-painting technique, Velas-quez. (In the early twentieth century, a suffragette recognized this symbolic status of the Velasquez nude when she slashed it with a razor in protest against men's attitude to women.) Rembrandt's *Bathsheba* is a little past her prime; she is developing a double chin and has large, washerwoman's hands. But as Lord Clark has observed, the round, solid body 'is seen with such love that it becomes beautiful'. He adds: 'The depth and subtlety with which he has rendered her emotions have never been surpassed' and remarks on the perfect balance of the composition. The actual technique of the painting could be called exemplary – though this is an example that nobody is likely to be able to follow. The effect that Rembrandt achieves with serene deliberation could not be achieved in any other medium; and no other artist could have achieved it.

BEST SCULPTURE *Michelangelo's Pietà, Rome*
Is it to be a work of classical antiquity? Some might choose the *Venus de Milo*, almost as 'pop' an image as the *Mona Lisa* (speculation about what her arms might be doing if she had them gives the same kind of *frisson* as trying to evade

'The one in the middle is paying for it.'

Mona Lisa's roving eyes and 'enigmatic' smile). Or the *Winged Victory of Samothrace*, also in the Louvre – carved with irresistible energy and a victorious swing of the exquisitely rendered draperies, to commemorate a naval victory of 306 BC by Demetrius Poliorcetes over the Egyptian general Ptolemy, off Cyprus. The *Apollo Belvedere*? The *Dying Gaul*? The snake-entwined *Laocoön and His Sons*? Executed by three Rhodian sculptors about 50 BC, the *Laocoön* was certainly regarded in the eighteenth century as the highest expression of Greek genius.

No, we will turn instead to the Renaissance, which took classical antiquity as its honoured model, but managed to infuse it with a new spirit. In one of his *Civilization* talks, Lord Clark well conveyed the working of this process of transmutation when describing Michelangelo's *David*: 'Seen by itself the *David*'s body might be some unusually taut and vivid work of antiquity; it is only when we come to the head that we are aware of a spiritual force which the ancient world never knew. I suppose that this quality, which I may call heroic, is not a part of most people's idea of civilization. It involves a contempt for convenience and a sacrifice of all those pleasures that contribute to what we call civilized life.'

Indeed, it is very tempting to choose Michelangelo's *David* as the supreme expression of aspiring man. Or, instead of this assertion of triumphant life, we might favour a totally different work by Michelangelo, the *Dying Slave*. Sir Ernst Gombrich has written of this sublimely modelled sculpture: 'There is unspeakable beauty in this last moment of final relaxation and release from the struggle of life – this gesture of lassitude and resignation. It is difficult to think of this work being a statue of cold and lifeless stone, as we stand before it in the Louvre in Paris. It seems to move before our eyes and yet to remain at rest.'

To eliminate masterworks of this order is painful; but the final choice must be Michelangelo's *Pietà* in St Peter's Basilica in Rome – a work he began in 1498 at the flabbergastingly early age of twenty-three. So far from being an apprentice work, it shows Michelangelo's powers at their most superhuman. It is the work of a religious fanatic (Michelangelo was a fervent follower of the fire-and-brimstone preacher and moralist, Savonarola). Yet this is not an evangelical work: its power lies in passivity. It allies the neo-Platonic ideal of human beauty with Christian doctrine. The carving is miraculous but the effect is not waxwork illusionism but something superior to, refined from, humanity.

It is the only one of his statues that Michelangelo signed. Vasari reports that the sculptor was enraged to hear that visitors to St Peter's Basilica were being told the *Pietà* was the work of Cristoforo Solari (d. 1527) of Milan, called 'il Gobbo' (the hunchback). But as Dr Josef Vincent Lombardo, who has made a study of the Rome *Pietà*, observes: 'It is more likely that he signed his name with full realization that this statue represented the zenith of his accomplishments.'

There was a public outcry in 1962 when it was agreed that the *Pietà* should be shipped to America for the New York World's Fair of 1964 – the four-hundredth anniversary of the sculptor's death. The Director of the Fogg Museum at Harvard University joined the protest. A group of Italian artists demonstrated in front of Florence Cathedral, soliciting signatures for a petition. A plaster cast of the *Pietà* was indignantly trundled round the streets of Florence. Those who supported the loan pointed out that in 1506 Michelangelo's *Bruges Madonna* was shipped from Florence to north-west Belgium without mishap. Archbishop Heenan joked that he hoped the *Pietà* would not suffer the same fate as the Elgin marbles! But, insured for six million dollars, the 6,700-pound *Pietà* left Naples (lowered by crane) on 5 April 1964 and arrived safely in New York on the *Cristoforo Colombo* on 13 April. If the ship had gone down, special transmitters attached to the outer case would have flashed light beams visible fifteen miles at sea level and fifty miles by air, and radio directional signals would have been broadcast: a Virgin of the Rocks indeed.

After the two transatlantic voyages were successfully over, the *Pietà* was horribly damaged by a maniac. The Pope, it was reported, had wept when he heard the news. But now this, surely the best loved of all Michelangelo's sculptures, has been brilliantly restored.

BEST LIVING PAINTER *Salvador Dali*

If Pablo Picasso had not died in 1974, he would have been the inevitable choice. Sir Herbert Read, in his collection of essays *A Coat of Many Colours*, depicted him at the head of an imaginary triumphal procession of modern artists. Even those who think the rot in modern art began with Picasso have to admit that his influence on the course of art was stupendous: the 'fragmentation' of art by cubism, of which Picasso and Braque were the leaders, was imitated by two whole generations of painters in a way that the fragmentation of literature by James Joyce was not (with a few isolated exceptions).

But with the master gone, who remains? Looking to the younger generation, some might pick David Hockney, already honoured, at just over forty, by a big one-man exhibition in the Louvre. A few lone critics might still point to the 'action painting' of Jackson Pollock as the most important new direction of European art since the launching of the cubist movement. Others, who in the 1960s applauded Pop Art, which fed on the popular kitsch of comic strips, advertising and musclemen magazines, might choose Andy Warhol as the most notorious immortalizer of junk culture. Aesthetic purists who are thrilled by pure patterning might even opt for Op – Bridget Riley.

But there survives one great leader of a European movement: Salvador Dali, a pioneer of surrealism. More than any other of the surrealists, Dali obeyed the dictate of the surrealists' manifesto: to translate one's subconscious into art without regard to ethics. (When he painted a canvas which seemed to some of his friends to hint at approval of Hitler, he replied that he could not help it if he dreamed about Hitler.) At the height of his powers, in the 1930s, he had a marvellously fertile imagination. He was able to look at conventional scenes and break them down into surreal components, exaggerating some of them to the ultimate degree. His autobiography, *The Secret Life of Salvador Dali*, proves that not all his eccentricity was a calculated showman's act: he genuinely saw life differently from most people, and he was able to make his vision physical in art. His best works, such as *The Metamorphosis of Narcissus* (1936), or another in which Houdon's bust of Voltaire suddenly resolves itself into two wimpled nuns, make brilliant play with optical illusion. Dali was born in 1904 and it is hardly suprising that his art has declined in recent years; the sketches sold to blue-rinse ladies in Los Angeles today do him no kind of justice. But he will always be remembered when surrealism is discussed – that movement most appropriate to the first century in which the theories of psychology and psycho-analysis were widely accepted and began to affect the artist's vision. We can accept him at his own estimate of himself: a genius.

BEST LIVING SCULPTOR *Henry Moore.*
Those who find Henry Moore a 'monumental' bore, one whose life is spent making big holes in big stones, might prefer to choose a more reassuringly representational sculptor such as William Redgrave, who is not only the finest living portraitist in bronze, but lived for many years on short commons to execute a heroic triptych in bronze called *The Event* (now at Waterfield School, Thamesmead, London).

But the international *réclame* of Henry Moore is so daunting that it would be perverse to choose anybody else. Unlike many artists, Moore is particularly articulate. He thinks representationalism unsatisfactory for a modern sculptor. He speaks of 'the intrinsic emotional significance of shapes' and suggests that 'sculpture in stone should look honestly like stone, that to make it look like flesh and blood, hair and dimples is coming down to the level of the stage conjuror'.

He also likes sculpture to be in the round, not carved as a relief. He prefers to see, and to sculpt, 'masses in opposition'. But he is not a purist abstract artist. 'Purely abstract sculpture seems to me to be an activity that would be better fulfilled in another art, such as architecture.'

'A sculptor,' he has written, with the directness and almost *faux-naïf* simplicity that marks his sculptures too, 'is a person who is interested in the shape of things ... the growth in a flower; the hard, tense strength, although delicate form, of a bone; the strong, solid fleshiness of a beech tree trunk.' Abstractionists may think Moore has settled for a tame compromise; but to him it has seemed essential to preserve the humanity of sculpture while not becoming a mechanical copyist.

Nobody has described better than himself the quality which gives distinction to his work. 'One of the things I would like to think my sculpture has is a force, is a strength, is a life, a vitality from inside it, so that you have a sense that the form is pressing from inside trying to burst or trying to give off the strength from inside itself, rather than having something which is just shaped from outside and stopped.'

But it is arguable that Moore's main contribution to the art of sculpture has not been the actual physical relics of his genius, the massive hewn stones themselves, but his placing of them in landscapes, 'converting the landscape itself into a masterpiece', as one critic has suggested. In an age when the word 'environment' has become a shibboleth, Moore's sculptures, often deliberately designed for a particular place in a particular landscape, have won even wider acclaim than when he first achieved his characteristic style in the 1930s. *Placement* – a genteel word sometimes used by hostesses in disposing their guests round the table – has been used in reference to Moore's *mise en scène* of his sculptures. Tony Keswick's *placements* of four pieces on his sheep farm in Dumfriesshire, Scotland – rearing out of the mist – are impressive. The Japanese, those masters of *placement* and landscaping, have seen the virtue of Moore. At Hakone, in the mountains near Tokyo, is *Reclining Figure: Arch Leg*, in the centre of an 'outdoor museum'. As they age and weather with the centuries, Moore's sculptures are likely to take on the mystic character of ancient dolmens and monoliths and be revered as twentieth-century Stonehenges. Perhaps men will wonder how our puny, primitive civilization managed to haul the great stones into such precise *placements*, and will wonder what part they played in our religion.

BEST EXAMPLE OF MODERN ART *Picasso's Guernica*

One of the basic ideas behind modern art has been that the artist should be representative of his own time; more than that, the idea that it is as much his duty to intervene as a politician's when there is an abuse of power by government, or a public catastrophe. Pablo Picasso subscribed to this point of view. 'What do you think an artist is?' he asked. 'A fool who, if he is a painter, has only eyes?... On the contrary, he is at the same time a social creature, always wide-awake in the face of the heart-rending bitter or sweet events of the world.... No, painting is not made to decorate houses. It is a weapon of offensive war against the enemy.'

On 28 April 1937 the Basque town of Guernica was reported destroyed by German bombers flying for General Franco. Picasso went into action at once. In January he had been commissioned to paint a mural for the Spanish Government Building at the Paris World's Fair. He began work on it two days after the news of the Guernica atrocity broke.

Never had a subject more terribly fit for the 'fragmentation' approach of cubism presented itself. The citizens of Guernica, and their homes, had been 'fragmented' all right. Picasso's picture shows a woman screaming, with supplicating upraised hands as her house burns with tooth-like flames; a dying horse poniarded with a spear; fragments of a warrior, the arm holding a broken spear. It is a synthesis and syncopation of suffering, a tableau of outrageous carnage. Juan Larrea has written of 'this horrified shuddering of light, this gnashing of teeth ... this canvas of sackcloth and ashes'.

It is a definitively modern work. Such mortal terror could never have been so eloquently represented by the academic art of the past: compare Stubbs's *Frightened Horse* with Picasso's dying one, or the potency of political message in David's solemnly staged *Oath of the Horatii* with the immediacy of the blurting, cinematic impressions of *Guernica*. The most advanced form of modernity is prophecy; and *Guernica* is a prophetic work – presaging the destruction of Warsaw, Rotterdam, Nancy, Coventry (and, at this distance, we can add Dresden). Juan Larrea claims it as the beginning of a 'new pictorial era' as well. 'For when there is an end of the pitiless deluge of fire which has levelled to the ground the buildings of the ancient world, we shall see, outlined at the horizon, a new alliance of Heaven and Earth. ...' Whether posterity has proved him right or wrong is a matter for debate; but few would dissent from his statement that *Guernica* is 'the most universally acclaimed painting of the century'.

BEST ART CRITIC *John Ruskin*

A century ago, there would have been no doubt about the answer: Ruskin was the commanding figure in art criticism, and it seemed that his judgments could never be reversed; they were to be engraved on the tablets of eternity. Ruskin was god to his own generation and – which is rare – he remained god to the next generation, that of William Morris and his followers such as Selwyn

Image, less this time as an aesthetic arbiter than as a social reformer, a proto-socialist. (The Working Men's College at Oxford, to which shifts of miners come to confirm their belief that university is for effete dilettantes, bears his name.)

But in the twentieth century the depreciation in his reputation was swift. It began with the qualms of some of his admirers, such as Laurence Binyon, who wrote:

> We all know, we are all irritated or perplexed by, his astonishing judgments on particular artists; we think of Michel Angelo disparaged, Rembrandt depreciated, Claude belittled, Constable contemned, Crome ignored; we remember the extravagances in his praise of Turner and Tintoret, the preference of men like William Hunt to men like Girtin, and the thousand self-contradictions of his wayward genius; and we feel sometimes inclined to ask ourselves whether this man can be a safe guide in anything.

And the depreciation continued because the twentieth century disliked fulminating moralizing (Ruskin believed art could only be aesthetically good if it was morally good); it distrusted rhetorical eloquence and a pontifical manner; it found irrelevant, rather than illuminatingly multifarious and 'universal', a mind that could not see a tangent without rushing off on it.

So what is the justification for choosing Ruskin as the best critic? First, he had one essential faculty of a great critic: the ability to store in the mind a vast range of visual (and literary) reference of which any part could at any moment be plucked out for a telling comparison. 'He pierces through the surface of things,' writes Lord Clark, one of Ruskin's few modern champions, 'seeing similars in dissimilars, and illuminating the familiar by some flashing analogy.'

Second, he had the asset of being a considerable draughtsman himself, with an artist's eye, incomparable in assimilating the beauties of landscape and geological formations (though admittedly a little deficient when it came to the nude body: his own marriage was unconsummated, and when he found a sketch of pubic hair by his idol J.M.W. Turner, he labelled it 'Brushwood').

Third, he had what few credit him with, a highly developed sense of humour, a dancing irony that could play on any unsatisfactory work of art and demolish it. Listen to him on a ramshackle mill painted by Clarkson Stanfield:

> Observe, that though all this ruin has befallen Stanfield's mill, Stanfield is not in the least sorry for it. On the contrary, he is delighted, and evidently thinks it the most fortunate thing possible. The owner is ruined, doubtless, or dead; but his mill forms an admirable object in our view of Brittany. So far from being grieved about it, we will make it our principal light ... we illumine our whole picture with it, and exult over its every rent as a special treasure and possession.

But finally, what singles out Ruskin from other critics and elevates him above them is his insistence on the human interpretation of art, on the primary duty of art to express life, vitality. L. March Phillips, who introduced an early twentieth-century edition of *The Stones of Venice*, wrote:

Art never was to him in any of its manifestations a matter of technique, of pigments, of mannerisms, of arrangements and patterns of paint, marble or stone; but, much more, of motives, of human passions, of impulses and tides of feeling which had animated the creators of it, or dwelt broadcast, as convictions and deep-lying beliefs, among the humanity of the age.... Things gave up for him the mood of mind in which they had been engendered.

BEST ART GALLERY *The Louvre, Paris*
Nominations to: the Boston Museum of Fine Arts (specially strong on the French nineteenth century); the Art Institute, Chicago (Bosch's *Garden of Paradise*, important collections of Eastern as well as Western art); the Frick Collection, New York (smallish, but a uniformly high standard within and a magnificent setting; great Rembrandts); the Metropolitan Museum, New York (a very strong contender; one of the most complete collections under one roof in

'*I don't wish to look too formal ...*'

the world); the Philadelphia Museum of Art (strong in Flemish works); the National Gallery of Art, Washington DC (hand-picked masterpieces, including one of the best Rembrandt self-portraits, and Vermeer's *Girl with a Flute*); the Rijksmuseum, Amsterdam (naturally, a fine representation of the Dutch school); the Uffizi, Florence (Vasari's noble building, centuries of the highest Italian genius); the Hermitage, Leningrad (paintings acquired by Russian rulers, including Catherine the Great, when the rest of Europe was on its uppers – Titian, Rembrandt, Rubens); the National Gallery, London (a superbly comprehensive collection of European art, mainly bought during the century of Britain's greatest power and wealth); the Prado, Madrid (unequalled for Velasquez, El Greco, Goya, Zurbaran, Murillo, but also rich in Flemish masters); the Alte Pinakothek, Munich (strongest on the early German School); the Künsthistorisches Museum, Vienna (Cellini's famous gold salt cellar; Spanish and Venetian Schools including Titian's *Woman in a Fur*; also world-beating Rembrandts and Vermeers).

But it has to be the Louvre. Apart from the classics almost hackneyed by illustration – *Winged Victory*, *Venus de Milo*, *Mona Lisa* – it has a vast arsenal of treasures, including Carravaggio's *Fortune Teller*, French masters such as Watteau, David, Géricault and Ingres, and some pleasant surprises like Whistler's *Mother*. And all in the grandiose palace begun by Francis I (who brought Leonardo to the Château of Amboise in France, where the artist died in Francis's arms, according to popular myth) and developed by Louis XIV's canny Controller-General, Colbert: the Grand Gallery was opened in 1681.

BEST AUCTION ROOM *Sotheby's*
This needs the judgment of Solomon! Novelists are able to use the pretty subterfuge 'Christaby's' to avoid giving offence to either of the two great auction houses. Sotheby's claim to be the older of the two (founded 1744) but Christie's who proudly display their foundation date, 1766, on all their catalogues, say that Sotheby's were at that time only book auctioneers, which doesn't count. Christie's can claim to have sold the most valuable work of art ever to come up for public auction – Velasquez's *Juan de Pareja*, which fetched £2,310,000 in 1970.

Both auction houses engage well-connected young men and women, presumably in the hope that they will induce their relatives and acquaintances to hock their family heirlooms; but Christie's young sprigs (the downstairs reception desk has been unkindly and no doubt unfairly called 'the Drones' Club') are slightly courtlier than Sotheby's – inspiring the now rather tired adage that 'Christie's are gentlemen trying to be dealers; Sotheby's are dealers trying to be gentlemen'.

In reality the two are very similar in the great reserves of first-class scholarship on their pay-roll; their ability to winkle out works of art from grand and not so grand country houses; their policies of expansion abroad – New York,

Geneva, Zürich and so on. (And certainly no foreign auction house compares with them.) But perhaps Sotheby's have the edge – undeniably in annual volume of business, and also perhaps in a certain *non*-Olde Worlde *élan* and flair for public relations. Successive chairmen of Christie's, Ivan Chance and J. Floyd, while both widely respected in the antiques trade, have lacked the headline–catching dynamism of Sotheby's chairman Peter Wilson. Sotheby's and Christie's among salerooms are like Oxford and Cambridge among universities: it is almost arbitrary to give one's allegiance to one or the other (though people passionately *do*) – but those two are way ahead of the rest.

Best Dealer *Joseph Duveen* (*Lord Duveen of Millbank, 1869–1939*)
S.N. Behrman, who wrote a sparkling life of Duveen, described him as 'the most spectacular art dealer of all time'. There is simply nobody else in the running.

Behrman admits that Duveen's 'knowledge of art was conspicuously exceeded by his enthusiasm for it', and to put a 'wheeler' in front of the 'dealer' is no libel on the dead. But no dealer in history bought and sold so many great masterpieces. To Andrew Mellon he sold the 'Wachtmeister Rembrandt' for $410,000; Donatello's *St John the Baptist*; and Botticelli's *Portrait of a Youth*, described by Bernhard Berenson as 'more Botticellian than any other Botticelli in existence'. To Mr and Mrs Henry Huntington, Gainsborough's *Blue Boy*; Lawrence's *Pinkie*; and Hals's *Balthasar Coymans*, later sold to Mellon. To Jules Bache, whom he called his 'pupil', Ghirlandaio's *Francesco Sassetti and his Son Teodoro*; Holbein's *Edward VI*; Velasquez's *Infanta Maria Teresa*; Crivelli's *Madonna and Child*; and Goya's *Red Boy* which Bache bought for his daughter. To Goldman and later Kress, Giotto's *Madonna and Child*. And many, many more. He bought and sold three times Rembrandt's *Aristotle Contemplating the Bust of Homer*.

Duveen developed perfect techniques with both the American millionaires to whom he sold and the English aristocracy from whom he often bought. With the Americans, who had learnt to speak with slow deliberation so as not to commit themselves first in any financial deal, he too was weighty and ceremonious. It was said they did not like him much. 'Why should they like me?' he once asked one of his many lawyers. 'I am an outsider. Why do they trade with me? Because they've got to. Because I've got what they can't get anywhere else.'

For them, no trouble was too much. He gained them entrée to noblemen's country homes, bookings in full hotels, passages on fully subscribed cruises. He even built them houses, making sure the architects left staring walls that cried out for Old Masters. With immense ceremony, he would usher them into his inner sanctum, saying, as they admired a great painting in the outer gallery in Paris, New York or London, 'Oh, you don't want *that*!' With the English dukes from whom he bought (Gainsborough's *Blue Boy* came from the Duke of Westminster) he was a different being – a brash Yorkshireman. Here his line would be: 'Greatest thing *I* ever saw. Will pay you the biggest price *you* ever saw.' That worked, too.

He did everything on a larger-than-life scale. Having admired the Ministry of the Marine in Paris, he had his architect build a replica of one of its wings as his New York gallery. He moved from the Ritz in Paris to Claridge's in London with a retinue of experts and a travelling gallery – not unlike the travelling menageries of eighteenth-century nobles. He 'exuded opulence'. He understood that paying the highest price for a painting could be a selling-point, not a deterrent. He was wise in his choice of experts. Berenson was for long his chief adviser, before the two fell out for ever over whether an *Adoration of the Shepherds* was by Giorgione or, as Berenson maintained, was 'a Giorgionesque Titian'. One of his experts was the only one who smelled out Van Meegeren's *Christ at Emmaus* as 'a rotten fake' (as he cabled Duveen.)

Behrman rightly claims that Duveen transformed American taste in art. At the beginning of the twentieth century, American millionaires collected French Barbizon paintings, English 'story' pictures, and mildly *risqué* French works by Bougereau. Duveen was quite prepared to sell them Bougereaus too; but gradually he infiltrated their taste and made them feel unsophisticated if they did not join the Old Masters club. 'How utterly duveen!' as Belle da Costa Greene, director of the Pierpont Morgan Library, said when she was first shown Jules Bache's art collection.

BEST ART FORGER *Han Van Meegeren* (*1889–1947*)

It is a sad fact that most people are more interested in fakes than in the real thing. If it could have been proved that the Tutankhamun treasures were forgeries, the queues for the British Museum exhibition would have stretched to Islington.

Han Van Meegeren, *probably* the most successful forger of all time (unless our galleries are littered with the undiscovered frauds of an even more expert malefactor), is widely regarded as a hero rather than a villain. He is the victorious underdog who took on the whole art-historical establishment and made monkeys out of them. He was only found out because he had to prove in court in 1946 that he had not been a Dutch collaborator with the Germans, selling national treasures to Goering: his defence was that as he had faked the paintings in question (and he painted one for the court to prove it) he had in fact played a patriotic jape on the Nazi leader.

It was in 1937 that, after long experimentation with colours and methods of achieving the 'crackle' of hard Old Master paint, Van Meegeren launched his first fake Vermeer, *Christ at Emmaus*, on the unsuspecting art world. The distinguished art historian Abraham Bredius went overboard for it, first writing a testimonial, then an article in the *Burlington Magazine* in which he said: 'It is a wonderful moment in the life of a lover of art when he finds himself suddenly confronted with a hitherto unknown painting by a great master. . . . We have here a masterpiece – I am inclined to say *the* masterpiece – of Johannes Vermeer of Delft.' The painting ended up in the Boymans Museum, where it was given a place of honour and Van Meegeren, going up close to the canvas to see what the restorers had made of his cunningly placed 'damage' and botched 'restorations', was roughly thrust aside by a guard. With equal cunning, Van Meegeren tried to convince his friends that the work was a fake, and told them – to their total disbelief – that he could do as well.

Van Meegeren's motive was somewhere between paranoiac revenge on the art establishment for the slights he had suffered as an academic portraitist; and the desire to make dishonest money. With hindsight, we can see that the 'Vermeergerens', as a wit called his fakes at his trial, are flawed; in particular, some of the women's faces look just like 1930s pin-ups of Marlene Dietrich. And as time went on he took less and less care over his forgeries of Vermeers and Pieter de Hooch works. But some art historians, against all the evidence, *still* maintain that *Christ at Emmaus* is genuine.

Honourable mention goes to Samson of Paris, who flooded the market with spurious Meissen and Chelsea porcelain; to Elmyr de Hory, whose fakes of Modigliani so fooled the Paris experts that when a genuine Modigliani was shown them they said it could not be 'right' as it was 'not in his usual style'; and Tom Keating, whose forgeries of Samuel Palmer and other artists were also, according to him, an attempt to score off the art-historical and art-dealing establishment – on behalf of 'my brothers, Palmer and Constable'.

BEST DRAWING *Leonardo's The Virgin and Child with St Anne and St John the Baptist (National Gallery, London)*
When the Royal Academy, London, to which this work had belonged since the end of the eighteenth century, decided to put it on the market in the 1960s, the British public eagerly paid its pounds and pennies to make sure it stayed in England. It now has a room to itself at the National Gallery.

If one had to draw up a hierarchical pyramid of draughtsmen, its tapering reaches would certainly contain Holbein, Dürer, Rembrandt, Rubens and, among later artists, Ingres, Seurat and Augustus John; but Leonardo and Michelangelo would be at the apex. By common consent, the National Gallery cartoon is among the most beautiful of Leonardo's works. Berenson wrote: 'There is something truly Greek about the gracious humanity of the ideals here embodied, and it is no less Greek as decoration. One can scarcely find draped figures contrived in a more plastic way without going back centuries to those female figures which once were clustered together on the gable of the Parthenon.' Lord Clark, who by contrast considered Leonardo 'essentially un-Greek', thought: 'The shadowy, smiling heads, the tender mysterious glances, the pointing hand, and those two high-sounding devices, chiaroscuro and contraposto, all are present in their most acceptable form.'

Not only is the drawing (unfinished as it is) a deeply moving work in its own right; it also represents an important new direction in art. It was painted about 1500 and in it we see the literal detail of fifteenth-century naturalism giving way to a more lyrical, fancy-free interpretation, the contours sensitively blurred. By a kind of early Impressionism, light is trapped between the fastidious yet nonchalant lines of black chalk.

BEST BOOK ABOUT ART *The Renaissance by Walter Pater (1873)*
As a writer on art, Pater is at the opposite pole to Ruskin. If, for Ruskin, aesthetics are always entwined with, dependent on, ethics, for Pater the two are and must be divorced. If Ruskin was the guru of the Pre-Raphaelite movement, intensely religious in inspiration, Pater was that of the Aesthetic movement (Wilde, Whistler, 'greenery-yallery' young men holding lilies) – the 'art for art's sake' movement. His disciples were urged to 'burn with a hard, gem-like flame' and to remember that 'all art aspires towards the condition of music': in other words, it aspires away from the anecdotal and moralistic towards an abstract perfection. Pater's philosophy of art is much more sympathetic to most people today than Ruskin's. It is freestyle versus authoritarianism.

Walter Pater treated art history as Thomas De Quincey had treated murder in a famous essay – as itself one of the fine arts. He first became famous through his article on Winckelmann published in 1867 and later incorporated in *The Renaissance*. Goethe had said, 'We learn nothing by reading Winckelmann, but we *become* something.' Pater was not quite as 'tremulously responsive' (to borrow Hugh Honour's phrase) as Winckelmann, but much the same can be said of his art history. He does not simply describe, as Ruskin does with genius attended by eulogy or denunciation; he lets his mind off the rein to graze in luscious metaphor. It is a form of verbal Impressionism which conveys what Pater's Oxford pupil, G.M. Hopkins, called the 'inscape', the especial distinguishing quality, of a work of art better than reams of pedantic description or intelligent analysis. Take the most famous passage in *The Renaissance* – which is also the most famous and quoted passage in all art history – his lines on the *Mona Lisa*. W.B. Yeats decided they were poetry and did them the honour of making them the earliest passage in his *Oxford Book of English Verse*, but here they are in their original form, as mystic but uniquely evocative prose:

She is older than the rocks among which she sits; like the vampire, she has been dead many times, and learned the secrets of the grave; and has been a diver in deep seas, and keeps their fallen day about her; and trafficked for strange webs with Eastern merchants; and, as Leda, was the mother of Helen of Troy, and, as Saint Anne, the mother of Mary; and all this has been to her but as the sound of lyres and flutes, and lives only in the delicacy with which it has moulded the changing lineaments, and tinged the eyelids and the hands.

We would not care for all art historians to write like Pater, any more than we would wish all political historians to write as apocalyptically as Carlyle, whose ability to plunge us into a riot or make us live through a revolution is not unlike Pater's impressionist technique. But it was open to one man in history to stake a claim to this exotic manner; and the sad little man with the droopy moustache who did so cannot be dislodged from his uniqueness and precellence.

BEST CARTOONIST/ILLUSTRATOR *Hokusai*

Bernini, the baroque sculptor, and Giovanni Batista Tiepolo, the painter, were both deft caricaturists. But their eminence in the grander branches of art would make it absurd to choose them as 'cartoonists'. One seeks an artist who has made cartooning his life work. Max Beerbohm's caricatures have perhaps the funniest (certainly the most sophisticated) captions, but he was an indifferent artist – the very maladroitness of his figures, with their flipper-like arms and hopelessly drawn feet, adds to the humour. Nominations might go to the eighteenth-century Thomas Rowlandson (who, besides being a dextrous caricaturist, illustrated *Dr Syntax*), George Cruikshank, Wilhelm Busch, Charles Philipon (whose 'Louis Philippe and the pear' caused a greater political scandal than any other cartoon in history), Daumier, the scourge of puffed-up lawyers and doctors, Sir John Tenniel (illustrator of the *Alice* books as well as a leading *Punch* cartoonist), or Phil May, whose linear satires were achieved with maximum economy of line. But for a pure cartoonist of incredible virtuosity, my vote would go to 'Caran d'Ache' (Emmanuel Poirée) who was also, incidentally, the cartoonist who introduced the pithy caption to replace laborious texts of several lines long.

The obvious choice of an illustrator, if the choice were from Europe only, would be Aubrey Beardsley, whose illustrations for the *Savoy* magazine, in particular, are miracles of sensitive draughtsmanship. Beardsley's illustrations are also remarkable for their *mise en page*, the deployment of blank space as well as black line and mass in the allotted space. But Beardsley would have been the first to acknowledge that the source of his own mastery in composition was Japanese art, especially the art of the Japanese woodblock print. And if we are looking for an artist who was at once a great illustrator *and* a great cartoonist – more adroit even than Caran d'Ache in line, more subtle even than Beardsley in composition – we must light on Hokusai, the great Japanese woodblock artist and illustrator, who in his old age gave himself a title which has been affectionately revived by his admirers ever since: 'The Old Man Mad about Drawing'. Only Rembrandt, perhaps, in European art approaches the instinctual *bravura* of his drawing.

BUSINESS

◆

Robert Heller

BEST MONEY *The Swiss franc*
Ever since the last war (during which they wisely stayed neutral), the Swiss have enjoyed one of the world's strongest currencies. After the oil price explosion of 1973, they excelled themselves by clamping down on the money supply. At one point, they reduced inflation virtually to zero, so making the franc even stronger, so reducing the impact of inflation still more – and getting richer and richer in consequence.

BEST SMALL BANK *Hoares Bank in London*
So minute as to be almost invisible, with only two branches, this venerable family bank preserves the type of institution from which all those big anonymous corporations have sprung. Going into Hoares is rather like buying your groceries from Fortnum & Mason: so much nicer.

BEST BIG BANK *The Bank of America, San Francisco and Los Angeles*
Partly because it's the world's biggest; partly because it still has something of the spirit of its founder, A.P. Giannini, the only great banker who wasn't greatly concerned with enriching himself and his family; partly because it invented the bank credit card; but perhaps above all because it confessed to its sins of the Great Banking Disaster: other banks also sinned, but kept it quiet.

BEST CENTRAL BANK *The Bank of Japan*
Difficult choice here, since central bankers generally have a terrible record,

including the Noblest of Them All, the Bank of England. But the Japanese monetary authorities did extremely well in turning the yen into a super-strong currency after oil-induced inflation had threatened to overturn the national apple cart.

Best Coin *Krugerrand*
For practical purposes, as opposed to numismatic or collecting ones, the best has to be the Krugerrand. It's no more than a way of buying gold in countries where the practice is officially banned, or in small quantities: but, financially speaking, that is the best reason by far for buying a coin. Collecting is another, much trickier matter.

Best Investment *Hoffman La Roche*
This drug company is a star in its own right, with a tremendous hold on the world supply of huge volume items like Vitamin C and tranquillizers. But what makes its shares so unique is that they are hideously expensive: so dear that only millionaires can afford them, and that dealings have had to be conducted in mini-shares, each representing a tenth of the real thing.

Best Company *International Business Machines*
No contest here. No other firm can offer IBM's combination of high technology, super-growth, business efficiency, internationalism and amazing generation of profits and cash. At the last count IBM's profits came to $5.8 billion; more than the reserves of some nations, and more than the total value of all but the top US companies.

Best Financial Paper *The Financial Times*
It may be that the Japanese equivalent, which is enormously successful, is better: but you have to read Japanese to find out. Meanwhile, not even the *Wall Street Journal*, let alone its European competitors, come near to the FT's blend of news reporting, features and general and cultural interest.

Best Status Symbol *The Seagram Building, New York*
Being among the world's biggest and best purveyors of hard liquor doesn't rank high in the prestige stakes. So Samuel Bronfman showed the inspired touch in getting Philip Johnson to build his set-back bronze tower on Park Avenue. It gave Seagram and the super-rich Bronfman family class: something you'll never get from a bottle of rye.

Best Advertising Campaign *Avis, by Doyle Dane Bernbach*
Not because it had stunning commercial results, but because the 'We Try Harder' campaign for No. 2 Avis not only gave Hertz at No. 1 a run for its money, but established a new, direct advertising style that altered the map of

'You know what I'd like when I retire?
A nice little office block by the sea.'

marketing. Also, it emphasized the vital point that you really can compete against giants.

BEST ADVERTISING AGENCY *J. Walter Thompson*
Not because it's the world's biggest, though that helps, but because you must be good to stay biggest that long in a fashion-conscious industry, with so many old and new rivals striving to topple the king from his throne. Despite (or because of?) a penchant for ex-Guards officers and the like, JWT has been as strong in Britain as in the US.

BEST ECONOMIST *Milton Friedman*
No contest. For years Friedman preached the basically simple truths about monetary growth and inflation to a totally unreceptive world. Then, when hyper-inflation struck, the prophet finally found honour. Friedman has changed the language of economic discussion and policy-making. No pundit ever deserved a Nobel Prize more.

BEST INSURERS *Lloyd's of London*
There may be risks you can't insure against at Lloyd's, but it's doubtful. The speed and informality with which the risks are accepted is as satisfying as the range – and as the financial rewards, which, because of a complicated system of delayed payments and tax reliefs, make membership of Lloyd's the most expensive but gratifying club subscription in the world.

BEST CLUB *Lloyd's of London*
See above. Unfortunately, the premises at Lloyd's don't offer premium creature comforts: for those the best bet is to seek out the bankers' club in any financial centre. Those who conduct their business in marble halls and the like don't approve of lowering their standards when they go out for lunch.

BEST FINANCIAL DISTRICT *Wall Street, New York*
London may have the tradition and the class, but you can't beat Wall Street for atmosphere, wheeling and dealing, contrasts of opulence and poverty, falling stockbrokers, rising whizz-kids and the other attributes of capitalism in the mixed modern economy. It also contains more gold (in the underground vaults of the Federal Reserve Bank) than any other financial centre.

BEST FINANCIER *Herbert Quandt*
This West German entrepreneur not only built one of Europe's biggest personal empires out of the post-war ruins, but has shown extraordinary flexibility in the running of enterprises like the Varta battery concern: and courage and imagination in operations like the rescue of BMW (by invitation) and turning the wreck into a great success in an industry dominated by multi-national giants.

BEST INVESTOR *General Georges Doriot*
His purchase of the largest stake in Digital Equipment, which made little computers as opposed to IBM's big ones, proved to be the most inspired technological foray in post-war history. Doriot's success – which even he couldn't repeat – also inspired a host of others to lose millions in the conviction that 'venture capital' was the name of the game.

BEST SWINDLER *Anthony de Angelis*
In a highly competitive field, Anthony de Angelis is the winner because of the extreme simplicity and great size of his salad oil swindle. De Angelis not only borrowed fortunes on the security of salad oil that wasn't there, he doubly defrauded the banks with which he was fraudulently connected, thus proving that, in a world where money is represented by pieces of paper, you can't always believe what you read.

BEST STOCKBROKERS *Merrill, Lynch, Pierce, Fenner and Smith*
Once again, sadly for advocates of the little man, biggest is best. But Merrill Lynch is so much the biggest, in a Wall Street where its competitors have been dying like flies and merging like melted butter, that its survival in such strength is testimony enough.

BEST MARKET *Chicago*
Not only is the Board of Trade, where dealers deal by shouting each other down in cockpits, a fascinating place: but Chicago's stock market innovators finally found a way of bringing the disenchanted American investor back to stocks and shares – by inventing an options market in which people trade not securities but the right to buy and sell them.

BEST COLLECTOR *Norton Simon*
After proving himself one of the best-ever collectors of companies, building up the conglomerate Norton Simon, Inc., Simon handed over the company and invested his millions, perhaps with even greater success, in first-rate works by Old Masters, paying horrendous prices which, of course, only served to reinforce the values of his previous buys.

BEST SURVIVOR *Charles H. Bluhdorn*
At a time when the big names of the conglomerate era are forgotten or devalued (James Ling, Litton Industries, etc.), Bluhdorn has kept Gulf & Western riding relatively high in its Manhattan skyscraper – partly by virtue of owning Paramount when the Mafia, in the shape of *The Godfather*, came riding to the rescue.

BEST WAGE-EARNER *Billie Wyllie*
Operating in one of the most exotic areas in world business, Hong Kong, and in one of the rarer fields of management, company doctor, he has turned round Hutchison, one of the colony's conglomerate giants, with such success that a modest share of the profits added up to half a million pounds of annual salary.

BEST MONOPOLY *De Beers*
The value of diamonds depends heavily on the supply. So the fact that De Beers, by virtue of its position in South Africa and arrangements with other diamond-producing areas, can control the supply means that it can also control the price. Moreover, since diamonds are not politically sensitive, nobody much seems to mind.

BEST ASSET *The Oilfields of Saudi Arabia*
It's a strange quirk of history that the Saudi Royal family, in a region awash with oil, should have so much more of it than the others. Although the oil will run out some day, the financial and other assets which the Saudis are

accumulating will mean that the Royals – or their successors – will always be among the richest property owners in the world.

Best Loser *Ross Perot*
In a single day, the founder of one of America's leading computer software houses lost, on paper, no less than $1 billion. The blow was no doubt softened by the fact that Perot remained one of America's richest men, having previously been a fabulously successful salesman for the mighty IBM.

Best Auction House *Sotheby's*
With a feel for modern trends that British manufacturing industry proved incapable of imitating, this Bond Street establishment not only played a crucial role in elevating fine art investment into the financial stratosphere, but made itself a dominant force both in America and on the Continent.

Best Retailer *Sears Roebuck*
Biggest is best again. Instead of going out with the times, like traditional mail orders, Sears converted itself into an aggressive and highly efficient retail operation working from both catalogues and stores, with a hugely successful insurance operation thrown in for extras.

Best Store Of Value *Gold*
The Muhammad Ali of commodities, gold, made a fantastic comeback from years in the doldrums after 1960. Long pinned down at $32 an ounce by the American government, in collusion with others, gold finally broke free and has been over $600, despite persistent efforts by misguided central bankers and politicians to eliminate its monetary role.

Best Family Business *Peugeot-Citroën*
While everybody has been predicting that the European car industry would be dominated by three or four big groups, nobody expected that one would be based on the family concern of the Peugeots – now Europe's Number Two after taking over both Citroën (from another French family business, Michelin) and the European interests of Chrysler.

Best Shipowner *Y. K. Pao*
While attention was focussed on the Great Greeks, Onassis and Niarchos, and other contenders, like the remarkable Daniel K. Ludwig of the US or Ravi Tikkoo from Kashmir, Pao, operating from a Hong Kong base, succeeded in building a fleet which is probably bigger than any of them – and strongly enough based to ride out the monumental post-1973 shipping slump.

BEST GURU *Peter Drucker*

As Friedman is to economics, so Drucker is to management lore: except that Drucker has never been a prophet without honour. His biggest contribution, apart from the idea of directing management towards articulated objectives, has been to infuse theory with practical observation, wry logic and a sense of human perspectives: all of them badly needed.

BEST EMINENCE GRISE *Felix M. Rohatyn of Lazard Frères*

Exactly how many strings this banker has pulled behind how many scenes nobody knows. He came to the forefront in major crises like the rescue of the bankrupt finances of New York City and the equally urgent salvation of the New York Stock Exchange, while also being credited with a major role in such triumphs of private enterprise as the creation and preservation of ITT.

BEST MERCHANT OF DEATH *James McDonnell*

While other great defence contractors, like Lockheed and Boeing, have had their troubles, Mr Mac (now an octogenarian) has kept his St Louis aerospace empire flourishing – despite taking on the civilian problems of Douglas. In fact, the military business has been so successful that efforts to diminish its contribution to the product mix have been negated.

BEST INVENTOR *Robert N. Noyce*

He first came to public attention as the genius behind the semi-conductors which elevated Fairchild Camera from Long Island obscurity into the electronic Big League. Now, as founder and boss of Intel, Noyce is the acknowledged Godfather of Silicon Valley and the entire micro-electronic revolution: out of which he has waxed exceedingly rich.

BEST ENTREPRENEUR *Edwin M. Land of Polaroid*

The choice is a matter of highly subjective taste. But Robert Bruce's maxim, 'if at first you don't succeed, try, try again', is an indispensable element: and Land, first in creating a sun-glasses business out of a failed enterprise, then in persevering until he had an instant camera he could market, and then in replacing both the film and the camera technology with new products, is an amazing example.

BEST ECONOMY *West Germany*

The *Wirtschaftswunder* may be over, but the memory, and in a way the miracle, lingers on. The Germans have maintained into an era of vast affluence and highly valued currency the attributes that took them out of post-war poverty: proving that stable money and real growth are not incompatible, but that the first is a precondition of the latter.

'A bit theatrical perhaps, but it's quite dramatic when he bursts through.'

Best Failure *Paul Erdman*

Having failed as a banker, to the extent that his bank crashed and he spent a spell in a Swiss gaol, Erdman turned his attention to books about banking and allied financial subjects: all of them – *The Billion Dollar Killing, The Silver Foxes, The Crash of '79* – have been world best-sellers.

Best Technique *Cash control*

Other techniques and theories of management may (and do) come and go, but the principles and importance of managing cash never vary – because the importance of cash to a business is fundamental. Effective (if sometimes hasty) adoption of cash flow forecasting by companies after the 1973 crunch partly explains why big bankruptcies were largely avoided.

Best Business School *Harvard Graduate School of Business*

Not because its professors are necessarily the best, or its methods (the famed case study method is looking a little dog-eared these days). But because Harvard has preserved that indefinable thing called *cachet*. Since that's the main benefit of a business school qualification, it makes Harvard the clear winner.

Best Qualification *President of Ford Motor*
A seat beneath Henry Ford II was too hot to occupy for long, but the position took Robert S. McNamara to the Pentagon and the top of the World Bank, while Lee Iaccoca again proved the value of a Ford diploma by landing one of the most lucrative contracts in US history as the new head of the troubled Chrysler Corporation – for what that's worth.

Best Perquisite *The US stock option*
Despite various curbs enacted by Congress from time to time, the option device still has the power to convert US executives (like Iaccoca, above) into dollar millionaires at a relatively early age. Since the executive has no downside risk, and doesn't necessarily have to perform well to cash in his chips handsomely, this beats any European perks – even the corporate Rolls-Royce – hands down.

Best Regulators *The French government agencies*
Not only are the French peculiarly adept at bending (or twisting) the rules of international business to their own advantage, but they succeeded in riding through the great banking crisis without suffering (or at any rate revealing) a major scandal; no other major financial nation in the West can say as much.

Best Bargain *Tax-free instruments*
For the high taxpayer. Whenever tax arises above the confiscation level of fifty per cent, tax breaks inevitably become perfect bargains for the taxpayer, who thereby avoids confiscation. He has little to lose (because most will be taken in tax, anyway) and everything to gain (because the benefit will be tax-free). The situation is thus perfectly free from risk.

Best Industry *Oil*
Crises come, and crises go. But the Seven Sisters, who dominate the world petroleum industry, have survived the nationalization of much of their oil and the pressures of governments in the consuming countries in remarkably good order. What they lose on the production swings, they gain on the marketing roundabouts. Hence the phenomenal profits achieved since 1973.

Best Doomsayer *Elliot Janeway*
This American sage has been predicting national and global economic gloom for many decades. Finally the seventies vindicated him triumphantly. Whether this is the reward of consistency or foresight, it has earned Janeway a place in history as the man who correctly called the turn.

Best Myth *Equities are a hedge against inflation*
This was so widely believed before the Second Great Crash that investors mostly wouldn't believe that, in many of the post-war years, cash was as good

an investment as ordinary shares. Even in the late seventies, after a disastrous decade, institutions and individuals hadn't completely escaped from a myth that has made millions – mostly for stockbrokers and the like.

Best Conference Centre *West Berlin*
The huge new complex in West Berlin, close to the airport and the lakes, is the latest marvel of a boom industry. Once inside the giant, every need is catered for. The only catch is that West Berlin isn't Paris, London or New York – which is why superior facilities were needed to pull in the international customers.

Best Exhibition Centre *Düsseldorf*
Another new development in a booming West German city. The vast halls cover an enormous area, and the surrounding city isn't totally devoid of charm for the visiting industrialist. The halls are so adaptable that you can show anything from the largest machinery to the minutest object of modern art.

'I'm thinking of calling it a "Rockamatic" or "Riverette" or something.'

Best Big Computers *Kray*

For some unknown reason, the large and established companies, headed by IBM, have never been tops at making the really huge number-crushers. Seymour Kray, a refugee from Univac, doesn't make many computers, but those he does produce are the equivalent of the Grosse Mercedes in cars – the biggest and most powerful around.

Best Small Computers *Digital Equipment*

In a desperately competitive industry, Ken Norris of the American company DE has maintained a leading market share by constant clever development. He can claim to run the IBM of little computers – machines which are now as powerful and versatile as the really big ones used to be.

Best Mini Computers *Hewlett-Packard*

With computers now being built on tiny slivers of silicon, the scientific calculators with which Messrs Hewlett and Packard first made their fortunes now look like antiques. But clever innovation has kept the HP range ahead in the specialized market including that for businessmen who like their calculators on their wrist, in a watch.

Best Gadget *The visual display unit*

Now that every schoolchild has an electronic calculator, there is still time for the VDU on the desk to operate as a status symbol – until everybody has one of these, too. But being able to summon up information (even if it's useless) from anywhere in the company in a flash, and to use the computer power on your desk, is at the very least a pleasant way of passing away idle office hours.

Best Name (American) *Rockefeller*

The name is excellent currency in banking, oil, politics and even fine art – since the late Nelson Rockefeller started selling replicas of his personal art collection: offerings which were the worst bargains of the seventies. But that piece of merchandising showed that after a century or so, the Rockefeller name still means money.

Best Name (European) *Rothschild*

In fact, the prominence of the Rothschild family in European business (like that of all merchants and investment bankers) has diminished markedly down the post-war years. But the family banks have enough presence in Britain and France, and the family carries enough prestige all over the world, to maintain the compelling drawing power of the name.

Best Speculators *The Murchison brothers*

Sons of an enormously rich oilman, the brothers figured in an abortive battle for possession of America's biggest investment fund company: left the headlines: then suddenly reappeared, having affected what came very near to a corner in silver. They have even been suspected of doing it again in the 1979–80 silver boom, which outdid even gold.

BEST BUSINESS WEEKLY *Business Week*
The flagship of the McGraw-Hill magazine empire, BW has an enormous staff who have always kept up a remarkable standard of accuracy, concise presentation and inspired selection of the right story at the right time. Perhaps strangely, there's no other weekly in the world which uses the same news-based formula.

BEST RIP-OFF *The Russian wheat deal*
Negotiating from the usual weak position of a poor harvest, the Russians took the Nixon Administration for one of the biggest rides in history, buying American wheat (heavily subsidized by the taxpayer) in secret talks shortly before the price took off. The Russians' super-bargain contributed heavily to American domestic inflation.

BEST BRIBERY *The US milk payola*
Again under the Nixon Administration, the US milk producers, both directly and through dummy organizations, gave $360,000 to the President's re-election fund. They got him to do the almost impossible or unthinkable – to reverse an announced decision by his own Agriculture Secretary and agree to higher milk prices that cost US consumers billions.

BEST ADVICE
When making financial investments, buy when interests rates are high and sell when they are low. The advice is so obvious that it's amazing to find people, even clever ones, doing the opposite. There's only one catch – how do you know what's high and what's low? But it's an easier question to answer than most of those in finance.

COMMUNICATIONS

David Taylor

BEST MEANS OF COMMUNICATION *Language*

Of which there are three main sorts: *kinetics*, *vocalization* and *speech*.

The first includes crude gestures and the so-called 'body language' of both voluntary and involuntary movements. Potent examples are showing a leg, coming out with your hands up, the two-fingers V-sign (for Victory, or else rude), the nudge and the wink, a policeman on traffic duty or those men with tangerine ping-pong bats directing aircraft on the ground. First man to use sign language to really good effect was Abbé Charles Michel Epée (1712–89) who pioneered the manual alphabet used by the deaf.

Vocalization includes the shouts, moans, snorts, whistles, grunts and squeaks of language favoured by such as chimpanzees, dolphins, infant children, primitive tribes and some drunks, not to mention people who insist on saying *uh-huh* or *mmm* instead of *yes*.

But *speech* is the versatile system of differentiated sounds arranged in significant sequence which only man can handle. There are about 3,000 spoken languages (not counting dialects) currently in use and, though nearly all of them can also be written down, most people in the world today are still illiterate.

BEST COMMUNICATOR *Humpty Dumpty*

'When I use a word, it means just what I choose it to mean, neither more nor less.' – Lewis Carroll, *Through The Looking-Glass*, 1871.

BEST SPOKEN LANGUAGE *Chinese*
Because you'll be understood by upwards of 650 million people, as against the mere 358 million who can speak English. In fact there are about fifty 'Chinese' languages but the one most millions speak is the Peking dialect we call Mandarin. The Chinese also used to call it Mandarin (*kuan-hua*) but these days that smacks of revanchist imperialism so they call it *p'u-t'ung hua* (meaning generally-understood language).

Chinese is hell to pronounce because pitch plays a part in determining meaning. The word *t'ang* pronounced with a high, level tone means soup, but with a tone rising from medium to high pitch it means sugar. The same word with a low, dipping, circumflex tone means lie down. And *t'ang* with a wide drop from high to low pitch is the word for hot. The tone-deaf should therefore never attempt to order 'hot soup' in China in case the waitress takes it to mean 'lie down, sugar'.

Writing Chinese is also nightmarishly inscrutable. Though it is the ultimate goal of the present Chinese leaders to introduce some form of alphabet, Chinese script has for centuries relied on characters (ideographs) representing whole words or ideas. Of the 2,000 commonest characters, only a quarter need fewer than eight strokes (a brush is best) and some have almost thirty. It is hard work writing Chinese, and even harder trying to come up with a Chinese typewriter.

BEST PUT-DOWN OF BAD WRITING
Attributed by Sir Ernest Gowers in *Plain Words* (1948) to Sir Winston Churchill, who is said to have written in the margin of an officialese document: 'This is the sort of English up with which I will not put.'

BEST COMMUNICATIONS CHESTNUT
'One picture is worth a thousand words' – everybody has heard this, nobody knows who said it. In fact it was one Frederick R. Barnard in 1927 in an obscure journal called *Printer's Ink*. Hoping to give his pithy comment a bit more clout, Barnard claimed mischievously that it was a Chinese proverb and to this day the classic *bon mot* is often credited to Confucius.

BEST-EVER BROADCAST COMMUNICATIONS
Went out on television on the afternoon of Sunday 20 July 1969 and featured interminable pictures of motionless grey dust – but was watched in fascination by an estimated world audience of 528 million. At precisely 4:17.42 Eastern Daylight Time, they heard the unforgettable message from Neil A. Armstrong – 'Houston, Tranquillity Base here. The *Eagle* has landed....'

Man was for the first time on the moon, inside the lunar module, *Eagle*, of Apollo 11. Later that evening, at 10:56.20, another historic message was transmitted the 50,000 miles back to earth by the first man actually to place a size

'I've always wanted my own chat show.'

$9\frac{1}{2}$ boot on the surface of another world. Said Col Edwin E. 'Buzz' Aldrin Jr – 'That's one small step for a man, one giant leap for mankind.'

BEST GARBLED COMMUNICATION
The First World War saw the first use of wireless telegraphy under battle conditions but the equipment was primitive and the operators unpractised. One crucial message from the front – SEND REINFORCEMENTS, WE ARE GOING TO ADVANCE – is said to have been received as SEND THREE-AND-FOURPENCE, WE ARE GOING TO A DANCE.

BEST BUSINESS COMMUNICATIONS INVENTION
On 7 January 1714, one Henry Mill was granted a British patent by Queen Anne for 'An Artificial Machine or Method for the Impressing or Transcribing of Letters Singly or Progressively one after another, as in Writing, whereby all Writing whatever may be Engrossed in Paper or Parchment so Neat and Exact as not to be Distinguished from Print.'

The trouble was, it was impossibly slow at 'engrossing' and not until 1867 and in America do we get the invention of one Christopher Latham Sholes appearing as recognizably a *typewriter*. Sholes had teething troubles and not until 1874 did he put his machine on the market – made for him by a firm of gunsmiths from Ilion, New York State, called E. Remington and Sons. It took donkey's years for the typewriter really to catch on, but one of the original Sholes/Remington machines was purchased by Mark Twain, the first author ever to submit a typewritten manuscript for a book.

There have been many recent advances in typewriter technology – most notably electric machines – but the next step ought to be the drastic rearrangement of the keyboard. The conventional layout – QWERTYUIOP is the top line of letters with ASDFGHJKL underneath and ZXCVBNM at the bottom – is by no means the most efficient for fast typing and was originally devised to *slow down* typists because early machines couldn't keep pace. Various alternative layouts have been tested but to date no-one has been able to contemplate the awful thought of all the world's English-speaking typists going back to square one at the keys.

Best Breakthrough In Mathematical Communications

Most people count with a system based on the fact we have ten fingers – *decimal arithmetic*. But there is another way, based on the fact we have two hands – *binary arithmetic*. Instead of counting 0–1–2–3–4–5–6–7–8–9, the binary scale uses only 0 and 1 and tots up 0–1–10–11–100–101 and so on. It may look clumsy but a German philosopher and mathematician, Gottfried Leibniz (1646–1716), devised a logical system of calculus based on the binary scale and one George Boole (1815–64), Professor of Mathematics at Queen's College, Cork, came up with a system of algebra using binary.

Now the great thing for modern science and communications is the fact that the figures 0 and 1 may be represented in an electrical circuit as ON and OFF. Applying the system of binary arithmetic and Boolean algebra, if you have enough switches (some of them ON, some of them OFF) you can do all sorts of fancy calculations with amazing speed and accuracy.

We call the modern, sophisticated boxes of switches *computers*.

Best-Ever Postal Communication *Pony Express*

Only operated between St Joseph, Missouri, and Sacramento, California, and took a minimum of ten days to deliver a letter (not exceeding $\frac{1}{2}$ oz) for a charge of $5. On the other hand, this was 1860 and the mail route was across 1,838 punishing miles of rugged trails through hostile Indian country, needing as many as 500 changes of mount for the indefatigable riders of the Pony Express who included William 'Buffalo Bill' Cody.

The completion of the transcontinental telegraph in 1861 closed down the loss-making service for good but the romance lingers on in a thousand Wild West movies and the name is still familiar in London, emblazoned on the backs of leather-clad contemporary cowboys who whisk urgent packages about the city on fast Japanese motor-bikes and are nicknamed 'Hell's Messengers'.

Best Short Communication

General Sir Charles James Napier (1782–1853) who, having missed the action at Waterloo by turning up three days late, did better when posted to India and, after a battle at Hyderabad in the province of Sind, despatched news of his victory to London in a single-word Latin pun – PECCAVI – 'I have sinned (*Sind*)'.

BEST HYSTERICAL COMMUNICATION

Broadcast on 30 October 1938 – the night before Halloween – when Orson Welles's *Mercury Theater* drama show on CBS hoaxed up H. G. Wells's *War of the Worlds* to sound like a real-life emergency and mass hysteria gripped America's listening public. Almost two million people, a survey later discovered, really believed that hideous, slimy, Martian monsters armed with death-rays had landed in New Jersey and zapped all resistance. More than a million people were so distressed they fled their homes. Telephone switchboards in every state were jammed and a woman in New York – one of hundreds of thousands calling the authorities for latest news of the 'invasion' – sobbed: 'Hurry, please – the world is coming to an end and I have a lot to do.'

BEST TRANSATLANTIC COMMUNICATION *Concorde*

It cuts conventional flying time in half and makes possible for the first time a trip from London to New York and back again in a single working day. Only place in the world where you can relish *boeuf Stroganoff* in idle comfort whilst travelling faster than a rifle bullet, at twice the speed of sound, ten miles above the earth's surface.

BEST PUT-DOWN OF NEWSPAPER COMMUNICATIONS

G.K. Chesterton (1874–1936) in *The Wisdom of Father Brown* – 'Journalism largely consists in saying "Lord Jones Dead" to people who never knew Lord Jones was alive.'

BEST COMMUNICATIONS EXPORT

The Premier Drum Company, of Leicester, won the Vladivar Vodka Incredible Export Award in 1975 with four shipments of tom-toms to Nigeria. The order included a complete tom-tom kit for the Nigerian Police Band and another for the country's top show-band, Dr Victor Oliyia and his All-Star Orchestra.

BEST ADVICE TO POLITICAL COMMUNICATORS

'The great enemy of clear language is insincerity.' – George Orwell (1903–50) in an essay on *Politics and the English Language*.

BEST VAIN ATTEMPT TO COVER UP A COMMUNICATIONS NIGHTMARE

Richard M. Nixon: 'I am not a crook.'

BEST RADIO COMMUNICATIONS BREAKTHROUGH *The transistor*

First put together in 1948 at Bell Telephone Laboratories by William Shockley and his associates John Bardeen and Walter Brattain who together shared a 1956 Nobel Prize for their achievement. The midget semi-conducting device was made by the carefully-controlled addition of certain impurities to a germanium crystal not unlike the ones used in early 'crystal sets', with the result that a current could be both rectified and amplified (as required in a radio receiver) far more efficiently than by the original crystals or by the valves which had succeeded them. The invention revolutionized electronics, made possible the miniaturization of computer circuitry (since further refined by integrated circuits and micro-processors) and gave the whole world small, portable, battery-operated 'transistor sets'.

BEST CONTRIBUTION TO COMMUNICATIONS COMFORT *The pneumatic tyre*
The principle was first patented by Robert William Thomson, an English inventor, in 1845. His patent showed a non-stretch outer cover and an inner tube of rubber to hold air. One of the earliest sets of Thomson's tyres covered 1,200 miles, fitted to a horse-drawn brougham. A quarter-century later, it was the popularity of the bicycle which made tyres big business and Thomson's ideas were taken up by a rubber manufacturer in Belfast called John Boyd Dunlop. The first tyres to be fitted to motor-cars came in 1895, on the French Panhard. They were made by another still-familiar firm of rubber manufacturers – Messrs Michelin.

BEST FORMULARIZED COMMUNICATION $E=mc^2$
Five simple characters which to the physicist put into a nutshell the interrelationship of mass and energy as worked out by Albert Einstein (1879–1955) in the Special Theory of Relativity. In the equation, E is energy, m is mass and c is the velocity of light. Since light fairly bats along at about 300,000 km/sec, it follows that a small amount of mass (multiplied by the speed of light squared) is equivalent to an awful lot of energy. One proof of the truth of it is the atomic bomb in which tiny amounts of matter are changed into huge amounts of energy. Einstein's complex insights showed that common-sense Newtonian laws of physics did not apply in the vastness of universal space or in the tiny world of the atom. But since few of us inhabit either world, most of us can get by without the trouble of unravelling Einstein's elegant mathematical communications.

BEST PLACE TO PLAY WITH TELEPHONES *America*
It is the world's most efficient system and the Supreme Court of the United States recently permitted subscribers to plug in their own phones to telephone company lines, making it the most fun system, too. Fierce competition between makers now means you have a choice of hundreds of different models from slim-line, push-button jobs to reproduction dime-in-the-slot machines to phones modelled on Mickey Mouse or custom-built to match your décor. Americans have always been phone-mad. As early as 1958, the American Telephone & Telegraph Co. (AT & T) claimed one hundred million telephones in service – half the world's total. Today the figure has almost doubled.

BEST GREETINGS TELEGRAM
Sent by American humorist Robert Benchley to his friend and fellow wit
Dorothy Parker when first he visited Venice: STREETS FULL OF WATER –
PLEASE ADVISE.

BEST UNLIKELY PHONE-CALL
Put through from Moscow to a tiny village in Cheshire in October 1957. The
occasion was the launching of the world's first artificial satellite – *Sputnik 1*.
The best-available antenna for tracking *Sputnik's* progress was at Jodrell Bank,
Cheshire, the site of Manchester University's radio-telescope. The Russians
rang Sir Bernard Lovell, the director, to ask how things were going. The 250-
ft dish at Jodrell Bank was built by the Sheffield engineering firm of H.C. Husband at a cost of around £1 million. At the time, Sir Bernard Lovell did not
have £1 million on him and was threatened with gaol for overspending on his
budget. Lord Nuffield saved the day with a handsome gift, supplemented by
a pile of sixpences collected by local schoolkids.

BEST ADVICE FOR NEWS COMMUNICATORS
Given in 1880 by John B. Bogart (no relation) who was City Editor of the New
York *Sun*: 'When a dog bites a man that is not news, but when a man bites
a dog that is news.'

BEST-EVER DAILY NEWSPAPER *The Daily News*
First published on 21 January 1846 from offices at 90 Fleet Street, price 5d
(undercutting the all-powerful *The Times* by 2d). It was Britain's first liberal
daily paper, the champion of free trade and the railway age, and years later
was to become the no less distinguished *News Chronicle*. In a leading article
in the first edition, the Editor (salary £2,000 p.a.) wrote: 'The principles advo-
cated by *The Daily News* will be principles of progress and improvement; of
education, civil and religious liberty and equal legislation; principles such as
its conductors believe the advancing spirit of the time requires, the condition
of the country demands, and justice, reason and experience legitimately sanc-
tion. Very much has to be done, and must be done towards the bodily comfort,
mental elevation and general contentment of the English people....'
  Recognize the Editor's style? It was Charles Dickens.

BEST BIBLICAL ADVICE ON COMMUNICATIONS
'To do good and to communicate, forget not.' – *The Epistle of St Paul to the
Hebrews*.
  'Evil communications corrupt good manners.' *The 1st Epistle of St Paul to
the Corinthians*.

BEST NEW IDEA IN COMMUNICATIONS
Without question, the *micro-processor*, or so-called computer on a chip.

'*Well, parlez-vous Français then? – or sprechen Sie Deutsch?...
parla Italiano? ... habla usted Español? ...*'

A tiny slice of silicon, this fragment of electronic wizardry can have as many as 100,000 miniaturized transistor circuits etched on to its surface with amazing precision and can handle as a result some hundreds of thousands of calculations *every second* with consummate ease. No human brain can touch it for sums.

Not surprisingly, it is fashionable to predict that the impact of the microprocessor will upturn electronics, telecommunications, automation and just about everything else in the next twenty years – it has been called the most significant invention since the wheel.

Twenty years ago, the things didn't exist. Today the world market is estimated at £3 billion a year. By the mid-1980s, some wit has reckoned up, every person in the world will need to have a micro-processing toy just to find an outlet for the industry's burgeoning output.

The fact is that, once designed, a silicon chip is ludicrously cheap to make. That's why everyone can buy for peanuts such sophisticated gadgetry as pocket calculators and complex TV games. And as well as being conveniently small and cheap, micro-processors are reliable – no connections to come undone. The potential applications are awesome.

Thirty years ago, the world's first electronic digital computer weighed about thirty tons and filled a room. Today's silicon-chip equivalent weighs a fraction of a gram, would disappear on your fingernail, and is twenty times more powerful than the original computer.

America is streets ahead of the field in micro-processing capability. Stanford University, just outside San Francisco, is where many of the best brains trained and the nearby area of Santa Clara County, where today they race each other to come up with the latest and greatest in silicon chips, is nicknamed Silicon Valley. So far, theory is in front of application. In only a few years from now, micro-processors will dramatically change everyone's life.

Best New Communications Frontier

Strictly for the boffins to date, *integrated optics* could well surface soon as yet another communications 'revolution'. It's another micro-miniature world of wonders, this time harnessing *light* instead of electronic impulses to transmit data in huge quantities at mind-bending speed by way of lasers, midget lenses, prisms and light modulators.

Already commonplace are *optical fibres* which, if swallowed, can send back pictures of your insides and which if fitted to your car's dashboard can illuminate umpteen knobs or instruments from a single bulb. Next thing you know, optical fibres thinner than a human hair will be carrying thousands of telephone conversations and millions of bits of computer data, making cables old hat.

Best Extraterrestial Communications

Until such time as Little Green Men make contact with us Earthlings, all the chattering in space is done via man-made *satellites*. At a rough count there are 850 of them now batting round the earth, not to mention over 3,000 bits of junk like spent rocket casings, bolts, springs and other fragments which were used to get them there and which also remain in orbit.

The *idea* of artificial communications satellites goes back thirty years to the science-fiction writings of Arthur C. Clarke, but it was 1957 before the first *Sputnik* began beep-beeping and 1962 before NASA launched the first *active* communication satellite (that is, powered by on-board solar cells) called *Telstar*. A year later came *Syncom* which, by matching its orbital speed to the earth's rotation, effectively stayed put in the sky.

First man to sit in on a satellite trip was Yuri Alekseyevich Gagarin on 12 April 1961. He had a ninety-minute ride in complete safety but, ironically, died tragically in an air-crash seven years later and never saw the first man on the moon.

The first heavenly body to be discovered from the use of telescopes was a satellite – one of a dozen natural ones circling the planet Jupiter. It was spotted on 7 January 1610 by Galileo and went on to feature in another scientific first, sixty-six years later, when the Danish astronomer Olaus Roemer watched the way it was periodically eclipsed and did a few quick sums to work out the speed of light. His answer was 227,000 km/sec whereas actually it is 299,792 km/sec. But not bad for a first attempt.

Today America leads the field in sophisticated artificial *comsats*, providing near-instantaneous global transmissions capability for such vital communications as the World Cup.

Best Silly Remark On Communications
Charles Prestwich Scott (1846–1932): 'Television? No good will come of this device. The word is half Greek and half Latin.'

Best Communications Statistic
During any manned space flight, there is extraterrestrial data transmission at the rate of fifty-two kilobits per second, as computer-buffs say. Or, as the rest of us say, the equivalent of an entire *Encyclopaedia Britannica* every minute.

Best International Communications Get-Together
Sponsored by the UN in 1974, 4,000 people from 72 nations used 38 ships, 13 aircraft, 6 satellites, 63 buoys, 1,000 surface stations and half a million balloons to survey an area of 29 million square miles from the bottom of the ocean to the top of the atmosphere. The purpose of the *Global Atmospheric Research Project Atlantic Tropical Experiment* was to improve weather-forecasts. Unfortunately, it failed to improve the weather.

Best Up-And-Coming Communications Toys *The home video recorder*
A box that sits next to your TV and records any programme, even though you may be watching another channel at the time or out of the house altogether. They're not cheap (yet) but video recorders, with their promise that you need never miss another episode of *Soap* or can watch and re-watch the best of *Monty Python* till your eyes go square, are proving brisk sellers.

Less popular to date, but long-term more likely to be rewarding, are TV sets equipped to receive *teletext* – news or information/reference at the touch of a button, night or day. The BBC system is called *Ceefax* and sends out regularly updated information on such things as the news headlines, stock market prices, weather or entertainment guides to be stored in the electronic memory of a user's TV set and retrieved at the push of a keyboard. The ITV system, *Oracle*, provides a similar service and the Post Office's new *Viewdata* system promises an even larger range of available reference sent over telephone lines and displayed on a terminal screen which is rented, just like a phone. For these (and other systems worldwide) it is still early days but eventually *teletext* seems likely to emerge as a powerful electronic competitor to conventional newspapers and magazines.

BEST EVERYDAY AID TO COMMUNICATIONS *The ball-point pen*
The use of quills for writing is reckoned to go back to the fifth century AD (goose or swan were the best) and not until the early part of the nineteenth century were they generally superseded by steel nibs. An Englishman named Bramah invented the fountain-pen and a Frenchman named Biro invented the ball-point.

BEST BIT OF FUN COMMUNICATIONS GADGETRY *The pocket television set*
Sinclair Radionics (St Ives, Cambridgeshire) make one that's not much bigger than a fat paperback. Called *Microvision*, it has a two-inch black-and-white screen but since you're looking at it from normal reading distance rather than across a room it's plenty big enough. The thing works off a set of penlight batteries, has built-in speaker and aerial, so is truly *pocketable* and provides a great sense of one-upmanship when used to watch the news on the bus home.

BEST UNSOLVED COMMUNICATIONS RIDDLE
How carrier pigeons find their way back home.

DRINK

Cyril Ray

BEST COOLING CUP

Take a bottle of claret in one hand and a bottle of champagne in the other (it doesn't matter if you use some other red wine and some other sparkler, and it doesn't matter which hand, either) and pour them simultaneously into a bowl. Pouring them simultaneously *does* matter: it gives you grand ideas. Add a glass apiece of brandy and one of the orange-flavoured liqueurs, such as Grand Marnier, with a long twist of the zest of a lemon and soft sugar to taste. Serve very cold, not by diluting the good creature with melting ice but by standing the bowl in a bigger bowl of crushed ice, or some such means. Not for young things unless you have designs on them.

BEST WARMER-UPPER

The Viennese *Lebensretter*, or Life-Saver, is simplicity itself: a bottle of port to half a bottle of brandy, sugared to taste and served very hot.

BEST RUM

As a mixer for Daiquiris and similar cocktails, the light Dry Cane.

As a mixer for long cold drinks, such as Planter's Punch, and for hot concoctions, a more flavoury Jamaica rum, such as Lemon Hart Gold.

As an after-dinner liqueur, taken straight, like a brandy, the Barcardi Anejo, aged in wood or, better still, if you can get it, the French Rhum Barbancourt, made and matured like a good cognac.

For blessed oblivion, the 90-degree Caroni Extra Strong Navy Rum, from Trinidad.

BEST VODKA

The best Russian vodka comes from near Leningrad, where the water of the lakes is said to be the softest in all the Russias, ideal both for distilling and for dilution to drinkable strength. Finnish vodka has the same virtue, the water for distillation being drawn from wells deep under the ice moraines. The Poles are particularly good at flavouring vodkas – their vodka Starka is aged in cask to a pale straw colour and a faint tang as of sherry; vodka Jarbeziak is tinted and flavoured by rowan berries; and vodka Zubrowka is the palest possible green from the zubrowka grass that gives it its slight herby taste.

But vodka can be made anywhere, and Smirnoff, now distilled both in Britain and the United States to a pre-revolutionary Russian formula, is as good as any. As the chief virtue of vodka is that however potent a potable it is, it bequeaths no hangover, there is much to be said for the strongest you can stand and still stand, so I plump not for the Smirnoff White Label, which is a little less strong than standard gins, nor for the Silver, only a little stronger, but for the Blue, a fairly formidable 80 degrees, which I would drink neat, ice-cold, and why not with smoked salmon or potted shrimps, as the Russians do with caviar?

Oh yes, there is also a splendid 'Commemoration' or 'Czarist' version, in a handsome replica – tall, slender, horizontally fluted and with Imperial eagles on its pretty period label – of the Russian bottle of the 1880s, but it is 100 degrees proof which, although mere mother's milk compared with the Pure Polish Spirit, or top-of-the-head remover, at 140, is a bit much for an effete Englishman such as me, and which I am reserving as a substitute for running away, in some as yet unforeseen crisis, to join the Foreign Legion, and forget . . . .

BEST GIN

Gordons and Gilbeys and Booths
All make a potion that soothes
The savagest breast,
Besides adding zest
To the amorous antics of youths . . .

– or so they tell me.

These are all 'London', or 'dry', gins and I cannot choose between them as admirable mixers for cocktails and gin-and-tonics. Sailors of my acquaintance prefer Plymouth gin for pink gin: as it is heavier and more aromatic than London gin, a pink gin made of Plymouth tastes more of gin, whereas made with London it tastes more of the Angostura bitters.

To drink for its own sake, and not as a mixer, Dutch gin – *genever*, or 'Hollands' – is best, and give me the *oude*, rather than the *jonge*, not necessarily

'*What really upsets him is that it was his father who did all the drinking.*'

longer matured but made to seem so in character, straw-coloured, a little sweeter and more aromatic than the young. An ice-cold Bols *oude* from its tall stone bottle goes well with a typical Dutch hors d'oeuvre of raw, pickled or marinaded herring, or before one of those hot, spicy Indonesian *rijstaffels* that you get almost anywhere in Holland.

BEST SCHNAPPS

All around the upper Rhine – in Alsace, Switzerland and the Black Forest – and also in Balkan and Central European countries such as Hungary and Yugoslavia, they drink the strong, dry, colourless fruit *eaux de vie* such as slivovitz and kirsch and black palinka as aperitifs. In Holland, it's gin; in the Scandinavian countries what is called aquavit or akvavit or schnapps or snaps, according to country. There are all sorts of these distillations from grain, usually flavoured with carraway, and the one I go for is the Norwegian Linie Aquavit, so-called to indicate that it has crossed the Line, which is to say the Equator – to Australia in oaken casks in the Wilhelmsen cargo ships, coming back a very pale golden colour, and with a suggestion of sherry in its delicate, subtle flavour. The Norwegian Ministry of Foreign Affairs, no less, published a pamphlet on how to drink the wine of the country: 'The bottle must be cold enough to be frosty with dew, the glass should be small enough to make it possible for the dram to get lukewarm before it is finished.' You say 'Skål!' And throw it back . . .

BEST VIN ROSÉ

Purists pooh-pooh pinkers: 'the wine of compromise'; 'neither one thing nor t'other'; and 'looks pretty and plays safe'. True of some but by no means of all – certainly not of Tavel rosé, which comes from near Châteauneuf du Pape, stronger in alcohol than most, which gives it staying power, and fuller in flavour, which a wine of Provence needs to be, to go with those rich, spicy southern dishes.

Pink champagne, too, can be firmer in character than the traditional pale gold. It is not simply a frivolous drink for frivolous young ladies, though it has that reputation. But it does carry with it a suggestion of lightheartedness and is none the worse for that: I recall a party at which my then octogenarian mother-in-law, handed her glass of pink champagne on arrival, held it up to the light and exclaimed, 'Pink champagne! How *very* pretty!' and a girl at her heels, a quarter her age, holding up *her* glass, and saying, 'Pink champagne! What fun!' There is a lot to be said for prettiness and fun: I cannot think of better reasons for serving or drinking a wine.

I have enjoyed pink Lanson and pink Moët and Chandon very much, but I think Veuve Clicquot the best of a delightful lot.

BEST BEER

The beer they brew in Pilsen might almost reconcile one to life in Czechoslo-vakia; Australian beer comes in cans specially designed for throwing at England's cricketers; Danish beers go down well after aquavit and with all sorts of pickled, smoked and salted bits of fish, but Guinness is best – draught Guinness, bottled Guinness, and canned Guinness, but what has long been sold abroad as 'Foreign Extra Stout', newly available in Britain as Triple X, is best of the lot, fuller and richer than the others, without being sweeter. It is half as strong again as bottled Guinness, and a half-pint bottle packs the kick of a double Scotch and a bit over – Guinness with teeth. . . .

BEST COCKTAIL

> *There is something about a Martini,*
> *A tingle remarkably pleasant;*
> *A yellow, a mellow Martini;*
> *I wish that I had one at present . . .*

So sang Ogden Nash, in the days when there was still enough vermouth in a Martini for the mixture to be yellow, however slightly, unlike those seventy-to-one knock-out drops of today, as colourless as vodka and at least as lethal – death to the taste buds, anyway.

Though it has neither so long nor so lovingly documented a history, the Sidecar is a better sharpener-up of pre-prandial appetite and, unlike the Martini, all the better for being drier now than when it was created, a couple of generations ago, when there were still officers of Pershing's army in Paris, to be driven in sidecars to Harry's Bar at Sank Roo Doe Noo, where and why it received its name.

It was equal parts in those days of lemon juice, Cointreau and cognac, but by some curious Lush's Law mixed drinks, if they survive at all, become stronger as the years go by, and now an American recipe calls for eight of cognac to two of lemon juice and one of Cointreau and there is an English one that is half cognac to a quarter each of the others.

The lemon gives sharpness, the Cointreau sweetness and the cognac kick, without quarrelling with the claret to come as the gin in a Martini does. The English version first, then the American, then every other proportion in between, to decide which is best, and see if I care. Or if *you* do, by then....

BEST SOFT DRINK
I have twice been concussed, once by jumping off a moving bus, once by falling off a jumping horse, which sounds grander, but is just as disagreeable. The first thing your doctor tells you is 'No alcohol!' – concussion is pressure on a blood vessel: alcohol distends blood vessels, and makes bad worse.

Neither time did I miss the alcohol, but I did miss the liquid intake. What to do? Not milk: I am not a calf. Not Coca-cola: I tasted it in 1936, the year I tasted cornflakes, and knew that neither was for me. Squashes and such were too sweet, orange-juice too rich, tomato juice too slimy. I settled on Shloer apple juice – a whisper on the sweet side, corrected by adding ice and a thick slice of lemon. If there's a drier brand than Shloer, that would be better still.

BEST LIQUEUR
Green Chartreuse is strong, sweet and subtle, and I wish I had a velvet smoking-jacket of the same colour. Yellow Chartreuse is sweeter and less strong. Take no notice of what the Almoner at the Grande Chartreuse told Oscar Wilde, who asked the secret of the serenity on the monks' faces: 'One third green, two thirds yellow.' Such namby-pamby mixtures are good enough for celibates: give me the green, straight.

BEST WHISKIES (SCOTCH AND CANADIAN) AND WHISKEYS (IRISH AND AMERICAN)
Single malt: Macallan when available – otherwise Glenfiddich, widely so.
Scotch blend: Islay Mist De Luxe (eight-year-old), otherwise Teacher's.
Irish: Old Bushmills Black Label.
Rye: Old Overholt.
Bourbon: Old Forester.
Tennessee sour mash: Jack Daniel's.
Canadian: Seagram's VO.

BEST BRANDY

There are all sorts of brandy, from applejack, which is apple brandy, to slivo-vitz, distilled from plums. But grape brandy is best, and there are all sorts of that, too, including the Iranian Grande Champagne Cognac Impériale, made by Ararat Limited and smelling – and tasting – like those chocolate creams that have crystallized violets on top.

The best grape brandy is cognac, and the best cognac commercially obtain-able is Delamain Pale and Dry – pale, because aged as long as any good liqueur cognac, and longer than most, in old casks that have lost most of their colour and their tannin, and big enough to offer less wood to more brandy than is usual. Dry, because not especially sweetened – a delicate digestif that has recon-ciled me to many a dinner in restaurants wise enough to know, at any rate, that good brandy can do something to make up for a bad cook.

BEST CHAMPAGNE

Idle to pretend that, of all the many delicious champagnes with famous names, Bollinger doesn't hold a special place in my affections: I once wrote a whole (unsponsored) book about the blissful beverage. In it I was able to record that I am the only begetter of what is now available – in small quantities and at a high price – as Bollinger Vieilles Vignes Françaises.

It happened thus. Ten years ago, I was shown the firm's two tiny vineyards that had withstood the phylloxera plague of a century ago. The blight was eventually conquered by grafting the classic European vines on to resistant American root stock, but here and there minute pockets of ungrafted vines still flourish, and Bollinger's are the only such in all Champagne – *vieilles vignes françaises.*

These grapes had always been included in the usual Bollinger blends, but I suggested that in suitable years their yield should be kept separate and made into a unique pre-phylloxera, *blanc de noirs* champagne. The vineyards are in the black-grape region of Champagne, so this new-old wine is a white wine made entirely from black grapes, whereas the classic champagne is a blend of black and white, and this is why the colour is deeper than that of other Boll-ingers – a greater richness of gold, with almost a suspicion of pink in the depths, and immense roundness and flavour, making it one of the few champagnes big enough to go with food as well as being a superb aperitif, a champagne for all seasons.

BEST RED WINE

Claret, for me, rather than burgundy, and the best claret I have tasted in the twelve months up to the time of writing has been the Cheval Blanc 1960 – a year generally considered rather light but, as Cheval Blanc is always full and flavoury, this has meant perfect balance and the staying power to make it still a mouth-filling miracle after the best part of twenty years.

'*What are IBM, Xerox and ITT drinking these days, Jack?*'

For a dessert red, then certainly the Taylor's 1955 for those who like port. I wish I had some in my cellar: I'd sell it, and buy brandy.

BEST WHITE WINE

Loire wines are crisper than hocks, lighter than burgundies and less earthy than the white Bordeaux – a Muscadet with the *appellation* 'de Sevre et Maine' goes uncommonly well with fish and shellfish, and the Château de la Galissionnière is a reliable example.

For a dessert white, Beaumes de Venise, from near Châteauneuf du Pape – sweet, orange-golden rather than truly 'white', which is to say colourless; with an intensely rich fragrance and flavour of the muscat grape it comes from, yet less unctuously cloying than the great Sauternes such as Yquem or a German *trockenbeerenauslesen*, and a great deal cheaper. The Galissionnière is cheap, too.

BEST SHERRY

Before dinner: Duke of Wellington Fino, failing which, La Ina.
After dinner: Don Zoilo Very Old Cream, which stands up better than port does to tobacco smoke, which is more than I do.

BEST BARS

There is no standing up at the Nicols Bar of the Café Royal, which may disqualify it as a bar in some eyes, but it suits me – I can have a drink, which takes a load off my mind, sitting down, which takes a load off my feet. David, head barman there, is an ingenious composer of subtly mixed drinks, too. But Nicols Bar is in London W1, whereas the bar of the Gritti Palace Hotel is on the Grand Canal, which brings it in an easy winner.

BEST BARMEN

David, at Nicols Bar – see above – is a creative artist with a cocktail shaker; Giuseppe Fontana, at the Gritti, has a singularly sympathetic manner and an extensive knowledge of the highways and byways – by which I mean the waterways – of Venice.

However, when Brooks's Club absorbed the St James's, it acquired not only a remarkable collection of eighteenth-century portraits but also Johnny, its barman for almost thirty years and worth the lot of them: he has the most welcoming smile I have ever seen on a barman's face, and it turns every drink into the equivalent of a double.

BEST HANGOVER CURES

At that civilized and companionable West End watering-hole, Jules Bar, there is a special 'Pick You Up' list from which, at eleven in the morning onwards, the morning-afterers of St James's may have their faith in divine beneficence restored by a Jules Reviver, a Wake Up and Die, or a Heart Starter.

The recipe for this last sounds terrible – gin, water and liver salts (Andrew's, say the cognoscenti, not Eno's) – but looks like a gin-and-tonic and is quite palatable, though a slice of lemon wouldn't come amiss. I think that its virtue as a hair of the dog is that the mere thought of it – or perhaps the crashing chords of effervescence – shocks the victim into sobriety before his trembling hand has even raised the glass. Ought to be available on NHS.

FILMS

◆

Alexander Walker

BEST FILM (RECENT) *Dr Strangelove or How I Learned To Stop Worrying and Love the Bomb*
(Dir. Stanley Kubrick: Britain, 1963). The largely unimaginable prospect of the extinction of the human race is turned into the satirical embodiment of its leaders' collective madness. Kubrick's *Dr Strangelove* is the most brilliantly conceived and executed post-war movie. The quality of its ideas and the speculations they set up in the appalled mind are extended and transformed into so many Jonsonian characters and evolving climaxes, so many Swiftian connections with man's generative urge to destroy himself, that the film can be approached from many points of view – farcical, semantic ('I'm not saying we wouldn't get our hair mussed. I am only saying ten to twenty million people killed, tops, depending on the breaks'), factual, nuclear. Yet like all truly great works, it gives an impression of perfect proportions.

BEST FILM (PAST) *Citizen Kane*
(Dir. Orson Welles: USA, 1941). In 1962 and again in 1972, this was the film that came top of the list of 'Bests' organized by the British critical quarterly *Sight and Sound*. Nearly one hundred of the world's critics voted. Innovative in its narrative techniques, its deep-focus photography, its ensemble acting by a company who had been stage- and microphone-trained to collective perfection, it was given superhuman dimension by Welles's own portrait of Charles Foster Kane the flawed genius – a role that Welles kept trying on for size on

screen and off in the years since. Herman Mankiewicz's hand in the script is now judged to be the guiding one, but Welles's is the line of fate imprinted on it.

BEST MALE PERFORMANCE *Marlon Brando in Last Tango in Paris*
(Dir. Bernardo Bertolucci : France/Italy, 1972). Until it opens out into the titular dance of death, this movie is an oppressively physical account of two (at first) nameless people pulled into genuine intimacy by their attempt at mutual degradation. Its audacious theme is matched by Brando's greatest performance. 'I suffer, therefore I am' may have been the dramatic rationale behind it; but he showed in his face the suffering in his guts – and more. He stripped himself figuratively nakèd to relate his own life and movie times to the washed-up Hemingway hero on the screen. The character melted into Brando the way – if one dare risk such a metaphor in such a film – that butter melts into its dish.

BEST FEMALE PERFORMANCE *Greta Garbo in Camille*
(Dir. George Cukor : USA, 1936). No other actress in one single film could range through the whole spectrum of womanhood and still keep the romantic line of her performance intact. Garbo was so unbelievably good in almost every film, even the most trumpery vehicle, that it's hard to come down on one performance alone – but *Camille* is not only her best film, it is her most dazzlingly elusive piece of acting, an imperfect human being who can laminate together the spiritual and the sexual without the join showing. 'So much heart, so little sense,' says her rich protector played by Henry Daniell (who, incidentally, was almost the only actor apart from Boyer able to abstract your eyes from Garbo in a scene with her). But he is wrong. She makes a perfectly balanced equation of heart and sense. And as for playing dead at the end – people swear they have seen, yes *seen*, the last breath go out of her body.

BEST CHILD PERFORMANCE *Shirley Temple in Bright Eyes*
(Dir. David Butler, USA, 1934). A few years ago it was smart and camp to mention Shirley Temple's name – people did it who couldn't even mention a film she'd made. But even that awful word 'moppet' can't extinguish retrospective recognition of her professionalism as a sort of miniaturized adult whose oddly gruff voice strained the cuteness out of her parts. In this film she played an orphan adopted by a flier who bails out of his plane with her clutched to his chest. But what's remembered is not her safe descent (never in doubt) but her rendering of 'The Good Ship Lollipop'. Hollywood gave her a special Academy Award in 1934, when she was only five, something it usually keeps for stars who are so old and enfeebled (like Chaplin) that they can hardly make it to the rostrum. The next day, Shirley put Oscar among her dolls – she knew its worth and where it belonged.

BEST COMEDIAN *Woody Allen*

He can distil pity out of misanthropy, make contact out of alienation – and a joke out of anything. Allen is the cinema's comic polymath who writes, acts, directs his films and carries more *schticks* (stand-up comic, monologuist, short-story writer) with which to chastise society than there are in a lictor's bundle. He is hilarious from the starting position – the long-distance runner of contemporary social comedy.

BEST COMEDIENNE *Mae West*

There is just no way round the fact that Mae West created herself more fully and lastingly than any other female talent in films. She was self-made and self-sustaining, a creative force in almost every department of her movies. Probably fewer women would agree with this choice than men. She is still the living embodiment of what a man regards as a 'good sport' whose ribald wisecracks can moderate into comedy what would otherwise be diagnosed as a raging case of nymphomania. She is at her very best in *I'm No Angel*, which came just before Hollywood censorship done her wrong and contains some of her best quips such as, 'It's not the men in your life, it's the life in your men that counts' and 'When I'm good, I'm very good. But when I'm bad, I'm better'.

BEST MONSTER FILM *King Kong*

(Dirs. Ernest B. Schoedsack and Merian C. Cooper: USA, 1933). There may have been more horrific, more realistic, more destructive monsters, but King Kong remains one of the great seminal myths of the movies as well as one of its most unforgettable sights. It is also an allegory of the movie-world as well as the jungle. Not by accident is the super-gorilla imprisoned by a Hollywood movie crew for the entertainment of the mob back home – beneath the tumultuous melodrama is the theme of the slave-actor kept in captivity so long as he accepted the ritual humiliations of the front office. But of course everyone loves Kong for the havoc he creates. Though today's special effects are more 'perfect' the creature's juddering progress by stop-action photography is nearer how we actually see things (or, rather, Things) in nightmare – which is why the simian monster with its suppressed sexuality stirs us to apprehension long after the sight of it has left the retina.

BEST SAGA FILM *The Apu Trilogy*

(Dir. Satyajit Ray: India, 1950–59). Humanism, lyricism and the ring of truth accompany a Bengali family from the village to the city, from childhood to early manhood. Three great films (*Pather Panchali*, *Aparajito* and *Apur Sansar* or *The World of Apu*) combine into a saga that brought India to the world screen – an achievement that outranks such contenders as Flaherty's *Nanook of the North* or Donskoi's *Maxim Gorki Trilogy* or Visconti's *La Terra Trema*, about the daily toil of Sicilian fisherfolk. *The Apu Trilogy* is also the best human document initiated, albeit inadvertently, by a government department, the West Bengal Bureau for Road Improvement, which thought it appropriate to be involved because the title *Pather Panchali* meant 'The Song of the Little Road'.

BEST SHOWBUSINESS FILM *A Star is Born*
(Dir. George Cukor: USA, 1954). This is the supreme example of Hollywood managing its own myth for public consumption. Maybe the 1937 version with Gaynor and March showed a more callous, exploitative, blameworthy side of fame and ruin in the movie colony; but Garland and Mason, as the rising and falling stars in this celebration of celluloid rites, perform impeccably at their respective ends of the see-saw and her 'Born in a Trunk' mini-musical remains the best catch-in-the-throat proclamation of what showbusiness is believed (by those not in it) to be all about.

BEST SCREEN MUSICAL *Gigi*
(Dir. Vincente Minnelli: USA, 1958). The last great Hollywood musical to be written directly for the screen (by Lerner and Loewe), this is a marvellous blending of wit, style, ingenuity and fidelity to its source in Colette whose dialogue is frequently preserved unchanged. A mere passing mention in the story to an elderly *boulevardier* results in Chevalier's vintage performance. Charm, elegance and Cecil Beaton's consummate period-pieces, plus a tolerant hedonism rare in an American movie, with or without music, are assets that time doesn't waste or repetition stale.

BEST DANCE FILM *Top Hat*
(Dir. Mark Sandrich: USA, 1935). 'Of all the Astaire-Rogers films,' wrote dance critic Arlene Croce, '*Top Hat* and *Swing Time* come closest to the level of the magnificent numbers they contain.' 'Top Hat, White Tie and Tails', 'Cheek to Cheek', 'The Piccolino' are three of the most famous numbers in cinema, rhythmically inventive compositions (by Irving Berlin as well as Astaire) that flow without pause; and the film's air of 'dolce far niente purposelessness' gives it an innocence that makes the 1930s seem, as Croce said, an era in which people never changed out of evening dress.

BEST PROPAGANDA FILM *Triumph of the Will*
(Dir. Leni Riefenstahl: Germany, 1934). The category 'best', it should be prudently observed, knows no morality. Although this account of the Nuremberg Rally is shot through and through with thunderous intimations of the Nazi Apocalypse, from Hitler arriving like a god in his aircraft to the masses sliding towards him with uplifted arms like a human moraine on the move, its orchestration of totalitarian power makes it a force to be reckoned with still, while the 'set dressing' of crowds, monuments, and Führer gives an effective lie to the

'But I don't want to see a truthful little film shot with a hand-held camera. I want to see a big lying movie made with the latest sophisticated equipment.'

belief that evil must be banal. *Pace* Hannah Arendt, here it is absolutely stunning.

BEST WESTERN *Red River*
(Dir. Howard Hawks: USA, 1948). With a heart sinking into one's cowboy boots, one has to pass over the claims of *Stagecoach*, *Shane*, *High Noon* and *The Searchers* and pick a picture that has virtually everything that makes a classic Western except, alas, John Ford as director. Here are cattle stampedes, epic scenery, Indian battles, gunfights and a father-versus-son relationship to give it true grit. Fortunately Wayne plays the father-figure – to have a 'Best Western' without him would be inviting trouble into town.

BEST FANTASY *Orphée*
(Dir. Jean Cocteau : France, 1949). It also manages to be one of the most poetic
films of all time : a marvellous use of contemporary emblems, images and artefacts, most of them from the immediate European post-war period, to embody
the eternal self-questioning of a poet who tries to penetrate the mystery beyond
mortality. Cocteau's trick effects, like the mirror of mercury which yields to
the touch, are less enduring than the whole *apparat* of timeless legend, or one
shot of Maria Casares's haunting figure of *soignée* Death.

BEST SURPRISE TWIST IN A MOVIE
The moment when the four burglars rob a jewellery store in *Rififi* (Dir. Jules
Dassin : France, 1955) and solve the problem of the falling plaster by thrusting
an umbrella through the hole they're making in the jeweller's ceiling – and
opening it.

BEST SCARE ON THE SCREEN
'Unexpectedness' has to be an essential part of this, though the fright ought
not to lose its power entirely on a second or more viewings. The moment when
the convict Magwitch grabs Pip at the start of *Great Expectations* : the sudden
rearing up of the shark in *Jaws* : the horrible moment at the end of *Carrie* (the
placing of the scare is vital and audiences are at their most vulnerable at the
end of a picture when they expect nothing more to happen) when the arm comes
out of the grave to snatch in the living ... all these are candidates. But the
winner must surely be the shower-bath sequence in *Psycho* (Dir. Alfred Hitchcock : USA, 1960), as it is not only sudden, horrifying and punctuated by Bernard
Herrmann's piercing shrieks of music which nail it to one's aural memory, but
it is also totally unexpected to see the person one had presumed to be the co-
star of the picture despatched so ruthlessly and so early.

BEST RELIGIOUS FILM *The Gospel According to St Matthew*
(Dir. Pier-Paolo Pasolini : Italy, 1964). The finest screen life of Christ yet
filmed, differing from all the others not only in its insistence on neo-realistic
personages and places, but because it is the only one to convey the feeling
that the people in it have not read the Bible before shooting began. To make
such a film, one has to put nearly 2,000 years of history behind one – which
is why such a film seldom gets made. It may have helped Pasolini that he was
a Marxist : his decline as a moviemaker began when he moved from the sacred
to the profane, but in this film he got the equation just right.

BEST FLASHBACK FILM *Rashomon*
(Dir. Akira Kurosawa : Japan, 1951). Not only one of the greatest films to come
out of the East, and the one that opened the West's eyes to the new cinema
there, but the best film to use its flashbacks for moral or metaphysical investiga-

tion and not just to construct a story. By continuously reconstructing a crime through the accounts of four people, the film demonstrates the truth that there is no 'truth' – what can one ever be sure of?

BEST THEME MUSIC *The Third Man*
Anton Karas's zither plucking at the nerves in *The Third Man* (Dir. Carol Reed: Britain, 1949) – it made the whole *film noir* resonate with impersonal evil.

BEST MYSTERY FILM *The Big Sleep*
(Dir. Howard Hawks: USA, 1946). This *must* be the 'best' of its kind, because it is a certified fact that Hawks admitted well after he had finished the film that 'neither the author (Raymond Chandler), nor the writer (William Faulkner et al), nor myself, knew who had killed whom'. It is the most byzantine plot ever committed to celluloid: a 'private eye' adventure in the night-city with monstrous aberrations in human form appearing at every corner of the mean streets down which Bogart goes. It also represents Bogart's apotheosis into trench-coated knight-errant.

BEST DOCUMENTARY *Man of Aran*
(Dir. Robert Flaherty: Britain, 1934). Anything with 'weather' in it gets tagged with the 'epic' label – but this account of islanders only a few miles from civilization, yet living on the bare subsistence of what they gather on the rocks and from the sea, has that quality. The sea possesses them without being able to extinguish them and a mode of film-making matches a way of life by its simplicity, endurance and courage. It is what every great documentary should be: a record transmuted by the recorder.

BEST ART FILM *Le Mystère Picasso*
(Dir. Henri-Georges Clouzot: France, 1956). Most 'art' films are stately peregrinations of finished pictures/sculptures/buildings, etc. Clouzot invented a method of demonstrating the artist at work by having Picasso use the screen as his canvas and paint directly on to it or on to a huge sheet of glass, so that the quality of the artist's mind becomes visible at the same time as the artist's eye and hand render it tangible.

BEST ANIMATED FILM (CHILDREN)
Snow White may be the cartoon that most people recall with special fondness, especially those old enough to have seen it when it first came out. But *Pinocchio* represents the high point of Disney's dazzling draftsmanship – it has more adventure, spectacle, plot ingenuity and animatable characters, and the great sequence when Pinocchio is swallowed by Monstro the whale outdoes anything else Disney designed before or after.

BEST ANIMATED FILM (ADULTS) *Heavy Traffic*
(Dir. Ralph Bakshi: USA, 1973). Picaresque social satire that got an 'X' (for eighteen-year-olds and over) in Britain on the grounds of the language and conduct of the cartoon characters – a dazzlingly limned cross-section of Manhattan ethnic types in which near-human animals and near-animalesque humans act out their kinky life-styles and real locations blend into cartooned ones. It is a cleverer film, and a more splenetic one, than Bakshi's earlier *Fritz the Cat*, a scatalogical satire of the underground culture based on Robert Crumb's comic strip.

BEST SHORT CARTOON *The Sand Castle*
(Dir. Co Hoedeman: Canada, 1977). Strictly speaking not a cartoon at all, but a stop-action *jeu d'esprit* in which bizarre shapes, discomfitingly like post-atomic mutations, form themselves out of sand and constantly alter appearance as incestuous and even cannibalistic traits develop in their tribe. It runs thirteen minutes, but it's as if Hieronymus Bosch had taken to playing on the beach.

BEST ANTI-WAR FILM *All Quiet on the Western Front*
(Dir. Lewis Milestone: USA, 1930). *Dr Strangelove* musters laughter as the antidote to the *folie de grandeur* that is nuclear war. In simpler, human terms this film recruits the immense power of post-war pathos to back up its pacifist message that war is waste – though as Pauline Kael has shrewdly remarked, war is always waste when it's told from the losers' point of view. But as the film has sometimes been banned in countries preparing to go to war, its resonance has outlasted the time (World War I) of its setting. As recently as 1978 it was the film that BBC TV chose to show on Armistice Day. It is the sense of waste it projects, rather than the 'madness' that later war epics like *Apocalypse Now* enshrine so vividly, which makes Milestone's ultimately a more moving experience than Coppola's.

BEST SCREEN GRAND GUIGNOL *Les Diaboliques*
(Dir. Henri-Georges Clouzot: France, 1955). Wife and mistress conspire to murder the headmaster of a seedy boys' boarding school – out of such a 'simple' plot unravels a particularly cold-blooded piece of sensationalism – a *crime de passion* which is also a *crime perverse*. The shot of the body getting out of the bath-tub is one of the queasiest in all cinema.

BEST SCREEN PETIT GUIGNOL *The Incredible Shrinking Man*
(Dir. Jack Arnold: USA, 1957). A man mysteriously shrinks in size till he finds his cosy domestic world of home and garden is full of hazards and horrors. Small may indeed be beautiful: but in this case it is terrifying. The film has a quality of loneliness and pathos rare in the genre.

BEST SF FILM *2001: A Space Odyssey*
(Dir. Stanley Kubrick: Britain, 1968). Spanning man's birth from the apes to his re-birth as a star child, this is the best science-fiction film to date. Its special effects are impeccable and beautiful: parts of the film, with the hardware orbiting in space, resemble an art gallery of the future. It puts awe of space in place of religious deity, yet reminds us how today's superstitions can become tomorrow's scientific facts. It also has the most memorable voice ever attached to a sentient being who is not quite human – HAL 9000, the mutinous computer. To seal so many tricks inside a fantastic envelope provides the satisfaction that the deliberately enigmatic ending denies us.

BEST SPORTS FILM *Downhill Racer*
(Dir. Michael Ritchie: USA, 1969). The making of a skier American-style. Starring Robert Redford, the film generated the same sort of obsession that winners must have – it also showed how near a winner can come to being a loser. A record is no sooner set than it is vulnerable: a champ is no sooner crowned than his head turns to hear the pursuing challenger.

BEST ALL-STAR FILM *Around The World in Eighty Days*
(Dir. Michael Anderson: USA, 1956). Forty-four all-star cameo roles, plus David Niven as Jules Verne's globetrotting hero Phineas Fogg, managed to fill producer Mike Todd's giant 70 mm screen without it looking underpopulated. It won an Academy Award as the year's Best Picture.

BEST ROMANTIC DRAMA *Gone With The Wind*
(Dir. Victor Fleming: USA, 1939). A romance of the American Civil War, this is one of the most happily cast films ever made as well as (for a long time anyhow) one of the longest (220 minutes). It was made at a time when Hollywood was absolutely confident where the audience was – and it shows in the tremendous certainty of the romantic blend. A remake is sometimes threatened and a sequel is in preparation; but the original *Wind*, in terms of sheer volume of people who have seen it, will always blow the strongest. And as the natural process of mortality seals off the stars from any fear of competition, their scarcity value as the full-flowering of the Hollywood system becomes apparent.

BEST ANIMAL STAR *Lassie*
Actually, Lassie's real sex was male, but the intelligent collie, represented by different dogs in different pictures since the first *Lassie Come Home* (1942), has consistently defeated all other canine challengers for the hearts and minds of dog-lovers.

BEST FILM TRAILER *Psycho*
(Dir. Alfred Hitchcock: USA, 1960). A marvellous example of fuelling the

audience's 'must see' desires by denying them satisfaction. It consists of Hitchcock taking film-goers through the set of the Old Dark House and hinting at the horrible happenings, without actually specifying what they are.

Best Comedy *The Gold Rush*
(Dir. Charlie Chaplin: USA, 1925). There are other claims for preferring the humanity and sweetness of the Tramp and his foundling child in *The Kid*, which contains so much of Chaplin's childhood as well as his maturity, but for sheer inventiveness in the genre of transforming the nature of things (the stewed boot that becomes a fish, its laces that turn into spaghetti) as well as the romantic longing of the Little Fellow (the lonely 'Dance of the Rolls' performed while waiting for his girl) and all set against a society that is (like Charlie) rootless but (unlike him) getting rich quick – then this is Chaplin's masterpiece. Purists will prefer Buster Keaton's *The General*, which cleaves to a subtler form of visual comedy altogether, but hasn't the resonant universality of this or half-a-dozen others of Chaplin's.

Best Nature Film *The Great Adventure*
(Dir. Arne Sucksdorff: Sweden, 1955). Oddly, and contradictorily, Nature looks her best in black and white, not colour – and this is one of the great evocations of the tones as well as the shapes of wildlife. It is also one of the finest 'wait and see' movies, where an infinity of patience has been expended to get the shot of fox, lynx, otter and others. Cartier-Bresson, who cultivated such 'moments', might have done just this had his pictures moved.

Best Horror Film *The Texas Chain Saw Massacre*
(Dir. Tobe Hooper: USA, 1974). The most authentic piece of Gothic horror in modern American cinema. An orgy of violence inflicted by meat cleaver and chain saw in a backwoods community of degenerates, it also manages to be a shudder-making comment on how some countries define themselves by their crimes – in this case, mass murder for a land that invented the factory production line. It is also one of the few films whose sound is frightening – the harsh, grating screech of the portable chain saw pursuing the victims through the undergrowth is the phobia of the dentist's drill – it strikes our nerve the same way.

Best Humanist Picture *Earth*
(Dir. Alexander Dovzhenko: USSR, 1930). The everyday story of country folk transposed into what critic Jay Leda called 'the philosophical sense of "the earth" or life and death' by a deep feeling for natural images and their connecting rhythms. Where other children of the Russian Revolution created an increasingly arid authoritarianism, Dovzhenko's own peasant origins maintained his view of man rooted in the element that gives him his living and his meaning.

BEST SCREEN SPECTACULAR *Ben-Hur*
(Dir. Fred Niblo: USA, 1925). Made with Herculean efforts in Europe and Hollywood, and at Babylonian expense, this version is superior to the 1959 one. Special effects in the 1920s had been perfected, scenic design was at its apogee, and somehow the sheer *movement* of silent cinema lent itself to the delineation of such spectacular highlights as the chariot race and the battle of the galleys. Acting is in the grand manner, which suits the turbulent fresco of Christian-Roman times better than the interior subtleties of the William Wyler remake. 'Nothing like it had ever been seen,' wrote historian Kevin Brownlow, 'nothing like it has ever been.'

BEST LAST LINE IN A FILM
It depends whether you are going for drama or comedy or romance. A really successful last line is one that makes its instant effect when heard, sums up the whole theme or mood of the movie, yet can be detached from the sound track and used by the myna-bird fans to recall the experience. Contenders are 'Mother of mercy ["God" was banned by the production code] is this the end of Rico?' from Edward G. Robinson as he lies dying in *Little Caesar* (1930); 'Oh, Jerry we have the stars, let's not ask for the moon', from Bette Davis in *Now Voyager* (1942); 'All right, Mr De Mille, I'm ready for my close-up' from Gloria Swanson in *Sunset Boulevard* (1950); and 'Mein Führer, I can walk' from Peter Sellers in *Dr Strangelove* (1963). But perhaps the quip-iest, pithiest last line that never fails to rouse a roar of laughter from audiences seized of its sexual ambiguities is Joe E. Brown's cheerful remark to Jack Lemmon who's just confessed at the end of *Some Like It Hot* (1959) that he's a man in drag and thus hardly an eligible wife – 'Nobody's perfect.'

BEST CREDITS DESIGN *A Walk on the Wild Side*
(Designer: Saul Bass: USA, 1962). Though his animated designs – the dismembered body for *Anatomy of a Murder*, the hinged dome of Congress in *Advise and Consent* – show him to be a master of the visual logo, it is with the design of the credits sequence for *A Walk on the Wild Side* that Saul Bass showed his flair for seizing the essence of a film (or what should be the essence). Simply a cat padding langorously along, its movements melting into each other with sensuous sureness. Everyone remembers the cat, nobody recalls the film.

BEST THEME SONG *Three Coins in the Fountain*
To be fair, one must exclude songs sung in films by the already famous vocalists and try for one that succinctly – or saccharinously – sums up what a film offers. The winner must be *Three Coins in the Fountain* (1954), which not only encouraged Hollywood to trek to exotic locations the world over, but established in the hearts and pockets of every tourist in Rome that the Fountain of Trevi was as indispensable a place of pilgrimage as the Vatican.

BEST SCREEN ADAPTATION OF A STAGE PLAY *Henry V*
(Dir. Laurence Olivier: Britain, 1944). It took the Shakespeare play and
extended it in three ways. One was a documentary recreation of what its production may have been like in the conditions of the Globe Theatre; another pushed
the relative crudities of the stage acting into the subtleties of Shakespeare's
verse married to screen dimensions; and the third, with the prelude to battle
around the campfire and the marvellously choreographed Battle of Agincourt
itself, took off into purely cinematic realms. No other adapter of Shakespeare
has managed to preserve respect for the text with such imaginative innovation
in the form.

BEST COMPILATION FILM *Hitler: A Career*
(Dir. Joachim Fest: West Germany, 1977). The best account yet of the sheer
charisma that allowed Hitler to rise to power. Based on the director's own biography, it used much hitherto unseen material from Goebbels's propaganda
archives which revealed not only how the great set-pieces of the Nazi era were
prefabricated but allowed a close-up of the Führer that took us into the man's
pores. It could, with justice, be called Close Encounters of the Third Reich.

BEST HISTORICAL FILM *La Prise de Pouvoir Par Louis XIV*
(Dir. Roberto Rossellini: France, 1963). A rigorously detailed, authenticated
reconstruction of the way Louis XIV put himself in a position of unchallengeable
authority over his court and courtiers. It was devoid of all theatricality, yet
remained engrossingly true to its subject's life and times. Financed originally
by French television, it has since achieved an independent life where it belongs,
on the cinema screen.

FOOD

◆

Clement Freud

BEST BANQUET
Best I have come across was at Hintlesham Hall, near Ipswich ... where they specialize in olde Englishe food beautifully and authentically served. The Savoy Hotel, London, is the only place where the banqueting department can cope with cheese soufflés for a thousand people.

BEST HAMBURGERS
The Elephant in San Francisco not only serves the best Hamburgers ... but serves a selection of classic French sauces like Béarnaise and Robert to go with them. In Europe, The Great American Disaster, Fulham Road, is possibly the best ... try Joe Allen's in Les Halles, Paris. There are some who feel that the secret is to mix ground beef with a little yoghurt ... and let the mixture stand.

BEST ICE CREAM
If there is a better mass produced ice cream than Baskin and Robbins, it would be good to know. On a national scale, Italian ices are the best in Europe.

BEST HOSTESS
If she exists, I am not on her list.

BEST SANDWICH
An artists' café in Cumaplatz, Vienna, serves the freshest rye bread spread with

'It's a great idea for a restaurant. Now if we
could only get them to pay ...'

the thickest application of butter upon which they pile the ripest Camembert
cheese, thinly sliced Mediterranean tomatoes and a lot of fresh chives.

BEST BREAD
Any Montmartre bakery ... preferably the one that has the longest queue.

BEST RECIPE
Whatever works best when you try it.

BEST RESTAURANT
The best restaurant is the one in which they know you best. In an effort to
find the all-time best restaurant in the world, an inspector was sent to Malagasy
from where we had had excellent reports. He has not returned.

BEST COOK BOOK
The Radiation Cook Book given away with pre- and just post-war gas cookers.
Factual, accurate and all-embracing. For style, try Elizabeth David (or me).

BEST BREAKFAST
At the lower end of the market, transport cafés; order coffee and bacon sand-
wiches. Roses at Ingatestone on the A12 and the caff at Scotch Corner on
the A1 are particularly recommended.
    The Connaught Hotel in Carlos Place, London W1, serves the best and most
expensive stylish breakfast. Try fresh orange juice, papayas in syrup, grapenuts
and cream with bananas before you go for pheasant kedgeree or mixed grill.
Beware of Brennans in New Orleans.

BEST CHEF
The best chef is the one who cooks in the best restaurant q.v. (Could he really
be Malagasian?)

BEST PORK PIE
Justin de Blank, London SW1.

BEST SNAILS
Thornbury Castle, Gloucester.

BEST CHELSEA BUN
Sagnes in Marylebone High Street, London, who also have the best Mont
Blancs, which is a confection made of puréed marron glacé flavoured with
liqueur, meringue and whipped cream.

BEST SMOKED FISH
Pinney's of Orford in Suffolk.

BEST SMOKED SALMON
Barnett's of Frying Pan Alley, London E1.

BEST SMOKED STURGEON
The Aviz Restaurant in Rua Serpa Tinta, Lisbon.

BEST KIPPERS
Isle of Man airport.

BEST MARMALADE AND JAMS
Elsenham Products.

BEST HAGGIS
I can never tell the difference between Haggis and Harris tweed.

BEST ENGLISH CHEESE
Blue Cheshire (Farmhouse).

BEST ITALIAN CHEESE
Dolcelatte.

BEST FRENCH CHEESE
Caprice de Dieu.

BEST FOOD DEPARTMENT
Harrods, London SW1.

BEST PRIVATE GROCER
Paxton and Whitfield, Jermyn Street, London SW1 ... who also sell the best
sausages (English variety). Saucisson de Toulouse is the best French sausage;
Feinste Bratwurst the best German.

BEST HOTEL
The best *appointed* hotel is the Lancaster in Paris.

BEST LOBSTER DISHES
The Hotel Bakoua in Martinique.

BEST GAME DISHES
Wilton's in St James', London SW1.

BEST HORS D'OEUVRES TROLLEY
L'Etoile, Charlotte Street, London W1.

BEST BEER
Adnams of Southwold, Suffolk.

BEST COCKTAIL
Bellini at Harry's Bar in Rome, made of fresh peaches and champagne.

BEST CHAMPAGNE
Louis Roederer's Crystal Brut.

BEST MINERAL WATER
San Pellegrino.

BEST SOFT DRINK
Vittel Framboise.

BEST EAU DE VIE
Poire William.

BEST BRANDY
Delamain.

BEST WHISKY (MALT)
Clynelish 95° proof.

BEST WHISKY (SCOTCH)
Chivas Regal twenty years old.

BEST WHISKY (RYE)
Overcroft 100° proof.

BEST RUM
Jamaican overproof (known on the island as 'Be rude to your mother-in-law').

BEST HANGOVER CURE
Fernet Branca mixed with crème de menthe and shaken with ice.

BEST BAR
Not the one on Liverpool Street Station, London.

BEST OLIVES
Come from Egypt.

BEST ALMONDS
From Majorca.

BEST SALT
From the Maldon Salt Company of Maldon, Essex.

BEST SAUSAGE
Made by mincing 2 lb of leg of pork when the pig has just been killed and the meat is still warm. Add 10 oz hard pork fat, minced; $\frac{1}{2}$ bottle of champagne and a quarter teaspoon of white pepper. Fill into casings and brush with melted butter before grilling under a very low flame.

BEST SUMMER LUNCH
Freshly baked wholemeal bread, unsalted butter. Parma ham, black figs, Egyp-

tian black olives, pâté of smoked eel; freshly grated horse-radish, peeled Mediterranean tomatoes sliced and dressed with olive oil, lemon juice, rock salt and fresh basil; wild strawberry tarts, fresh cream; Framboise eau de vie, iced Provençale rosé, Château du Marquis de Selle.

BEST WINTER LUNCH
Oysters Rockerfeller, fillet of lamb baked in pastry, Chanterelle mushrooms, pommes salardines, soufflé of Parmesan cheese.

BEST SUPPER
Baked potatoes stuffed with Beluga caviar and sour cream.

BEST SUMMER DRINK
Pimm's Number One made with champagne where they tell you to use lemonade ... and a measure of apricot brandy per glass where they don't tell you to add anything at all.

BEST CHRISTMAS PUDDING
The best Christmas puddings are bought from Marks and Spencers, ideally a year ahead. To make them even better, flare pudding in brandy and serve with brandy butter and lightly beaten double cream spiked with ground ginger.

BEST SAVOURY
Devils on horseback: prunes soaked in port until almost tender; then wrapped in streaky bacon and grilled. Serve on slices of white bread crisply fried in olive oil. Angels on horseback are oysters wrapped in streaky bacon grilled and served similarly.

BEST DRINK TO TAKE TO BOTTLE PARTY
Your favourite single malt whisky ... and take a candle which you insert and light when you have opened the bottle. (Somehow no-one ever expects anything drinkable to be in a bottle which has a candle stuck in its neck.)

Law and Crime

Fenton Bresler

BEST JUDGE
Solomon, third king of all Israel, son and successor of David, reigning from *c.* 970–931 BC and, to all lawyers' shame, he wasn't even a lawyer.

BEST REASON FOR NOT BECOMING A JUDGE
'I would rather talk to the damned fools than listen to them.' – Philadelphia lawyer John C. Johnson, quoted by Martin Mayer in his 1966 book *The Lawyers*.

BEST EXAMPLE OF JUDICIAL WIT
Mr Justice Swift (1874–1937) in a 1935 High Court 'running down' action. A motorist was being cross-examined about what he first said when he realized he had caused an accident. He was embarrassed, did not want to say it in open court. 'Come now, my man,' said counsel. 'We are all men and women of the world here. What did you say?' The motorist replied, 'Well, I said "I'll be buggered!"' 'What did you mean by that?' persisted counsel. 'It's very simple, Mr Robinson,' interposed the judge. 'He was taken aback.' Regrettably we don't have judges like that any more.

BEST PHRASE COINED BY A JUDGE
'An Englishman's home is his castle.' – Sir Edward Coke (1552–1634), Lord Chief Justice of England in the reign of James I.

BEST ABSENT-MINDED JUDGE

1st Lord St Leonards (1781–1875), a British ex-Lord Chancellor who carried judicial absent-mindedness to the level of mislaying his own will so that when he died there was no available written record of his Lordship's last wishes. His unmarried daughter had been accustomed to read the will to him as he lay in bed every night, but her powers of recollection were no greater than her father's and when she tried to recite the will from memory in the witness-box, she could not get it right. Whereupon counsel had a brilliant notion and sipped his glass of water rather noisily, which reminded her of her aged father sipping his regular nightcap and brought back to her mind the exact terms of the will, which was thus duly able to be admitted to probate.

BEST MODERN EXAMPLE OF JUDICIAL IGNORANCE

It's a toss-up between Mr Justice Cantley, then aged sixty, in an October 1970 High Court case and Mr Justice Caulfield, then also sixty, in an October 1974 case. In the earlier case, when a QC said that a twenty-five-year-old man's sex life had been affected in a bulldozer accident, Cantley asked if the man was married. 'No,' replied the QC. 'Well, I can't see how it affects his sex life,' said the judge. In the later case, an ex-model was explaining why she could not get a Bunny Girl's job after being injured in a car crash. 'I have no boobs,' she said modestly. 'You have no what?' asked the judge. 'Breasts, my Lord,' explained counsel swiftly.

BEST STORY ABOUT AN OFTEN-APPEALED JUDGE

'My Lords, this is an appeal from a decision of Mr Justice Kekewich but I hasten to add that there are also other grounds of appeal,' said counsel rising to his feet in the Appeal Court in the early years of this century. Sir Arthur Kekewich (1832–1907), a High Court judge for twenty-one years until his death, still has the reputation among British legal *cognoscenti* of being the most often reversed judge ever to sit on the High Court Bench. 'Grandpa has been upheld in the Court of Appeal today! Isn't it wonderful?' is supposed to have been the reply of the judge's small grandchildren when once asked why they were having cream cakes and jelly for tea, even though it was no-one's birthday.

BEST HANGING JUDGE

Undoubtedly, *Sir Horace Avory* (1851–1935), who sat as a High Court judge for twenty-five years until his death at the age of eighty-four. The seeming relish with which the aged judge – known as ' 'angin' 'orace' because of his in-ability to pronounce his 'h's' – used to pronounce sentence of death in his high-pitched, reedy voice upon young prisoners sometimes a third or a quarter of his age was obvious to all those who saw him in action. Typical example of his style: in July 1922, before sentencing Thomas Henry Allaway, a young chauffeur, to death for the murder of a girl, he told him, 'The jury have found you guilty of a foul and brutal murder. Such a verdict can be followed only by one judgment – *that you also shall die!*'

BEST UNKIND REMARK BY A JUDGE
The punch line in a squabble between a Los Angeles judge and a long-haired attorney over fixing a trial date, related by Joseph C. Goulden in his 1974 book *The Benchwarmers*:

'I am not here to play games,' said the judge. 'I am not here to play games either,' retorted the attorney. 'Well, you look like it. From your looks, I can't tell whether you are a girl or a boy. Are you a man?' asked the judge.

'I think the moustache can reflect . . .,' began to reply the attorney. But the judge interrupted: 'I am talking about the long hair. I wasn't sure whether you were a man or a woman.'

'I don't know what proof your Honour requires,' said the attorney.

'Relax,' said the judge. 'You don't need to strip. I'd have had you take down your pants and resolve this question of gender once and for all, but judging from the way you look I'd have to rule there was not sufficient evidence to render a decision.'

BEST UNKIND REMARK BY JUDGE ABOUT OTHER JUDGES
By Samuel I. Rosenman, former judge and adviser to Presidents Roosevelt and Truman, speaking as President of the Association of the Bar of New York in October 1964: 'Let us face this sad fact that in many – far too many – instances, the benches of our courts in the United States are occupied by mediocrities – men of small talent, undistinguished in performance, technically deficient and inept.'

BEST UNKIND STORY ABOUT JUDGES
Told to the author in New York by a local attorney about one of the New York City judges who called in counsel to see him before the start of a highly contested commercial dispute and told them: 'I feel it only right to inform you that last night a representative of the plaintiff corporation came to see me with a bribe of $20,000. This morning a representative of the defendant corporation came to see me with a bribe of $25,000. Naturally, I have returned to the representative of the defendant corporation the sum of $5,000.'

BEST SHORT JUDGMENT BY A JUDGE
In a case at Whitechapel County Court a defendant was protesting to Judge Albert Rowland Cluer (1852–1942): 'As God is my judge, I did not take the money' – only for his Honour to rule: 'He's not. I am. You did.'

BEST PUT-DOWN OF COUNSEL BY JUDGE
A somewhat ponderous counsel was trying to discredit a witness and asked him, 'Are you a married man?' 'I am,' said the witness. 'How many children have

you got?' 'Two,' replied the witness. Counsel asked some more questions, then said with awesome solemnity 'You have two children, you say, and you are married?' – whereupon Mr Justice Darling (see above) could contain himself no longer and broke in: 'He told you he had two children a few moments ago. There are hardly likely to have been any fresh arrivals since your first question!'

Best Put-Down Of Judge By Counsel

The young and brilliant F.E. Smith, later to be the 1st Lord Birkenhead and Lord Chancellor (1872–1930), was appearing for a tramway company being sued by the father of a boy who had been run over and blinded. The county court judge was clearly showing his sympathy for the plaintiff: 'Poor boy, poor boy,' he said, 'stand him on a chair and let the jury see him.' 'F.E.', as everyone called him, bridled: 'Perhaps your Honour would like to have the boy passed round the jury box?' The judge: 'That is a most improper remark.' F.E.: 'It was provoked by a most improper suggestion.' The judge: 'Mr Smith, have you ever heard of a saying by Bacon, the great Bacon, that youth and discretion are ill-wedded companions?' 'I have,' retorted F.E., 'and have you ever heard the saying of Bacon, the great Bacon, that a much-talking judge is like an ill-tuned cymbal?' 'You are extremely offensive, young man,' spluttered the judge. 'As a matter of fact we both are,' replied F.E. languidly. 'The difference between us is that I am trying to be, and you can't help it.'

Best Definition Of A Lawyer

'A legal gentleman who rescues your estate from your enemies and keeps it himself.' – Lord Brougham (1778–1863), barrister, KC and later Lord Chancellor.

Best Piece Of Cross-Examination

By Sir Edward Marshall Hall, KC (1858–1927), in his successful 1907 Old Bailey defence of young artist Robert Wood on a charge of murdering prostitute Phyllis Dimmock. A prosecution witness had described a man he saw leaving the girl's lodgings soon after the murder and had later identified Wood. So –

> Marshall Hall: 'Did you describe the man as of stiff build with broad shoulders?'
> Witness: 'Yes.'
> Marshall Hall: 'Wood, stand up!'
> The accused rose in the dock, a slight figure with narrow shoulders.
> Marshall Hall: 'Now, do you describe that man as broad shouldered?'
> Witness: 'He looked broader with his overcoat on.'
> Marshall Hall: 'Then he shall wear it!'
> Wood put on his overcoat, and still looked a slight figure.
> Marshall Hall: 'Would you describe that man as broad shouldered?'
> Witness: 'He has broader shoulders than I have.'
> Marshall Hall: 'Would you call a bluebottle an elephant because it is bigger than a fly?'

Best Reply By Witness To Cross-Examining Counsel

By Oscar Wilde (1854–1900) on the first day of cross-examination by Edward
(later Lord) Carson (1854–1935) in April 1895 in Wilde's private prosecution
for criminal libel of the 8th Marquess of Queensberry for having left a card
at his club accusing him of 'posing as sodomite'. Carson, a heavy, dour man
with an uncompromising Northern Irish brogue, had been reading some of
Wilde's writings, with more obvious homosexual overtones, to him and inviting
his comments, and was now reading a private letter that Wilde had written
to Lord Alfred Douglas, nearly twenty years younger than him and Lord
Queensberry's son:

Carson: 'I can suggest for the sake of your reputation, that there is nothing
very wonderful in this "red rose-leaf lips of yours"?'
Wilde: 'A great deal depends on the way it is read.'
Carson: '"Your slim gilt soul walks between passion and poetry." Is that
a beautiful phrase?'
Wilde: 'Not as you read it, Mr Carson. You read it very badly.'
Touché. But alas ....

Best Question To Witness By Cross-Examining Counsel

By Edward Carson on the second day of his cross-examination. He was questioning Wilde about a succession of working-class young men, whom Wilde

'... *and this is your defence counsel!*'

had befriended and entertained, and the witness had had a great deal of fun with his adroit handling of the barbs. Wilde had become over-confident. So –

Carson: 'Do you know Walter Grainger?'

Wilde: 'Yes.'

Carson: 'How old is he?'

Wilde: 'He was about sixteen when I knew him. He was a servant at a certain house in High Street, Oxford, where Lord Alfred Douglas had rooms. I have stayed there several times. Grainger waited at table. I never dined with him. If it is one's duty to serve, it is one's duty to serve; and if it is one's pleasure to dine, it is one's pleasure to dine.'

Then suddenly out of the blue – Carson: *'Did you ever kiss him?'*

Wilde: 'Oh dear no. He was a peculiarly plain boy. He was, unfortunately, extremely ugly. I pitied him for it.'

And that was the give-away to Wilde's sexual appetites. Carson immediately followed: 'Was that the reason why you did not kiss him?' 'Oh, Mr Carson, you are pertinently insolent!' replied Wilde weakly, assuredly realizing the damage he had done. Carson now persisted: 'Did you say that in support of your statement that you never kissed him?' – 'Did you ever put that forward as a reason why you never kissed the boy?' – 'Why, sir, should you mention that this boy was extremely ugly?' – 'Why did you mention his ugliness?' – 'Then why did you mention his ugliness, I ask you?' – until finally, in the words of the 'Notable British Trials' report, 'the witness began several answers almost inarticulately, and none of them he finished. His efforts to collect his ideas were not aided by Mr Carson's sharp staccato repetition: "Why? Why? Why did you add that?"'

At last, Wilde answered: 'You sting me and insult me and try to unnerve me, and at times one says things flippantly when one ought to speak more seriously. I admit it.'

But the case was virtually over. When Wilde eventually left the witness-box, he accepted his counsel's advice to withdraw his prosecution and the following month he was sentenced to two years' hard labour for gross indecency with various young men – not including the 'unfortunately extremely ugly' Walter Grainger.

BEST DEFENCE

By Sir Patrick Hastings, KC (1880–1952), at the Old Bailey in June 1932 when wealthy Mayfair beauty Mrs Elvira Barney, one of the Bright Young Things of the twenties and thirties, was acquitted of murdering her lover Michael Stephen. It was a tale of sordid, drunken quarrels: the prosecution alleged Mrs Barney had deliberately shot Stephen because he was threatening to leave her; she said the gun went off by accident. The case abounded in what the Press of the time called 'dramatic incidents' – but perhaps the best was when 'Pat'

Hastings was questioning his own client. A neighbour had claimed that a few days before the murder she had seen Stephen leaving Mrs Barney's Knightsbridge mews house with Mrs Barney screaming at him out of the window, 'Laugh, baby, laugh for the last time!' – whereupon she fired a revolver at him which (on that occasion) missed. She said Mrs Barney had the gun in her left hand. Now, as Hastings questioned the accused woman in the witness-box, with the revolver lying on the ledge in front of her, he broke off as if to say something to the judge, then suddenly whipped round and commanded: 'Pick up that revolver, Mrs Barney!' She gave a start and picked it up – with her *right* hand.

BEST EXAMPLE OF A CROOKED LAWYER
Richard Nixon (b. 1913), President of the USA, 1969–74.

SECOND-BEST EXAMPLE OF A CROOKED LAWYER
John Newton Mitchell (b. 1913), Attorney-General of the USA, 1969–72.

THIRD-BEST EXAMPLE OF A CROOKED LAWYER
Any of the clutch of Presidential lawyers involved in Watergate.

BEST POST-ACQUITTAL REMARK
After attractive Adelaide Bartlett, thirty, had walked free from the Old Bailey dock in April 1886, having stood trial for the murder of her husband Edwin. An entire bottle of chloroform had been discovered in his stomach after his death, but how had it got there? How had he been prevailed upon to drink the searing liquid? 'Now she's acquitted,' said surgeon Sir James Paget, who had given evidence for the Crown, 'she should tell us, in the interests of science, how she did it.'

BEST POST-ACQUITTAL POEM
About Lizzie Borden, the thirty-two-year-old Massachusetts spinster, frequent visitor to the Corcoran Art Gallery in Washington, Sunday School teacher, secretary of the Christian Endeavour Society, member of a Fruit and Flower Mission, a supporter of the Women's Christian Temperance Union and a sensitive painter of decorative pictures on porcelain, who was acquitted in June 1893 of the brutal murder with a hatchet of her ageing father and step-mother. The evidence of her guilt was overwhelming and few people have ever understood how she managed to get off – including the unknown author of this rhyme:

> 'Lizzie Borden took an axe
> And gave her mother forty whacks
> When she saw what she had done
> She gave her father forty-one.

BEST ALIBI

That of Harold Loughans, forty-seven, who in March 1944 convinced an Old Bailey jury that he could not be in two places over eighty miles apart at the same time. The estimated time of death of widowed Mrs Rose Ada Robinson, sixty-three, robbed and strangled Portsmouth publican, was between 2 and 4 am on the night of 28/29 November 1943. When long-time thief Loughans was picked up by the London police a month later, there was a great deal of circumstantial evidence against him – but at his trial he called five independent and completely honest witnesses who swore they had seen or talked to him as fellow shelterers from the wartime Blitz in a London Underground station at various times between 12.30 am and 5.15 am on the night of the murder. He was acquitted.

Sixteen years later, the late J.D. Casswell, QC, the prosecuting counsel, wrote in his memoirs, serialized in a British Sunday newspaper, how he had organized a test-ride in a police car through the night from London to Portsmouth and back, which showed that Loughans *could* have committed the crime by a fast expedition down to Portsmouth, if only one of the vital witnesses was mistaken in her timing – but the judge had, for technical reasons, ruled the evidence inadmissible. He called the crime 'a perfect murder' in the newspaper. Loughans, newly released from gaol for another offence, sued both QC and newspaper for libel. In January 1963, for the first time ever in a British court, the murder trial was, in essence, fought out again as a libel action – only this time with the police giving their evidence of the test-ride. Result: the jury said the defendants were 'justified' – Loughans *had* committed the murder. Then came the final twist: three months later, dying of cancer, Loughans walked into the newspaper's office and said, 'Before I die, I want to make a confession. I did kill the woman in the public house at Portsmouth.' What about his alibi? 'The stories I told about being at Warren Street tube station were lies ... I was broke at the time ... I stole a jeep and drove to Portsmouth to rob the place.'

BEST FALLACY ABOUT MURDER

That at the moment of death the killer's image is imprinted on the retina of his victim: it isn't – although in September 1927 the belief that it might be made British get-away thief Frederick Guy Browne shoot again through the eyes at close range PC George William Gutteridge, already lying dying at his feet. 'For God's sake, don't shoot any more!' cried Browne's henchman William Henry Kennedy. 'The man's dying.' Kennedy's concern did not save him: both he and Browne were hanged.

BEST COUNTRY TO AVOID IF YOU DON'T WANT TO BE MURDERED

Mexico, with 46·3 per cent homicides recorded for over 100,000 of the population in 1970. Only malaria and heart disease cause more deaths.

Best Last Words By A Murderer

Neville George Clevely Heath, twenty-nine, handsome British sex-murderer who within two weeks seduced two attractive girls then brutally killed them, mutilating the bodies. When his counsel's plea of insanity failed and the Old Bailey jury convicted, he did not appeal – almost alone among modern capital offenders. On the morning of his execution on 26 October 1946, when asked if there was anything he would like before being led out on to the scaffold, he said, 'Yes, a Scotch', then thought again and said, 'You might make it a double.'

Best Example Of Making The Punishment Fit The Crime

In the case of Richard Roose, a cook who poisoned two of his master's guests with a compound of hemlock and other fatal herbs, whom Henry VIII (1491–1547) condemned to be boiled alive. A huge cauldron, slung from a strong iron tripod, was set up over some logs in London's Smithfield and the murderous chef was placed in it. It took two hours for him to be cooked to death.

Best Executioner *Albert Pierrepoint*

Son and nephew of the two previous British Official Executioners, who in the twenty-five years until his resignation in 1956 executed 433 men and 17 women. A perfectionist, proud of the family tradition, he travelled extensively abroad, teaching his skills to apprentices in other countries. Finally, in his autobiography in 1974, he summed it all up: 'I now sincerely hope that no man is ever called on to carry out another execution in my country ... It is said to be a deterrent. I cannot agree. If death were a deterrent, I might be expected to know. It is I who have faced them last, young lads and girls, working men, grandmothers. I have been amazed to see the courage with which they took that last walk into the unknown. It did not deter them, and it had not deterred them when they committed what they were convicted for. All the men and women whom I have faced at that final moment convince me that, in what I have done, I have not prevented a single murder.'

Best Reason For An Execution

'To encourage the others.' Voltaire's famous remark on the execution of Admiral John Byng, shot on the quarterdeck of the *Monarque* on 14 March 1757, having been found guilty by court martial at Portsmouth of negligence under the British naval Articles of War for his failure to raise the French siege of Minorca the year before. And so to—

Best Legal Nonsense

Regulation 14 of the Bread and Flour Regulations of 1963 which lays down that all bakers in Britain, when marketing fruit loaf or any other bread containing fruit, must specify the fruit on the wrapper. It states that the description

'He's willing to settle out of court for six ounces of flesh.'

of the fruit 'shall be clearly legible and shall appear conspicuously in dark block type upon a light coloured ground or in light block type upon a dark coloured ground so that in either case every letter in that description shall be –

'(a) of uniform size, save that the initial letter in any word in that description may be larger than the other letters in that word, and

'(b) not less than one-quarter of an inch in height or of such size that the area of the smallest rectangle capable of enclosing each letter in that description, not counting for this purpose the initial letter of any word, is not less than nine-sixteenths of the area of the smallest rectangle capable of enclosing the largest letter in any word of more than one letter appearing on any label or show ticket relating to the bread to which the description relates, whichever is the larger.'

BEST NEWSPAPER REPORT OF A CASE
This appeared in the London *Times* for 8 December 1971: 'Hackensack, New

Jersey, Dec. 7 – A man who spent 14 years on death row, and escaped the electric chair 19 times on appeal, has finally confessed to killing a girl of 15. He was immediately set free.'

BEST TRAFFIC LAW
Section 78 of the Highway Act of 1835 which still makes it an offence on any road in Britain for 'the driver of any waggon, cart or other carriage' (which by a subsequent Act also includes 'a motor vehicle or bicycle') to 'quit the same and go on the other side of the hedge'.

BEST PROSECUTION FOR BREACH OF A LOCAL BY-LAW
In August 1977, three suspects were hauled into court at Ocean Beach on Fire Island, New York, for contravening a local by-law that bans eating in public or carrying open containers of food or drink on the walks or beaches so that litter may be dropped. The charges were: eating a slice of crumb cake in public, nibbling a chocolate chip cookie in public and holding a glass of water in public – and all three cases were dismissed.

BEST SUCCESSFUL PLOY IN COURT
By Melvin Belli, American attorney and self-styled 'King of Torts', in a plastic surgery case. The operation – on her breasts – had gone wrong and she was suing the surgeon for damages. Half-way through the hearing, Belli suggested to the judge that perhaps his Honour and the members of the jury would care to inspect the unsatisfactory nature of the surgeon's work in the privacy of his Honour's own room. The idea met with favour and judge, jury, counsel and the plaintiff adjourned to the judge's private room. Shyly the girl removed her blouse and then, with even greater embarrassment, her brassiere, then, to quote Belli's words to the author in his San Francisco office in May 1970: 'As she stood there the tears flowed down her face, between her poor misformed breasts – and straight into the cash register.' Her award: $150,000.

BEST FAILED PLOY IN COURT
By the bullying cross-examiner in a New York court who met his match, as recounted by Francis L. Wellman (1854-1942) in his classic study '*The Art of Cross-examination*', in this tale of an altercation between witness and attorney in a dispute between an Italian contractor and a householder who had engaged him to build a masonry wall for his garage. The contractor was suing for his money and the defence was that the wall had been poorly built and not in accord with proper masonry standards. The defendant's attorney was trying to cross-examine the contractor on the witness stand to show that his employees, all Italian masons, were an inferior grade of workmen and knew little of the jobs required of them:

Q.: 'Was Domenico a good mason?'

A.: 'Oh, yes, verra fina mason.'
Q.: 'And Giuseppi, was he a good mason?'
A.: 'Even better.'
Q.: 'How about Giovanni?'
A.: 'Best of the three.'
Q.: (Slurringly) 'I suppose then that you claim *all* masons are good masons?'
A.: 'No – no – justa like lawyers – soma good – soma rotten.'

BEST LEGAL DEFINITION
By the late H. L. Mencken: 'A judge is a law student who corrects his own papers.'

BEST STORY TO KEEP A CASE OUT OF COURT
By a Milwaukee citizen arrested in September 1978 on being found naked in his car, except for his shoes and socks, after a woman motorist had complained to the police that he had been following her through the streets. He explained that he had met his girlfriend in a park earlier that evening. They had quarrelled and she drove off in her car – with his clothes inside. He said that he could not go back to his wife without them and had cruised around hoping to spot the girlfriend. It was gathering dusk and the woman he followed drove the same model and colour of car. Hence, he had tailed her. 'His story is so weird that there has to be some truth in it,' said the Assistant District Attorney, explaining the decision not to prosecute him for any offence.

BEST LEGAL STORY ABOUT JUDGES
Shortly before the official opening of the Royal Courts of Justice in the Strand, London, by Queen Victoria in 1882, Lord Selborne, the Lord Chancellor, called a meeting of the judges at which an address to the Queen was considered. It contained the phrase, 'Your Majesty's judges are deeply sensible of their many shortcomings', whereupon Sir George Jessel, the Master of the Rolls and a very senior judge, protested strongly: 'I am not conscious of "many shortcomings" and if I were I would not be fit to sit on the Bench.' The nearest thing to a judicial row then occurred – in the course of which Lord Justice Bowen suggested unavailingly the compromise: 'Instead of saying that we are "deeply sensible of our own many shortcomings", why not say that we are "deeply sensible of the many shortcomings of each other"?'

BEST LEGAL REASONING
By the California Appeals Court in October 1975, when ruling that a law requiring women to cover their breasts at city parks and beaches while men were allowed to go bare-chested was not unconstitutional, because: 'Nature, not the legislative body, created the distinction between that portion of a woman's body and that of a man's torso.'

Best Police Force

It has to be the Metropolitan Police, 150 years old in 1979. In modern times, always under strength – 22,923 against its authorized establishment of 26,589 at the last official counting – it yet contrives to police with world-wide acknowledged efficiency the 786 square miles of London's Metropolitan Police District. Still today called 'Bobbies' after Sir Robert Peel (1788–1850), the Home Secretary whose brainchild it was, although an earlier popular nickname was also 'Peelers'.

Best Traffic Cops

The West German, not because they are necessarily any better in themselves than any other of their misanthropic colleagues, but because they have the best popular nickname for their autobahnen division: 'White Mice after their scrupulously clean white Porsches. It is more descriptive – and accurate – than the euphemism 'Angels of the Road' used by the more volatile French and Spaniards.

Best Device To Stop You Parking

In Mexico City, where the police remove a parked car's front number plates so that the motorist, on returning, has to drive straight to the nearest police station to get them back and pay the (exorbitant) parking fine.

Best Gaols

Again in Mexico where, though in no way wholesome, they do have the advantage of permitting conjugal visits. At weekends wives and girl-friends queue up for an hour or two of delight with their loved one, while cell-mates on the rota system patiently wait their turn.

Best Escape From Gaol

By Leonard T. Fristoe, convicted of killing two sheriff's deputies in 1920, who two years later escaped from Nevada State Prison, USA, and was at liberty for forty-six years, living under an assumed name, until finally his son turned him in to the authorities at Compton in California aged seventy-seven.

Best Way Of Preventing A Successful Escape

Put the gaol on an island, as with the French penal settlement that existed on Devil's Island for ninety-nine years (1854–1953) and with the much shorter-lived maximum security US Federal prison on Alcatraz Island in San Francisco Bay that was in service from 1934 to 1963. There were *some* successful escapes from Devil's Island but none from Alcatraz.

Best Detective Of All Time *Eugène François Vidocq (1775–1857)*

The first modern police detective and also the classic instance of 'poacher turned

*'... fortunately, however, there appears to be
one law for the rich and another for the poor.'*

gamekeeper'. Scoundrel, adventurer and prison escapee (from an eight-year term as galley-slave for forgery), he joined a gang of highwaymen whom he eventually betrayed to the authorities. From 1808 to 1812, he was in regular service as a police spy informing on his associates until finally he achieved 're-spectability' and was put in charge of the newly-formed *Brigade de Sûreté* in Paris. This ex-criminal was thus virtually the founder of the modern *Sûreté*, the CID of the present-day Parisian police. He survived Napoleon's defeat and continued to build up his Department until forced to resign in 1827, when at last the truth dawned on his colleagues that his brilliant track-record for the apprehension of villains was at least in part due to the fact that he was himself the originator of many of the burglaries he showed himself so clever in hunting out. Thereafter, he started a paper mill, ran a private detective office (using mainly ex-convicts as his agents), had a brief spell as Chief of the *Sûreté* under King Louis-Philippe, was a friend of many famous men such as Victor Hugo, Balzac and Alexandre Dumas, wrote several books on crime – and eventually died penniless. A remarkable man.

Best Private Detective *Allan Pinkerton (1819–84)*

Born in Glasgow, who emigrated to Chicago, USA, where in 1850 he founded the Detective Agency that still bears his name. The founder of many modern techniques, such as drawing up a Rogues' Gallery containing full details of wanted suspects, he used to boast that a case was never closed until the criminal was officially declared dead. Feared by Wild West villains and modern bank robbers alike, the Agency continues today as a superlative private security service.

Best Modern Arrest

Of veteran Canadian burglar Georges LeMay in Miami, Florida, in 1965, four years after he had pulled off an audacious bank robbery in Montreal, Canada, where, on Dominion Day weekend with the city deserted for a national holiday, he blasted a two-hundred-square-inch hole through the two-foot concrete vault floor of the Bank of Nova Scotia building. After prising open nearly four-hundred safe-deposit boxes, he crawled back to safety with an amount of loot it will never be possible definitely to quantify but estimated to be in the region of *at least* $633,000. He was the first known criminal to be caught with the help of the Early Bird satellite which relayed his photo to television screens all over the world. On being arrested, he immediately married his girl-friend to prevent her testifying against him but he was still extradited back to Montreal where on 17 January 1969 he was sentenced to eight years in gaol. None of the loot has been recovered. And finally –

Best Chamber Of Horrors

At Madame Tussaud's in London. Not only the best and the first but also the only genuine one in the world in that, apart from the normal waxwork effigies of famous killers and their victims, it contains real-life, original, grisly relics and not merely copies – such as the actual death masks cast from the severed heads of Louis XVI and Marie Antoinette, the very blade that formed part of the guillotine set up in the Place de la Concorde in Paris during the Reign of Terror, the gallows brought from Hertford Gaol in 1878 after over fifty years' use and the actual bell used to toll at executions in London's Newgate Prison. Originally called 'The Separate Room' by Madame Tussaud (1761–1850) herself, it was *Punch* magazine that in 1846 coined the phrase 'Chamber of Horrors'.

LITERATURE

Anthony Burgess

The most *comprehensive* dictionary is the *Oxford English Dictionary*, but the best of the English dictionaries is still Dr Samuel Johnson's, which is human, hence imperfect, hence lovable. The OED is too great to be loved. But Johnson has definitions like:

Net: Anything reticulated or decussated at equal distances, with interstices between the intersections.

and

Pension: An allowance made to anyone without an equivalent. In England it is generally understood to mean pay given to a state hireling for treason to his country.

and

Patron: Commonly a wretch who supports with insolence, and is paid with flattery.

The best dictionary, and perhaps the most idiosyncratic, from English to a foreign language is Sir Richard Winstedt's *English-Malay Dictionary* (Kelly and Walsh, Singapore, 1952). Its playfulness sometimes goes too far, but that is part of its stylishness. Thus, for *mustard* we get *sawi-sawi* and *sesawi*, but we also get *tahi tikus*, literally *mouse-turd*, which is not helpful. *Copulate* is well served. You can use *jamah, berjima, jumaat, bersatu, satuboh, asmara, mengurut*

'*Hey, this is a serious poetry reading, God damn it! In Russia I could go to jail for this stuff.*'

and *berhamput* and, if you wish to be vulgar, *beranchok* or *berbaka* or *bekak* or *ayut* or *ayok*. The polite word for copulation with a male is *berbini*. When hens do it it is *berjantan*, and frogs *bertindeh*. To perform coitus after circumcision with an older woman is *menyepoh tua*, but only in the State of Perak. There are other words too. If the best dictionary is one you can read, for pleasure, in bed, then Windstedt's is the best.

BEST LIBRARY IN THE WORLD

In a truly desirable and *human* library you can smoke, drink, treat books like expendable and serviceable *things* to be scribbled on, dog-eared, torn, and not like holy vessels of learning and enlightenment. The best library in the world is thus one's own. But, if you really want a great bibliothecal institution, the British Museum Reading Room is the best. There are ghosts of men and women who, with books, travailed to bring new systems of thought into being – Karl Marx, for instance. The best too, in that its total comprehensiveness of amenity reminds you of the total folly of using books at all for anything except passing the odd quarter of an hour between television programmes. The *really* best library was the one at Alexandria that Julius Caesar destroyed.

BEST MYSTERY WRITER

Not Agatha Christie, a deplorable stylist. Probably, alas, the Father Brown stories of G.K. Chesterton reveal him to be the best post-Sherlock Holmes mystery writer. Why *alas*? Because there is a sneaky eschatological overtone riding about *mystery* in GKC, and you are getting theology without having ordered it. But he was the best at this genre as he was the best at all the other literary genres. And what does one say about Conan Doyle? That he produced Sherlock Holmes and then left it to him to call into being the cases he was best endowed, by intellect and instinct, to solve. When you talk of Holmes you don't talk about *writing*. Damn it, the man *existed*.

BEST NOVEL OF ALL TIME

The *Ulysses* of James Joyce has to be the best, whether one wants it to be or not. It evades most of the problems of novel-reading by confining itself to a few hours of dull life in a dull Irish city, hence making it impossible for the characters to develop, see life, experience catastrophe, realize previously un-dreamt of potentialities. But as a narrative artefact, a mammoth verbal jigsaw, an example of literary creation in which every adverb and every crumb of tobacco is accounted for, it is the ultimate and unbeatable professional fictional performance against which all other novels (including *War and Peace* and *Don Quixote*) have to be measured.

BEST NOVEL (IN ENGLAND)

The best novel produced by a British writer (and *British* has everything to do with culture, nothing to do with blood) is the tetralogy by Ford Madox Ford (previously named Ford Madox Hueffer) called *Parade's End*. It is also the finest novel about the First World War. It is also the finest novel about the nature of British society. Ford is neglected. The finest editor of his time, he not only encouraged Joyce and Lawrence but actually wrote a good deal of Joseph Conrad's fiction for him. If this judgment on the supremacy of *Parade's End* be cavilled at, I am prepared to yield and to submit Ford's *The Good Soldier* as the best novel ever produced in England.

BEST AMERICAN NOVEL

Mark Twain's *Pudd'nhead Wilson* – a fine study of crime and detection, of Mississippi small town life, of the relationship between blacks and whites, the first book genuinely to reproduce black speech, a brilliant fictional fusion of plot-artifice and fresh smoking realism – remains unbeatable. F.R. Leavis thought highly of it. This may not be a recommendation.

Best French Novel

François Rabelais's *Gargantua and Pantagruel* seems to me to be a genuine novel: it has characters, conversations, incidents, conflict, dénouement. If the captious prefer to call it by some other genre-name, such as philosophical fantasy, scatograph, comic strip, then I have an alternative book ready. This is Gustave Flaubert's *Bouvard et Pécuchet*. That may not be a novel either.

Best Italian Novel

The best is the one that Italo Calvino does not propose writing. Having given us the plan, he feels free to abandon the hard work of construction. This is the plan. After an atomic war the denizens of a fall-out shelter find themselves struck dumb. They want to do a kind of static *Canterbury Tales* but can only put their stories together by pointing at odd frames in a tattered comic paper that happens to be lying around. They do not get very far, but they get further than Calvino has got or gotten. But, of course, the best books are always those that are going to be written and never are. In the absence of this masterpiece of Calvino's, the palm might go to Carlo Emilio Gadda's *Quer Pasticciaccio Brutto de via Merulana*, translated by William Weaver but really untranslatable, since the solidity resides in the language, an astonishing macaronic confection, a neo-dialect of immense verve and humour. If it were possible to accept a sequence of two and a quarter thousand sonnets in the Roman dialect as a novel, then the *Sonetti* of Giuseppe Gioacchino Belli would win the inter-national prize. Here we have, in the mouth of a blasphemous Roman, a minute survey of his city and its philosophy, lack of faith, joys and suffering, sardonic humour. It is the proto-novel of city life, with the city itself the hero. But, perhaps by definition, 2,279 sonnets cannot be a work of fiction.

Best Japanese Novel

Junichiro Tanizaki's *Diary of a Mad Old Man* is what it says it is. There may be other and better Japanese novels (and are not some of those ancient pillow-books really perhaps delicate Proustian master-or-mistresspieces?) but I have not read the whole of Japanese fiction. This one is a great novel, and it is the best in Japanese that I know. It is also very much what it says it is. Arigatu, Tanizaki.

Best Novel In German

Nothing by that fake Indianist Hermann Hesse. Nothing by that guzzling flounder Günter Grass. How about Robert Musil's unfinished and unfinishable

The Man Without Qualities? Don't make me laugh. (Credit where it's due, Musil doesn't try.) No, it has to be something by Thomas Mann. It has to be *Doktor Faustus*, his last novel, grim, of the solidity of a Hanseatic warehouse, but the only work of fiction which understands the nature of both music and Germanic morality and has the courage to see Germany's artistic achievements as an aspect of a national endowment which contains Hitler as well as Luther. Adrian Leverkühn, the composer-hero, has genius and syphilis. So, thought Mann, had Germany.

BEST NOVEL ABOUT WORLD WAR TWO

Let's award *ex aequo* prizes. In England, Evelyn Waugh's Crouchback trilogy, published eventually as a single novel called *Sword of Honour*. This comes close in achievement to Ford's *Parade's End* and undoubtedly owes something to it. In America, Norman Mailer's *The Naked and the Dead* said most about the Pacific side, while Waugh concentrated on Europe. If I have to choose between the two, Waugh must win.

BEST POET OF ALL TIME

It could have been Shakespeare if he'd written less hastily and used more self-control – cared more, in a word, for literature and less for New Place and raising his rents. It has to be Dante, who had, moreover, the advantage over Shakespeare of being born to a coherent system of theological thought and not the mixed scrappy bag of bits of Seneca, Montaigne and Machiavelli that Shakespeare had to make do with. *The Divine Comedy* is always physically sharp, lucid, concise, controlled, sardonic, moving, awe-inspiring, elevating, and a great linguistic glory.

BEST POET OF THE 1970s

Where? In England? In America? The English language doesn't make good poets any more, it produces Yeats and Betjemans. It's a pity that the best English language poet of the seventies should also be the best of the forties, fifties and sixties – namely, W.H. Auden. Eugenio Montale (born 1896) is old, but he, an Italian, is the best living poet.

BEST REVIEW

One must avoid giving the palm to mere flippant trickery, like Dorothy Parker's admired '*The House Beautiful* is the play lousy'. Sir Thomas More came close to delivering the best brief review when he advised a young writer to rewrite his prose as verse and then was able to say: 'Yea, marry, now it is somewhat, for now it is rhyme; before, it was neither rhyme nor reason.' But, of the long written reviews, the best were in the old *Edinburgh Review*, and Thomas Babington Macaulay wrote the best of those best when he reasonably and kindly considered the poems of Mr Robert Montgomery, saying, among other things, that 'Mr Robert Montgomery's readers must take such grammar as they can get, and be thankful,' and, of one of the poet's images, stating:

We take this to be, on the whole, the worst similitude in the world. In the first place, no stream meanders, or can possibly meander, level with its fount. In the next place, if streams did meander level with their founts, no two motions can be less like each other than that of meandering level and that of mounting upwards.

This is the kind of criticism even bad writers should be glad to get.

BEST TITLE FOR A BOOK
The anonymous Elizabethan pamphleteers had some of the best titles, like *A Comb for the Lousy Locks of the Ungodly* or *A Just Gibe at the Whole Tribe of Poetified Sneerers*, but the playwrights did well too, with *If You Know Not Me, You Know Nobody* and John Ford's *'Tis Pity She's a Whore*. Of all plays ever written, Goldsmith's has the best title – *She Stoops to Conquer*. Of all poems, Milton's title is best – *Paradise Lost*. Of all books of prose, James Joyce wins with *Finnegans Wake*, a title containing a whole bookload of ideas, from the apostrophized ballad title *Finnegan's Wake* to (all the) *Finnegans Wake* (up again), with *fin* (end) and *egan* (resurrection) on the way.

BEST HUMORIST
Here is a difficulty. It would not be difficult to state what is the best humorous book – *Augustus Carp Esq., by Himself* (published anonymously by King George V's personal physician). But the best humorist must be capable of many humorous books, and very few humorists have produced more than one good one – Jerrold with *Mrs Caudle's Curtain Lectures*, Jerome K. Jerome with *Three Men in a Boat*. I think Max Beerbohm achieved the greatest consistency consistent with the greatest variety – *Zuleika Dobson* is very different from *A Christmas Garland* – and ought to be accounted England's, if not the world's, best humorist. But none of Max's funny books is the funniest book in the world, unless he served quietly as King George V's personal physician.

BEST BIOGRAPHY
Yes, but can we regard Boswell as sufficiently objective? Hero-worship and a tape-recorder brain are probably not enough for a great biographer. I have thought, for at least twenty years, that the best biography in English is Rupert Hart-Davis's of Hugh Walpole, in which steady if not overwhelming affection drips on to a subject rather less than worthy of a massive biographical tribute – which, nevertheless, that subjects gets. I have read the book at least ten times and have not yet done with it, yet I have read hardly a line of Walpole. The study of a literary man, rather thinly endowed with talent, on the make in the London *d'entre deux guerres*, is as fascinating as a novel (Maugham's *Cakes and Ale*, for instance) and it is all true.

Best Epigram

How remarkable is Oscar Wilde (our best epigrammatist, and so one must look in his works for the best epigram). Quite casually in *The Importance of being Earnest* he throws in the following: 'All women become like their mothers. That is their tragedy. No man does. That's his.' Unprepared, unfanfared. Then we get on with the play and more epigrams.

Best Repartee

Dr Samuel Johnson, railed at by a bargee, said: 'Sir, your wife, under pretence of keeping a bawdy house, is a receiver of stolen goods.' But he could have had that in readiness for years, and it is not a particular and apt response to an insult. It is, in a word, merely abusive. So the prize goes to Richard Brinsley Sheridan who, in a speech in the Commons in reply to Mr Dundas, said 'The right honourable gentleman is indebted to his memory for his jests, and to his imagination for his facts.'

Best Opening To A Book

The *Memoirs* of Harriette Wilson (1789–1846) begin: 'I shall not say why and how I became, at the age of fifteen, the mistress of the Earl of Craven.'

Best Literary Magazine

It was *Blast*, edited by Wyndham Lewis. I have a copy of the second and last number, 1915. When, covering the date, I show it to young ignorant literary people, they think, from the revolutionary look of it, that it came out a few years ago. But it is pure rich modernism right out of the modern, as opposed to contemporary, period. It contains poems by Eliot and Pound. It has Lewis hammering away at important things like aesthetics. The horror and emptiness of war are caught for ever in vorticist sketches. There has never been a magazine like it.

MEDICINE

◆

Richard Gordon

BEST ADVICE TO ALL DOCTORS
'First do no harm.' Hippocrates (460–?355 BC).

BEST ADVICE ABOUT HOSPITALS
'It may seem a strange principle to enunciate as the very first requirement in a hospital that it should do the sick no harm.' Florence Nightingale (1820–1910).

BEST CURE FOR A COLD
A bottle of whisky and a hat. Go to bed, stick the hat on the bedpost and drink the whisky until the hat moves. It is no more effective than other cures but it takes your mind off the cold.

BEST CURE FOR A HANGOVER
Jeeves prescribed Bertie Wooster a raw egg whole in Worcester sauce. Take plenty of (non–alcoholic) fluid. Try a brisk walk, followed by a steaming mug of meat or yeast extract (rich in salt and potassium). Remember that aspirin can cure a headache, but irritate the stomach. Vow never to risk another one, like everyone else.

BEST WAY TO STOP SMOKING
Improve yourself socially. Smokers in Social Class I are fewer than in all other

classes. Death from coronary heart disease – which is linked with smoking – fell in Social Class 1 from 327 for each 100 among the rest of the population in 1932, to 88 against 100 in 1972. An equally good way to stop smoking is taking up medicine. Deaths from lung cancer in doctors have fallen to thirty-five per cent of the non-medical population. Smoking by doctors has fallen to half that of everyone else.

Best Amount Of Nightly Sleep For Any Individual
The amount he actually has.

Best Way To Slim
Eat less. Best method comes from Germany – *Fressen die Hälfte* (guzzle only half). And stop drinking. All alcoholic drinks are heavy with calories and anyway shed your inhibitions towards the roast potatoes and marmalade pudding. It is possible to slim and still drink, but difficult – like playing the piano in boxing gloves.

Best-Avoided Diet
Whole-wheat, stone-ground, compost-nourished, chemical-free, home-baked bread. Ratafia, ginseng, carob powder. Sesame seeds, mung beans, comfrey. Sea salt, birch beer, parsnip wine. Bee-collected pollen, acorn coffee. Nature's foods, like ground elder, lungwort, plantain, fenugreek, goatsbeard, lady's bed-straw, wild angelica, meadowsweet, salsify. Tenderized prunes and dandelion leaves. All have no specific nutritive value. Most are expensive. All are unnecessary. Just eat a normal mixed diet with some roughage. Almost everybody does, except health cranks. Vitamin tablets are as unnecessary as an umbrella for a scuba diver.

Best Medical Advice Which Is Ignored
Always clip on your seat belt. This would prevent 1,000 deaths and 10,000 injuries on the road every year. About one in four drivers and front-seat passengers buckle their belts in towns, about one-half on motorways. Best remember that built-up areas have the higher accident risk.

Best-Ignored Medical Advice
Cast ne'er a clout till May be out. Feed a cold and starve a fever. An apple a day keeps the doctor away. A potato in your pocket (or a copper clasp on your wrist) wards off rheumatism. Oysters are aphrodisiac. ('Only ten of them worked,' traditionally complained the debutante who was advised to feed her boy-friend a dozen for supper.)

Best-Forgotten Medical Fallacies
Brown eggs are more nutritious than white. Broiler fowls are less nutritious

'He was a dreadful hypochondriac.'

than free-range ones. A man is as old as he feels and a woman as old as she looks. A green winter makes a fat churchyard. Wet feet give you a cold in the head. Port gives you gout. Sitting on cold stone gives you piles. Lavatory seats give you VD.

BEST ADVICE FOR LIVING A LONG TIME
Select long-living parents and grandparents.

BEST ADVICE TO PEOPLE WORRIED ABOUT BEING 'REGULAR'
Samson Wright's *Applied Physiology* records the case of a man who did not 'go' at all from 18 June 1900 to 21 June 1901.

BEST CURE FOR GOUT
'Live on sixpence a day – and earn it,' according to London surgeon John Abernethy (1764–1831). Alternatively, a plucked and drawn owl, salted, hung for a week, roasted in a closed pot, pulverized and mixed with boar's grease, as prescribed by herbalist Nicholas Culpeper (1616–54). Or a clove of garlic eaten night and morning. (Garlic is praised by modern German doctors for lowering the blood cholesterol. Eaten regularly, it could surely be an effective contraceptive.)

BEST CONTRACEPTIVE
Traditionally, a glass of water. Neither before nor after, but instead of. The female pill is reliable and acceptably safe. The male pill has small chance of widespread popularity. It reacts violently with alcohol.

BEST (PSYCHOLOGICAL) APHRODISIAC
'Ah! Sire! Change is the greatest aphrodisiac of all.' – his doctor, to Louis XV (1710–74).

BEST EXCUSE FOR FIRST TAKING OPIUM
'It was a Sunday afternoon, wet and cheerless, and a duller spectacle this earth of ours has not to show than a rainy Sunday in London.' – Thomas de Quincey (1785–1859).

BEST WAY TO SNATCH A BODY
Dig a small hole at the head of the grave, smash open the coffin, and slip out the corpse using the ears as handles. Employ a wooden spade, to reduce noise. This method was used by William Burke (1792–1829) and his fellow resurrectionist William Hare, who turned King's evidence in Edinburgh and escaped hanging. Have care not to take the shroud, which is theft. Sacking up a human body, which belongs to nobody, is not.

BEST MEDICAL CHESTNUT
'How much did you charge for his operation?'
    '£184.62.'
'That's a very odd sum.'
'It was all he had left.'

BEST NAVAL SURGEON *James Lind (1716–94) of Edinburgh*
Joined the Royal Navy aged twenty-three, served at sea for nine years, mostly in the tropics. Appalled by living conditions and diet afloat – 'putrid beef, rancid pork, mouldy biscuits and bad water'. And by the inescapable scurvy as the voyage progressed. Noticed that scurvy was cured by green vegetables and fresh fruit. Eliminated it from the Fleet, seemingly magically, with a daily ration of lemon juice. Lemon juice acts by providing the antiscorbutic vitamin C. Lind published *A Treatise of the Scurvy* in 1753, 153 years before Sir Frederick Gowland Hopkins (1861–1947) discovered the necessity for vitamins in a healthy diet.

BEST MILITARY SURGEON *Dominique Jean Larrey (1766–1842)*
Born in the Pyrenees, studied medicine in Paris at the Hôtel-Dieu. 'The most honest man, and the best friend to the soldier that I ever knew. Vigilant and indefatigable in his exertions for the wounded ... he scarcely allowed a

moment's repose to his assistants, and kept them eternally at their posts. He tormented the generals, and disturbed them out of their beds at night whenever he wanted accommodation or assistance for the wounded or sick. They were all afraid of him, as they knew he would instantly come and make a complaint to me.' – said Napoleon. Larrey was at Aboukir, Borodino, Waterloo. He invented the flying (horse-drawn) ambulance. He was made a Baron for daring to slaughter officers' horses to brew bouillon for the wounded.

BEST POLITICAL DOCTOR *Dr Georges Benjamin Clemenceau (1841–1929)*
Born in Nantes, studied in Paris, jailed in Montmartre for shouting '*Vive la République!*' Went to the United States, did not practise but taught girls French. Prime Minister 1917–20. 'Tiger' Clemenceau resuscitated an exhausted France for victory in World War I, though his influence on the Treaty of Versailles in 1919 probably contributed to World War II.

BEST ROYAL DOCTOR *Sir Frederick Treves (1853–1923)*
Shortly before his Coronation Day, 26 January 1902, King Edward VII was struck with abdominal pain. Treves diagnosed acute appendicitis, advised immediate operation. The King refused. A Coronation was not a postponable event. 'In that case, Sir,' said Treves, 'you will go to the Abbey as a corpse.' Instead of being crowned, the King had an appendicectomy, and reigned another eight years. Second best was Robert Keate (1777–1857), who wanted William IV out of the room while he examined Queen Adelaide's knee. 'I'm hanged if I go,' said the King. 'Then, your Majesty, I will be hanged if I stay,' said Keate. 'You doctors can do anything,' grumbled the King, obliging. 'But if a Prime Minister or a Lord Chancellor had presumed to order me out of the room, the next day I should have had to address his successor.'

BEST SURGICAL SPRINTER *Robert Liston (1794–1847) of University College Hospital, London*
Could amputate a leg in half a minute – he had his students time him, like some prizefighter, which he physically resembled. Liston operated before the discovery of anaesthetics, when surgery was a matter of more haste, less pain. In his enthusiasm, he is said during one leg amputation to have whipped off the patient's testicles as well. In another, he removed the leg in record time (though the patient died later in the ward from hospital gangrene – they nearly all did in the 1840s), plus the fingers of his assistant (who also died later in the ward from hospital gangrene), and the coat-tails of a watching doctor, who, fearful that the knife had pierced his vitals, dropped dead from heart failure. This was the worst operation in history, with a 300 per cent mortality.

BEST MEDICAL BENEFACTOR *Lord Nuffield (1877–1963)*
Inventor of the bull-nosed Morris Oxford car. Gave £10 million to the Nuffield

Foundation, financing many medical advances at the famous Radcliffe Infirmary and the University of Oxford.

BEST PATIENT *Alexis St Martin*
A Canadian of nineteen, had his stomach split open by duck-shot at close range, in an accident on 6 June 1822. The wound healed with the inside of the stomach exposed to the air. 'The case affords an excellent opportunity for experimenting upon the gastric fluids and process of digestion,' wrote his doctor, William Beaumont (1785–1853) of Mackinae, Canada. 'Various kinds of digestible substances might be introduced into the stomach, and then easily examined during the whole process of digestion. I may, therefore, be able hereafter to give some interesting experiments on these subjects.' Alexis revealed much about gastric physiology, of lasting value to doctors and their patients. He passed his life as a log-chopper.

BEST DOCTOR NOVELIST *W. Somerset Maugham (1874–1965)*
Who qualified at St Thomas's Hospital, London. He said, 'I do not know a better training for a writer than to spend some years in the medical profession.'

BEST DOCTOR PLAYWRIGHT *Anton Chekhov (1860–1904)*
Who studied at Moscow. Chekhov referred to medicine as his legitimate wife, but the stage as his flashy mistress. He was lucky, his mistress kept him.

BEST POETIC DOCTOR *John Keats (1795–1821)*
Son of an ostler at the Swan and Hoop, Moorgate, London. Qualified at Guy's Hospital in 1816 (with credit). Wrote *Ode to a Nightingale* in a morning in 1819. Died of TB, aged twenty-six.

BEST MUSICAL DOCTOR *Dr Alexander Porphyrievich Borodin (1833–87)*
Graduated at St Petersburg. Died at a masked ball.

BEST DOCTOR FOR SELF-HELP *Dr Samuel Smiles (1812–1904).*

BEST DOCTOR FOR FINDING THE RIGHT WORD *Dr Mark Roget (1779–1869).*

BEST WORD COINED BY A DOCTOR *Anaesthesia*
By Dr Oliver Wendell Holmes (1809–94). In Boston, after the first use of ether at the Massachusetts General Hospital there in 1846. During the late 1840s, many girls born after painless childbirth narrowly avoided being lumbered with the name.

BEST TRAVELLING DOCTOR *David Livingstone (1813–73)*
From Blantyre, Lanarkshire. Became a cotton-spinner, saved his wages to study

medicine, qualified in 1840. Immediately explored Africa. Went three times. Discovered the Victoria Falls in November 1855. Finally got lost, found by Henry M. Stanley (1841–1904) in October 1871.

BEST FAILED MEDICAL STUDENTS
Hector Berlioz (1803–69). Took up music.
Charles Robert Darwin (1809–82). Could not stomach the operating theatre. Propounded the law of natural selection.
Sir Humphry Davy (1778–1829). Invented the miners' lamp.
Galileo Galilei (1564–1642). Unravelled the universe.
C. S. Forester (1899–1966). Created Hornblower.
Johann Wolfgang Goethe (1749–1832). Indulged in the arts.
Christopher Isherwood (b. 1904) was a student at King's College Hospital 1928–29.
John Leech (1817–64). Drew for *Punch*.
Sydney Smith (1771–1845). Became a wit.

BEST BRITISH MINISTERS OF HEALTH SINCE WORLD WAR TWO
Nye Bevan (1897–1960). Enoch Powell (b. 1912). No other contestants.

BEST AMERICAN DOCTOR *Dr Benjamin Spock*
His Baby and Child Care sells almost as well as the Bible, from which many young parents find it indistinguishable.

BEST FICTIONAL DOCTOR *Dr Watson*
Without whom Sherlock Holmes would be as commonplace as a village bobby. Watson reflects Holmes's thought-process, because Conan Doyle (1859–1930) modelled him closely on Dr Joseph Bell (1837–1911), who taught Doyle medicine at Edinburgh. The great detective's reasoning in solving crime is exactly that used in diagnosing disease.

BEST OBSTETRICIAN *Sir James Young Simpson (1811–70)*
Seventh son of a Scottish baker, Professor of Midwifery at Edinburgh aged twenty-nine. On 5 November 1847, after a dinner-party in his house (still standing) at 52 Queen Street, he passed round tumblers of chloroform instead of the port. Simpson and two young doctors sniffed, passed out and ended under the table. A powerful anaesthetic had been discovered.

Simpson's giving chloroform to abolish labour pains was attacked by the Church sanctimoniously and acrimoniously – 'In sorrow thou shalt bring forth children' (Genesis 3.16). Scripturist Simpson retaliated, 'And the Lord God caused a deep sleep to fall upon Adam, and he slept; and he took one of his ribs' (Genesis 2.21). He delivered with equal skill and consideration the wives of Edinburgh artisans and English aristocrats.

BEST GUINEA-PIG *Queen Victoria (1819–1901)*
On 7 April 1853 took chloroform for the birth of Prince Leopold. The anaesthetic was given on a handkerchief, in quarter-teaspoonful doses, for fifty-three minutes. Chloroform was still a drug of unknown danger and suspect propriety. *Chloroform à la reine* made it unassailably respectable. 'Her Majesty was a model patient,' said the anaesthetist, Dr John Snow of St George's Hospital. He was also the –

BEST EPIDEMIOLOGIST *Dr John Snow (1813–58)*
Lived in Soho, a district ravaged regularly by epidemics of cholera. In August 1854, 500 inhabitants of its slums died in ten days. London's panic recalled the Great Plague of 1665. Dr Snow accused infected water from the pump in Broad Street. The vestrymen of St James's refused to believe him. It was their pump and their water. Dr Snow removed the pump handle. The cholera stopped. He was the first to connect impure water with disease, almost twenty years before the germ theory was established by Louis Pasteur (1822–95) at Lille and Robert Koch (1843–1910) at Wollstein in the Rhineland.

BEST HEALTH SERVICE
Despite its being an industrial battleground, a structural Stonehenge, an administrative Scutari, an ideological Charge of the Light Brigade and a political circus-ring, the British National Health Service. It is the world's most experienced. It is the only one financed almost wholly from central taxation, and more or less free at the point of delivery. It spends over £6 billion a year. It treats 2,500,000 hospital in-patients a year, with an average stay of 21·5 days. It has a waiting list of 600,000. It takes 5·3 per cent of the British gross national product, compared with 7·4 per cent for health in the United States, 7·3 per cent in Sweden and 6·4 per cent in West Germany. It is health on the cheap. Its employees are more devoted to a health *service* than they sometimes seem, than the public recognizes or the Government deserves.

BEST HEALTH FARM *Forest Mere, Liphook, Hampshire, England*
(Americans do not need health farms; they are health-conscious without having to pay for it.)
   Has lake, lovely views, swimming-bath, horses, beauty parlours, sauna, colonic massage, sitz-baths, steam cabinets, resident hypnotist, yoga. Prunes, apricots, yoghurt progressing to salads and cheese. Nearby Enton, near Godalming, Surrey, is more homely. Hot water with slice of lemon progressing to apple juice, salad, wheat germ, muesli, fruit and yoghurt. Enton is best health farm for compost-fed-soil buffs. Best for scientifically-minded slimmers, Ragdale Hall, near Melton Mowbray, Leicestershire. Ragdale counts the calories, 500 a day, doubled as a treat on Sundays. Melon, ham salad, apple baked in cider, mëringue, chicken casserole and – of course – yoghurt. Swimming pool, saunas,

massage, facials, yoga, computer-controlled artificial sun. All health farms are as dry as Salvation Army hostels.

BEST HOSPITAL *The Wellington, St John's Wood, London*
Modern, smallish, three operating theatres, intensive care unit, Elemaschö-mander skull X-ray unit, radio-isotope diagnostic department. Ninety-eight private rooms all with bath and thermostatically controlled shower, outside telephone, colour TV, resuscitation facilities, drinks refrigerator, ninety with own balcony. No restrictions on visitors (snacks available). Interpreters, chaplains, view of Test Matches at Lord's. Menu offers low fat, soft, low sodium, restricted calories, diabetic diets. A la carte has thirteen items from hors-d'œuvre (smoked salmon pâté, egg in aspic) to cheese board, via fillets of sole Waleska, chicken à la Kiev. Sound wine list, including chateau-bottled Mouton Rothschild 1964. Gin and scotch come in miniatures, like airlines. Champagne, Dom Pérignon 1966, but Bollinger non-vintage best value. Clientele largely foreign and rich. One patient was robbed by a sneak-thief of £150,000.

Best hospital in the USA: The most expensive. It follows.

BEST MEDICAL INVENTION
In 1816, Dr René Théophile Hyacinthe Laënnec (1781–1826) was consulted by a young woman with heart disease 'in whose case percussion and the application of the hand were of little avail on account of the great degrees of fatness'. Laying his ear flat against the chest 'being rendered inadmissible by the age and sex of the patient,' Dr Laënnec had the inspiration of rolling up a quire of paper and listening to the heart through it. This became the stethoscope, the doctor's inevitable hand-prop.

BEST MEDICAL LABOUR-SAVING DEVICE
Professor Carl Wunderlich (1815–77) of Leipzig invented the temperature chart – 'he found fever a disease and left it a symptom'. But his clinical thermometer was a foot long, and took twenty minutes to read. In 1867, Sir Thomas Clifford Allbutt (1836–1925), Regius Professor of Physic at Cambridge, invented the short, portable, quickly read thermometer which is today poked under everyone's tongue. Sir Clifford had spent thirty years as a Leeds GP, and was the model for the first medical hero in fiction, Dr Tertius Lydgate in *Middlemarch* by George Eliot (really, Mary Ann Evans, 1819–80).

BEST NON-MEDICAL LABOUR-SAVING DEVICE *The guillotine*
Invented in 1789 by Dr Joseph Ignace Guillotin from Saintes, a graduate of Rheims, Professor of Anatomy at Paris and member of the National Assembly.

BEST STROKE OF MEDICAL LUCK
Sir Alexander Fleming's (1881–1955) discovery of penicillin at St Mary's Hospital, London, depended on six chances all coming up. This is the equivalent

*'He's much better. Receiving the last rites seems
to have been just what he needed.'*

in betting of going through the card. (1) Fleming was examining staphylococci germs for colour changes, which required their being exposed to the air instead of shut in an incubator. (2) He went for a month's holiday in August, 1928, leaving his glass dishes of germs to sterilize in disinfectant – but one escaped on top. (3) It was a cool summer, and the dishes were piled away from the sun. The temperature encouraged the correct growth of both staphylococci and penicillin mould. (4) The penicillin mould did not float through the laboratory window, which was always shut. It came up the stairs. Immediately below was the laboratory of a scientist studying moulds. (5) The mould fell on the plate at exactly the right time and place to kill the germs. (6) When Fleming came back to work, he happened to notice the top plate – now in the British Museum – and murmured, 'That's funny'. Fleming did little to develop penicillin, which was virtually rediscovered in Oxford in 1940 by Lord Florey (1898–1968).

BEST PLACE FOR PLASTIC SURGERY *Los Angeles*

Only 1,300 doctors are certified by the American Board of Plastic Surgery as competent. But in California, any doctor can set up as a plastic surgeon. They guarantee to 'get rid of that exhausted, dissipated look' in fiftyish executives, generally seeking employment. They specialize in nose-jobs, face-lifts and the 'turkey wattle operation'. Hair transplants – fifty plugs of skin from growing to barren areas on the scalp – have recoated Senator Proxmire and Frank Sinatra. Phyllis Diller confessed to a boost professionally and psychologically from a silicone face-lift. Plastic surgery is popular with Californian school-teachers, to help relate better to the young. Cost the same as a summer holiday in Europe, but less fun.

BEST-SELLING DRUGS

In Britain antibiotics, anti-inflammatories, bronchial dilators, anti-hypertensive drugs, diuretics, pain-killers, anti-depressants, tranquillizers. NHS prescriptions for tranquillizers are now 45 million annually. In USA oral contraceptives, anti-depressants, anti-psychotics, coronary artery dilators, diuretics, oestrogens, antibiotics. Best promotion of drugs in USA, West Germany, Italy, South Africa – the manufacturers' advertising expenditure is 22 per cent of the sales. In Belgium and Canada it is 21 per cent. In Indonesia 16 per cent, in Britain 15 per cent.

BEST MASS HALLUCINATION *The Loch Ness Monster*

Sighted regularly since a road was built alongside the loch in 1933. Despite the photographs, which could be birds and logs, the sonar graphs, which could be fish, and the underwater pictures, which could be anything, neither skin nor bone of a monster dead or alive has ever been found. The possibility of a prehistoric or unknown creature inhabiting an insignificant stretch of water in Scotland is negligible compared to the infinite capacity of human beings for seeing things not there. UFOs, ghosts, the Angels of Mons, the Devils of Loudun, illustrate the powerful overall effect of the brain on human vision. Seeing is unfortunately not believing. It is only seeing what we believe we see. Meanwhile, Nessie offers a bonnie boost for the Scottish economy.

BEST TIME TO COMMIT SUICIDE

May and June are the most popular months, according to Douglas Kerr's *Forensic Medicine*. Twenty-five per cent more people kill themselves in the springtime compared with gloomy November. There is a jump over Christmas and the New Year.

BEST SPECTACULAR END FOR A DOCTOR *Dr Jean Paul Marat (1743–93)*
Who had practised in Paris and London, died instantly when stabbed in his
bath on the evening of 13 July by twenty-four-year-old Charlotte Corday. Distinction shared with Dr William Palmer (1824–56), who studied at Bart's and
murdered thirteen people with strychnine (dreadfully painful). Palmer was the
last doctor to be executed in public, on the wet morning of 14 June outside
Stafford Jail. Dr Roderigo Lopez, also of Bart's, was hanged, drawn and
quartered at Tyburn in 1594 for trying to poison Queen Elizabeth 1. But at
the time, this end was commonplace.

BEST CURE FOR HICCUPS *Listening*
The sufferer stands up, and everyone else in the room listens in silence for
the next hiccup. It never comes.

BEST PLACE TO HAVE A BABY *Japan*
Infant mortality rate: 1 per 100 live births. Next best, the Netherlands: 1·03.
Then Denmark: 1·04. United States is 1·48 for whites, 2·49 for blacks. Britain
is 1·4.

BEST PLACE TO AVOID HAVING A BABY *Rochdale, Lancashire*
About 70 out of 3,000 babies born there every year fail to survive the week,
the highest proportion in Britain. Rochdale's first-year mortality rate is halved
on the other side of Manchester, at Trafford.

BEST PLACE TO BE HEALTHY IN EUROPE *The Netherlands*
The mortality rate is 7·9 per 1,000 population. Next, Italy: 9·6. Then France:
10·1. Scotland's mortality rate is 12·6 per 1,000, England and Wales' 11·0. The
Netherlands has 132 doctors for every 100,000 population, Italy 185 for every
100,000, France 139, Scotland 156, England and Wales 127.

BEST PLACE TO BE HEALTHY IN AMERICA
New York State has the highest ratio of doctors to patients in the USA – 193
per 100,000 inhabitants. But this is not the place. *Nebraska* has only half the
proportion, and everyone lives two and a half years longer.

BEST PLACE FOR A DOCTOR TO PRACTISE (FINANCIALLY) *France*
Doctors' earnings are 7 times average manual earnings. Next best, Italy, 6·8
times. The Netherlands, 6·3 times. Germany is 6·1, USA 5·6, Belgium 4·2,
Sweden 3·5. Bottom of the OECD countries is Britain – 2·7 times.

BEST HOSPITAL FOR DINING *Southampton General*
Staff canteen is 'The Truffles'. Recommended – champignons à la greque,
entrecôte béarnaise, brochettes de langoustine. Prices reasonable.

BEST HOSPITAL FOR BREAKFAST *Heatherwood, Ascot*
Renowned scrambled eggs.

BEST PIECE OF USELESS ANATOMICAL INFORMATION
'The average American male has a penile length of 6·3 inches in erection.'
(Alfred C. Kinsey.)

BEST NASTY CLINICAL REMARK

> Here lies wrapt up in forty thousand towels
> The only proof that Caroline had bowels.
> *On Queen Caroline's Death-bed,*
> by Alexander Pope (1688–1744).

BEST DYING WORDS
William Pitt (1759–1806) – 'I think I could eat one of Bellamy's veal pies.'
Possibly misheard for, 'I think I have eaten one of Bellamy's veal pies'?

BEST APOCRYPHAL DYING WORDS
When Viscount Dawson of Penn (1864–1945) on 20 January 1936 encouraged his patient George V that he was recovering from a second attack of pneumonia, and would shortly be convalescing again at the Sussex seaside resort of Bognor Regis, the King said 'Bugger Bognor' and died. Officially, His Majesty uttered, 'How is the Empire?' Perhaps somebody else misheard.

BEST EPITAPH

> All you that do this place pass by
> Remember death for you will dye
> As you are now even so was I
> And as I am so shall you be
> Thomas Gooding here do staye
> Waiting for Gods Judgment Daye.

> In Norwich Cathedral.

BEST RULES FOR HEALTH
(1) Do not smoke. (2) Keep your weight down. (3) Take regular exercise. (4) Look both ways before stepping off the pavement.

MEN'S FASHION

John Taylor

BEST DRESSED MAN

It has to be George Bryan Brummell. Not only for his unique fastidiousness, but for the fact that he entirely changed the whole direction of male dress.

He introduced 'adult' clothing to the scene of aristocracy though he was not himself an aristocrat. He really started modern menswear on its trends into the subfusc and the understated, and its concern with detailed esoterics of restraint, quality and cleanliness.

Against a background of general garish flamboyance, he concentrated on line. After him the norm was to dress in woollens and worsted rather than silks and satins. His personal uniform of blue coat and buff trousers became in shape the basis for modern formal wear, though it is to be suspected he used his clothes simply for purposes of personal PR rather than for any real love of creativity.

Together with the effects of the Industrial Revolution, he simplified men's clothing into the three-piece basis of the present-day suit. He made way for the manly reticence typified by the Duke of Wellington and the sober seriousness of Prince Albert. These latter really established modern dress, but Brummell started it.

BEST DRESSED MEN

Choose your own list. Far from welding us all together into one great society, the march of democracy has simply swopped the old vertical dress structures, based on prosperity and breeding, for new horizontal classifications based on age and vocation. The 'slob seventies' rejected the importance of a concern with appearances – and interests have been divided into three sectors – AC or DC or BC.

AC (After Carnaby) is composed of men crucified to an image of labouring – though they are possibly the generation responsible for less work than any previously in history. There could be no list of Best Dressed Men in this age grouping without absurdity. The Dirtiest T-shirt? The Most Patched Denims?

DC (During Carnaby) is the Lost Generation which came to an appreciation of clothes during the anarchy of the swinging sixties. Their yardstick was simply flamboyance, and no ruling measures of elegance can confine the choice.

BC (Before Carnaby) is an age category composed of men over the age of fifty years nowadays – and their standards are those of the reticent brainwashing of the *mores* of the 1930s. They respect good tailoring, cleanliness, neatness, understatement, consideration and a search for effect in pleasing terms. None of these is currently in fashion, and there is therefore no logical standard by which a list of Best Dressed Men can currently be chosen.

BEST BOUTONNIERE *The carnation*

Best because its *calyx* (the cup beneath the bloom from which the petals grow out) is bulky enough to be held firmly in place by the best buttonhole – which should be between one inch and one and an eighth inches long.

The best suits always have a lapel buttonhole. Small buttonholes, false buttonholes, and the absence of a buttonhole mark only the cheaper suits.

A rose is best only on St George's Day – which is the only day on which a gentleman would wear one. Cornflowers and orchids are respectively (a) twee, (b) high camp.

Best carnation for day-wear is the clove or deep red. A white carnation is best for formal evening wear or functions such as weddings. Any colour may be worn with a dinner suit.

A white carnation can be tinted to almost any shade by placing it overnight in a bottle of coloured ink. It will suck up the colour, though its life will be shortened.

Whatever colour, the bloom must be pulled through the buttonhole so the petals lie flush against the lapel. Small buttonholes do not allow this and expose you to the trauma of being approached by strangers and told: 'Excuse me, sir, but your calyx is sticking out.'

BEST TAILORS TODAY

There are four, depending upon what image you are pursuing. They are all in the Savile Row area of London.

Most sociably acceptable must be Hawes and Curtis of Dover Street, W1. They make for Prince Philip, Prince Charles and Prince Andrew, due to the fact that Prince Philip was recommended there by Lord Louis Mountbatten.

Most expensive London tailor is Huntsmans of Savile Row, where one of the firm's directors – Colin Hammick – has himself been voted on several Best Dressed Men listings. Aspiring clients must take their place on a waiting list.

Most successful tailor, in business terms, is probably Kilgour, French and Stanbury of Dover Street, W1, which has an enormous international clientele and can boast making the most famous set of tails ever – the suit worn by Fred Astaire in *Top Hat*.

Most famous tailor is probably Pooles and Cundey of Cork Street. They moved there when Savile Row was redeveloped, but were originally the first tailors to open in The Row. Other tailors moved in around them in the nineteenth century to share the aura of their fame.

Previously, Savile Row had been the habitat of London surgeons – but as the influx of tradesmen sent amenities plunging, they all moved off north westward to Harley Street. Savile Row thus swopped one set of cutters for another.

The superiority of Pooles at one time induced a certain arrogance in their attitude towards other craftsmen. 'We are Pooles,' was their slogan; 'the others are only puddles.'

'It's always the same, Dad – you never understand the latest gear!'

BEST FOREIGN TAILORS

Lanvin, in Paris, is admirable; Caraceni of Rome too. There used to be a good tailor in America, called Harris, but he's dead.

BEST TAILOR EVER *Henry Poole*

The Prince of Tailors. Poole was the great tailor of the late Victorian and early Edwardian era. He virtually 'started' Savile Row by opening premises there, and making the street famous.

A brilliant craftsman and stylist, Poole pursued as expensive a social life as his aristocratic clientele and was constantly on the verge of bankruptcy. He first introduced the idea of the men's club type of atmosphere for the tailor's shop and was famous among the *bon ton* for 'Pooley's claret', which he dispensed freely and at great hazard to the firm's economy.

An arrogant eccentric, he took lip from nobody. Once, submitted to a rude haranguing concerning the fit of one of his suits by the Prince of Wales (later Edward VII), Poole listened for a while with mounting irritation. Finally he produced a piece of tailor's chalk from his waistcoat pocket, drew white alteration marks all over the black jacket of the furious Prince, snapped 'Bring it in for alterations,' and stalked off.

BEST DRESSED BRITISH KINGS IN MODERN DRESS

Edward VII. He first brought the Homburg hat to Britain. He first applied double-breasted lapels to a single-breasted jacket. He first creased trousers up and down the front and back of the trouser leg; previously they were creased either at each side or pressed cylindrically without creases. He first formalized the double-breasted jacket. He first wore a white waistcoat and stiff dickey shirt for evening dress. He first popularized the bowler hat for wear in town.

Edward VIII. He first popularized turn-ups on trousers. He popularized the wide spread shirt collar and the wide 'Windsor' tie-knot. He popularized the Fair Isle sweater. He first wore 'midnight blue' instead of black for evening wear. He popularized the double-breasted dinner jacket. He first gave royal approval to suede shoes in the 1930s. Previous to his accolade they had been worn only by consenting adults in private.

BEST MEN'S FASHION DESIGNERS EXTANT

Hardy Amies (Britain).
Pierre Cardin (France).
Georgio Armani (Italy).
Jeff Sayre (American in Paris).
Bruno Piatelli (Italy).
Tom Gilbey (Britain).

BEST SHIRT-MAKER

We could get in trouble here, but the bespoke shirtmaking trade seems to have deteriorated. Or, at least, the ready-made shirt, with the vast improvement of fused collars, has improved so much that the price discrepancies of shirt-makers off Piccadilly hardly seem worth it.

Too, the traditional bespoke shirt-maker retains his blind faith in the 'two piece' collar – which does not afford the low sit of the shirt collar emerging fashionwise as we go into the 1980s. Hand-inserted linings give a much greater chance of a 'bubbling' collar too. John Langford, Rocola, Carven of Paris – are a better bet because they avoid the expensive gamble of wondering whether you'll like a made-to-measure shirt when it's made up.

BEST OVERCOATING MATERIAL *Vicuna*

Vicuna fibres – from an animal which is related to the camel – are the finest animal fibres that exists. They measure about 2,500 to the inch, which is about half the thickness of the very finest merino sheep wool. The natural habitat of the *Llama Vicunia* is the high uplands of the Andes between Lake Titicaca and the coast, and currently the animals are protected because the wide desire for their coats has threatened extinction.

Possibly the nearest rival to Vicuna is fibre from the coat of the related Guanaco, but the animal is even rarer and its coat not quite so luxurious. After them, fine Chinese Cashmere is next in the luxury line – but Vicuna makes the 'mere' in Cashmere ring true.

BEST EVENING WEAR INNOVATION *The dinner jacket*

On 10 October 1886, a Mr Griswold Lorrilard startled New York's 'Four Hundred' by appearing at the autumn ball of the Tuxedo Park Club in a short jacket with satin lapels. All other gentlemen present were wearing tails, but American society being what it was, he was not thrown out but won so many disciples that the 'tuxedo' was adopted officially by the club's menfolk for evening wear when ladies were not present. This was the birth of the dinner jacket.

BEST DAY-WEAR INNOVATION *The drape*

Scholte, a tailor in Heddon Street, off London's Regent Street, used to make the officers' uniforms for the Brigade of Guards in the 1930s. He noticed that the full hanging greatcoat, when belted in tight, gave the impression of much fullness of chest and a great impression of masculinity therefore.

He incorporated fullness into the upper portion of the jacket at the area in front of the 'scye' (the tailor's expression for the armhole – derived from the arm's eye) – adding an inch or two of unnecessary material over and above the 'fitting'. This was made to blouse out at front and back and achieved the same fullness effect.

'Drape', as he called it, made him famous and he died just after World War

II, leaving more than a quarter of a million pounds. Its exaggerated use by film stars in the post-war period gave the innovation the title 'American Drape' but it was a thoroughly British invention.

Best Men's Underwear *Sulka of New Bond Street*
First established in New York in the 1880s, they opened up in London about fifty years ago, and then in Paris.

Clientele includes crowned heads (and bottoms?) for made-to-measure silk underwear. They also make a highly specialized men's shirt with a camiknicker fastening under the fork for perfectionists who hate their shirts to ride up when they are jacketless.

They modestly forbear to name the Cabinet Minister who likes to smoke in bed, and insists on a pocket for his pipe in his made-to-measure pyjamas.

Best Riding Boots *Henry Maxwell, New Bond Street, London W1*
Founded in 1750 by spur-maker Henry Maxwell of Worcester.

Ambitious, he moved to Soho in 1756, where he established his forge in his garden; thence moved to Piccadilly in 1820. In the 1900s the company seemed threatened by a tendency for bootmakers to start manufacturing their own spurs – so Maxwell hit back by going into the boot business.

They supply a semi-fitted boot: a standard foot, but the back seam is not finished until the customer's foot has been measured.

They still have a pair of spurs originally ordered by Napoleon, but which he never got round to picking up.

Best Dressed Film Stars
Fred Astaire.
Adolphe Menjou.
Cary Grant.
Terry-Thomas.
Jack Buchanan.
Franklyn Pangbourne.
Edward Arnold.
David Niven.
Rex Harrison.

Best Hatter *Locks of St James's*
Veddy British. A beautiful anachronistic old shop with a great tradition. Locks it was who produced the first bowler hat. They had been given drawings of the shape by a Mr William Coke, a kinsman to the Earl of Leicester, who in the early nineteenth century began to fret at losing so many tall top hats when riding.

Locks subcontracted the design to a hatting family named Beaulieu, anglicized descendants of Huguenots, and it is from their name and not from its bowl shape that the name derives.

Locks themselves have clearly resented the fact that their hat deified a mere subcontractor, and to this day themselves refer to the hat as a 'coke' or a hard felt.

BEST NECKTIE KNOT *The Windsor knot*
Named the Windsor after the man who popularized it – the Duke of Windsor. Its advantage derives from the fact that it applies equal tension on either side of the knot and does not therefore give a lopsided effect, as with the traditional wrap–over method.

BEST MEN'S HATS
The boater. Though relegated to school uniform nowadays, the boater has a shape which quite curiously suits *everybody*. It is highly attractive on both men and women; the only truly unisexual shape in that it can be worn by women without the lesbian associations induced by women in top hats, bowlers or cloth caps. The boater was seen at its best when worn by Maurice Chevalier – with the seemingly contradictory formality of a dinner suit. *Insouciance!*
The bowler. This attained its pinnacle of elegance with the curly-brimmed version popular in the revived Edwardian look of the 1950s.

It is interesting to note that both the boater and the bowler are 'hard' hats, i.e. shaped to the cranium in manufacture rather than being stretched to fit the cranium via the material of the soft felt or cloth cap.

BEST MALE FASHION ERAS
The late Plantagenet period.
The Regency period.
The revived and modified Edwardiana of the 1950s.

Note that all these idealized the 'natural' but virile shape – emphasizing masculinity with shoulder focus and hose, breeches or trousers which revealed the shape of the leg.

BEST RAINCOAT *The trench coat*
It is intensely practical, elegantly dashing via its militaristic connotations, and has shown itself adaptable to all kinds of materials – proofed cloths, leather, suede, tweeds, fur, cashmere or Vicuna.

BEST UMBRELLA *The telescopic*
Easily carried in a brief-case, or in a deep pocket, its cover can also be used as a male handbag. It avoids that rather Neville Chamberlainesque association which bespeaks dull Victorianism, middle-class morality, the effeminacy of a fear of the elements, and an arrogant tool to prod the proletariat.

BEST MEN'S SHOE *The Chelsea boot*
A derivative of the original Wellington Boot – which title has now been vulgarized to be associated with children's waterproof rubber footwear, and which was launched by the famous Duke – these boots first became popular in this century with the revived Edwardiana of the 1950s. Because of their lack of lacing they did not impede the hang of narrow bottomed trousers.

Because of their depth, they hide what is perhaps the most unattractive area of a man's *ensemble* – the sock-revealing gap between the top of the shoe and the bottom of the trouser. They have the merit, indeed, of allowing any coloured socks to be worn with any coloured suit – because they hide the sock entirely.

And not having laces, they allow the foot to swell naturally and comfortably without laces cutting into the instep.

BEST READY-MADE TROUSERS FOR THE FAT MAN *Sansabeli*
These are high-rise trousers which boast patented waistband with triple-stretch webbing which controls the *embonpoint* with comfort and firmness. Originally of French design, the idea has been developed by the US firm of Jaymar-Ruby, who sell five million pairs a year to chubby Americans.

The high rise – the 'rise' is the distance in a pair of trousers from fork to waistline – covers the very paunchy, and even improves the look of a flat stomach. Those distributed in Britain are manufactured in Italy.

BEST READY-MADE TAILOR
Probably the Chester Barrie range, manufactured by the firm of Simon Ackerman. The industry generally acknowledges that it sets a standard of manufacture for all ready-made tailors to emulate – and long-time boss Myron Ackerman was acknowledged for many years as the Father Confessor of the trade. The firm was in financial trouble not long ago, but seems to be coming through okay now, via absorption by the Austin Reed group. The range is retailed through many top class men's stores around the world.

BEST YEARS OF OUR LIVES – MENSWEAR-WISE
Study of fashion suggests that basic psychologies change roughly every decade and elegance reaches a peak approximately every half century.

If we take the twentieth century, we see that it started on a wave of elegance and imperial formality during the years up to World War I.

Following upon the social shake-up of World War I, we descended from the formal tens into the mad twenties and followed up with the sober reaction of the depressed thirties.

Another reaction brought the emphasized sexuality of the big shoulders and drape shapes of the aggressive forties – aggression obviously underlined by World War II.

The fifties calmed down into the considered, even affected, Edwardian nostalgia which reflected the dandyism of half a century previously. The swinging sixties went into a throwback to the flamboyant anarchy of the twenties, and the slob seventies became the anti-fashion decade (even sadder than the thirties) of the twentieth century – with a general acceptance of clothes for digging a hole in the road in.

The eighties were ushered in hand in hand with a return to the physical emphases of the forties – big shoulders and the padded attributes of masculinity. The nineties seem set to start reflecting elegance again.

The best years of our lives, therefore, have been the 1910s and the 1950s; with the natty nineties still to come.

BEST SHOEMAKER *G. J. Cleverley*

In London's Cork Street, first started making shoes at the famous house of Tuczecs. The first pair he actually ever cut as a journeyman were for Rudolph Valentino, for wear in the original *Blood and Sand*.

Since then he's also made for Rex Harrison in *My Fair Lady*, for Sir Ralph Richardson, Ray Milland, and a cast of thousands.

BEST MEN'S TOILETRY RANGE *Knize 10*

Necessarily a subjective choice. Knize 10 was one of the very first men's toiletries – possibly *the* first. It was launched by the famous Viennese tailoring house Knize (established 1858), more than fifty years ago, and initially it was simply given away to important clients as an exclusive present, to heads of state and rich industrialists. Knize were appointed grooming and tailoring purveyors to the Imperial Austrian Court before World War I, but the firm had financial difficulties soon after World War II and ceased making Knize 10 in 1950. But manufacture has been recommenced recently and Ettinger have exclusive UK distribution. Toilet water, cologne, after-shave, deodorant and hair lotion are available – for a price – as well as bath and body foam soap and shaving cream.

BEST DRESSED US POLITICIAN

Undoubtedly Ronald Reagan. His theatrical background has impressed upon him the need to project a pleasing image, and he manages a natural elegance which must be at least partly due to his experience as a male model in early years.

In the world league, US politicians are placed Second in the Best Dressed List. Best, on average, are the Italians. British politicians, for all that country's sartorial traditions, come nowhere.

BEST DRESSED THEATRICAL DESIGNER *Cecil Beaton*

His own clothes were always as impeccable as the designs he produced in a dozen directions. Pointless to look closer in time for a younger man. Modern designers study aesthetics in every aspect but their own appearances.

Best Dressed Tailor *Colin Hammick*
Design Director, H. Huntsman and Sons, Ltd, 11, Savile Row, London W1.

He has at his disposal the excellent facilities of a fine tailoring house, of course, but has also the tall, slim figure from which men's clothes can most elegantly hang.

He is, too, an example of the fact that at least sixty per cent of being well dressed depends upon the personality of the wearer rather than on the clothes themselves. He has an elegant personality.

The reason why great tailors are not themselves apparently well dressed (with a few exceptions) is because they have necessarily the self-effacement of the tradesman – whereas being well dressed needs a strong personal projection of charm and self-confidence.

Best Defunct Male Fashion Accessory *Spats*
These not only had the commendable function of protecting part of the boot from mud splashes (hence the name – Spatterdashes), but they hid from view the ugly ankle section where shoe or boot top is not met by the lower section of the trouser.

Too, their contrast effect around the top of the boot undoubtedly gave visual conception to the two-tone shoe of the 1920s, which were so favoured by the racy set that they became known as 'co-respondents' shoes'.

Best U.S. Contribution To Men's Fashions *Jeans*
These have now become an international uniform which can be traced back to the tent-fabric inventions of Levi. They are probably the *only* entirely original contribution to the man's wardrobe from America – and have an indigenous aspect which is not widely known. Sociologist Pearl Binder says that tight-bottomed jeans are psychologically attempting to reproduce the effect originally achieved by the Red Indians, who did not cover their buttocks but whose trousers were like '*chaps*' covering the shin, thigh and groin, but giving no protection to the rear. In attempting to establish an indigenous identification with the surroundings, says Pearl Binder, early settlers adopted very tight trousers – though the Red Indians, when they first bought Paleface trousers, used to cut the seats out for proper comfort. This is possibly why Sitting Bull always chose a warm spot. There may be some connection here with the fact that the Horse was not indigenous to North America. Only when the Spaniards took horses to the new continent and redskins learned to ride, did the natives realize the good sense of a good seat.

THE MILITARY

Alun Chalfont

BEST PISTOL *The Stechkin APS* (USSR)
The German Walther PPK 9 millimetre automatic, in spite of the awful nonsense written about it by Ian Fleming, was a very good hand-gun; and the best pistol available today is a development from the Walther PP series – the Russian 9 mm APS, known as the Stechkin. It has a cyclic rate of fire of 750 rounds a minute and a practical rate of ninety rounds a minute. The magazine takes twenty rounds, and by converting the wooden holster into a stock and raising the backsight the pistol can be used with reasonable accuracy up to two-hundred metres. A far cry from Wyatt Earp and the other heroes of the Wild West who, whatever may have been written about their legendary skills, would have had trouble hitting the side of a barn at fifty paces.

BEST RIFLE
Difficult to choose between the Russian Kalashnikov (now the chosen weapon of every Bedouin tribesman and Arab terrorist), the French 5·56 mm Clairon, the Israeli Galil (also 5·56 mm) and the British Army's Enfield 4·85 mm Individual Weapon. The verdict goes by a small margin to the Enfield, because of its lightness (7 lb 7 oz empty), excellent optical sight and its combination of rifle and sub-machine-gun qualities. Still in the experimental stage.

BEST SOLDIERS
For jungle operations, the Gurkhas; for armoured warfare, the Germans; in

the mountains, the Swiss; for undercover operations, the British Special Air Service; for tunnel warfare, the Chinese People's Liberation Army; for ceremonial parades, the band and drums of the Royal Marines; for any task requiring patience and unshakeable determination, even under the most miserable, dangerous or boring conditions, the British infantry of the line.

Best Generals

Some people say the choice lies between three Alexanders – Alexander the Great, Field Marshal Earl Alexander of Tunis and General Alexander Haig, once Chief of Staff at the White House and Supreme Allied Commander in Europe. Although any of these is better qualified for the Hall of Fame than some of the more familiar candidates (such as Napoleon, a much overrated commander who made a complete mess of Waterloo, or Marlborough who made very heavy weather of Blenheim), there are others who have to be considered very seriously – Wellington, the sadly neglected Blücher, Rommel and our own Montgomery who, for all his faults, was one of the best battlefield tacticians in modern warfare. In the end, however, the soldiers' Oscar for the best general in the history of war must go to Alexander the Great, who died at the age of thirty-three, and who was, apart from being an outstanding military commander, a man of great moral and intellectual stature. He introduced into warfare new standards of humanity, tolerance and compassion.

Best admirals: Nelson (by a distance); Gorshkov (USSR); Rickover (USA).

Best Aircraft

In the short history of the military aircraft a number of names have passed into the language and become legends – the American Flying Fortress bomber, the German Stuka dive-bomber, and the British Spitfire fighter. Today the military aeroplane is a complicated weapon-system, packed with electronics and modern weapons. The best are probably the Russian Tupolev V-G strategic nuclear bomber (known to NATO intelligence officers as the 'Backfire'), the Tu 28P fighter, the largest fighter aircraft in service in the world today, the F-16, an American-designed air combat fighter, and the British Hawker Siddeley 'Harrier', a fighter ground-attack aircraft which can take off vertically or from very short runways. Each is almost certainly predominant in its class. There are, however, aircraft on the drawing board which will make them all obsolescent in a few years.

Best Tank

A close contest between the British Chieftain, the Russian T72, the American XM-1 and the German Leopard 2. But look out for Britain's new main battle tank, due to replace Chieftain in the late 1980s. It will be fitted with the new Chobham armour, making it virtually invulnerable against current anti-tank weapons (although possibly not against those of the late 1980s!) It will have

'Aw c'mon, Genghis – we need one more to make up a horde!'

a top speed of 70 kph compared with Chieftain's 45 kph; and will be equipped with the British-designed 120 mm gun – the best tank gun in the world. It will, for those interested in these matters, cost about £1 million per tank to develop.

BEST SUBMARINE
Attack submarine: Russian Victor class.
Ballistic missile submarine: American Trident class.
Small submarine: German 206 class (450 tons).

BEST FRIGATE
Guided missile frigates *Tromp* and *de Ruyter* (Netherlands).

BEST MOBILE NUCLEAR MISSILE
Russian SS 20.

BEST MILITARY HELICOPTER
Boeing Chinook (USA).

BEST MILITARY BRIDGE
Fairey Medium Girder Bridge (Britain).

BEST MILITARY ACADEMY *West Point* (USA)
First year cadets ('plebes') are treated like a lower form of animal life (cf. fags in *Tom Brown's Schooldays*). The 'honour system' requires cadets to report on other cadets who betray the Academy's idiosyncratic standards of ethics and discipline. The atmosphere is a cross between an open prison and a British public school – but it turns out some of the best officers in the world.
   Runners-up: St Cyr (France); Sandhurst (Britain).

BEST STAFF COLLEGE *The Royal College of Defence Studies* (*London*)
Known as the Imperial Defence College when Britain had an Empire to defend. A highly civilized year-long seminar at which senior British officers, usually destined for the highest ranks in the armed forces, are given a chance to place their military expertise in a broad political and strategic context. The pink gins in the officers' mess bar are memorable.

'I know we've been here for four hundred years, but we'll certainly pull out as soon as the Britons show they're able to defend themselves.'

BEST MILITARY MUSEUM
1. The Kremlin Armoury (Moscow).
2. The British Army Museum (Chelsea, London).
3. The Battlefield of Isandlwhana (Kwa Zulu).

BEST MILITARY UNIFORM
1. Chinese People's Liberation Army. Cool in summer, warm in winter. No badges of rank. Cheap, rugged and workmanlike.
2. French Foreign Legion. A combination of functional design and Beau Geste glamour.
   (The *worst* Army uniform ever invented was the British battle-dress of World War II.

BEST MILITARY JOKE
'Cuban forces in Africa are a force for stability.' – Mr Andrew Young, court jester to the US Administration.

BEST MILITARY DRINK *Gin Piaz*
A version of the traditional Royal Navy drink, pink gin, much favoured in Army cantonments in India in the days of the Raj. Gin, angostura bitters, a little water (very little) and two or three small pearl onions ('piaz' in Urdu). Five or six to be drunk before a huge curry lunch on Sundays – lunch to begin about 4 pm when the worst heat of the day is passing.

BEST MILITARY RANKS
Lieutenant-Colonel (or the equivalent in other services). At this rank an officer usually gets his first genuinely independent command. The ratio of subordinate people to be ordered about and looked after to the number of superiors and staff officers wishing to interfere is just about right at this level.
Corporal (or the equivalent in other services). As for Lieutenant-Colonel (above), with the added advantage of not having to dress for dinner.

MUSIC

Alan Blyth

BEST COMPOSER (SEVENTEENTH CENTURY)

Without question the outstanding composer of the pre-classical period was Claudio Monteverdi (1567–1643), whose three extant operas and *Vespers* of 1610, not to mention his vast output of madrigals, created an individual and original style of vocal writing, more vital and broader in range than any of his predecessors. His invention and his expressive powers, in delineating both comedy, love and tragedy, were unsurpassed in his time. He also led the way in the development of instrumental writing that was to flower in the work of his successors.

BEST COMPOSERS (BAROQUE ERA)

Bach (1685–1750) and Handel (1685–1759) must share this honour. Bach, working in a primarily sacred context, Handel in a secular one, were both supreme masters of their idioms, capable of almost endless melodic and contrapuntal invention, as skilled in the writing of vocal music as they were in the instrumental field, both almost as fecund in their output while maintaining an almost incredibly high standard of writing. Bach's forty-eight preludes and fugues have rightly been dubbed music's Old Testament. Handel's oratorios remain unique masterpieces of their genre.

BEST COMPOSER (CLASSICAL ERA)

Mozart – need one say more?

BEST COMPOSER (ROMANTIC ERA)

Although a hundred years after his death still a controversial figure, Richard Wagner (1813–83) has undoubtedly entered the Valhalla of the greatest composers by dint of his operas, which stand as one of the most towering achievements of civilized man, both in their originality of textual and musical thought and in their sheer all-embracing universality of concept. Wagner's influence was also wholly dominant over his successors.

BEST COMPOSER (TWENTIETH CENTURY)

Igor Stravinsky (1882–1971) has certainly been the most influential composer of the century, chiefly on account of the rhythmic and melodic innovations of his early ballet works. After *The Rite of Spring* (1913), nothing in music could be the same again. For the next fifty years, he remained a seminal figure, constantly changing his style and absorbing the work of others into his own special idiom, and changing that of those younger than himself.

BEST COMPOSER (MODERN AGE)

The palm here must go to Karlheinz Stockhausen because, after his works came into prominence, nothing could quite be as it was. His advances (?) in the techniques of producing sound, using the most up-to-date scientific devices undoubtedly altered the perspective of music. Whether his influence becomes a lasting one remains to be seen – and heard.

BEST SYMPHONY

In an over-populated area, Beethoven's Fifth must cling to its pre-eminence for its achievement above all other achievements in the arts, *multum in parvo*. No other symphony says so much in such a short space of time – less than half an hour – or is so successful at plucking triumph out of tragedy.

BEST CHAMBER-MUSIC WORK

For its profundity of utterance and depth of feeling, Schubert's C major Quintet remains supreme, with its slow movement perhaps the most searching music ever composed in this genre (although Mozart's late quintets offer a serious challenge to Schubert's supremacy).

BEST PIANO WORK

In another overcrowded field, the choice must be arbitrary, but for resourcefulness in exploring the instrument's possibilities and for inventive virtuosity, Beethoven's 'Diabelli' Variations would be hard to surpass unless it be with the same composer's 'Hammerklavier' Sonata.

BEST CHORAL WORK

For its integrity of purpose and technical inspiration, Bach's Mass in B Minor is unlikely to be outdone. Those with a less severe taste might choose Verdi's *Requiem*.

BEST CONCERTO
Breadth of expression combined with the need for extreme virtuosity on the part of the soloist have never been achieved in greater measure than in Brahms's Second Piano Concerto. Most pianists consider it to be the Everest among concertos, a work in which spirit and flesh must be in ideal balance.

BEST UNCATEGORIZED WORK
The nineteenth century, in particular the romantic era, produced many works of genius that fit into no particular category. Among these Mahler's *Das Lied von der Erde* for mezzo and tenor soloists and orchestra holds a special place for its conviction, orchestral variety and musical beauty.

BEST COMIC OPERA *Così fan tutte by Mozart*
The perfect ensemble opera, it sets off three pairs of characters in a study of human emotions put to music of surpassing eloquence and beauty in the context of humorous situation. A cynical, practical joke is here transformed into profound comment on human failings and young love by Mozart's sublime score.

BEST DRAMATIC OPERA *Otello by Verdi*
Librettist Boito's finely tempered condensation of Shakespeare's play provoked from Verdi, in his penultimate work, a tightly knit score that fuses recitative and aria into an ideally flexible and expressive language that is tailored to the needs of the dramatic situation. The action moves swiftly and inevitably to its tragic close while allowing time for the illumination of character by subtle, pungent vocal and orchestral phraseology. No wonder many consider the piece superior to the original play.

BEST EPIC OPERA *Tristan und Isolde by Wagner*
Following his studies of Schopenhauer's philosophy, Wagner (setting, as usual, his own text) here extended the scope of opera to include psychological study of the eponymous hero and heroine through a musical language, continuous in structure, that peered beyond the conventional world of tonality through the extreme use of chromaticism and the profound and extended use of *leitmotiv*. The unconscious mind is here revealed as never before and seldom since in music of poetic, intense richness.

BEST TWENTIETH-CENTURY OPERA *Pelléas et Mélisande by Debussy*
Based on Maeterlinck's tragedy of the same name, Debussy's only opera creates a haunting world all its own, a twilight atmosphere and mood in which a continuous and delicate orchestral tissue underlays a new kind of vocal utterance,

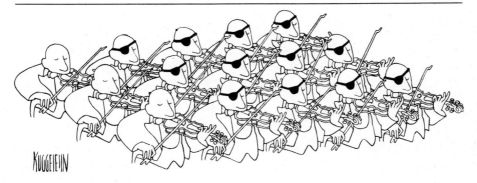

KUGGEEIN

at once lyrical and conversational, exploring the minds and actions of the three principals (the girl and boy of the title and Golaud, Mélisande's jealous husband) and expressing their emotions in music of infinite and unique subtlety.

BEST OPERA SINGER OF THE PAST
Although her vocal technique was far from perfect, Maria Callas was able to sing and act with greater dramatic truthfulness than any of her many rivals of the past or present. She brought to bear on all her roles an intelligence and understanding that enabled her to bring words and music into ideal accord, thus raising operatic interpretation to the highest art.

BEST MALE OPERA SINGER OF TODAY
Few tenors of the past or present have achieved so much in such a wide repertory as Placido Domingo, whose interpretations are as notable for their musicality as for their vocal opulence.

BEST LIEDER SINGER
In boxing the compass of German song, Dietrich Fischer-Dieskau has achieved more than any other singer in this field. He has recorded all the songs of Schubert, Schumann, Brahms, Richard Strauss and Hugo Wolf that are suitable for the male voice. His interpretations pierce to the heart of poem and music alike.

BEST FEMALE SINGER
For the sheer variety of her art, the power and intensity of her utterance and the thoroughness of her study, Dame Janet Baker has been outstanding in our time. She is as accomplished at interpreting Bach as Britten, Schubert as Massenet. She has distinguished herself in the opera house, on the concert platform and in recital. She has won the admiration of her colleagues, the devotion of her audiences, the unanimous praise of critics.

BEST PIANIST OF THE PAST
Legend credits Liszt with prodigious feats, but regrettably we have no evidence to support his claims. Artur Schnabel left records and the word of his many still-living pupils and admirers to testify to his intellectual control and mastery of phrasing. He is the supreme musician's pianist as opposed to pianist's pianist.

BEST PIANIST OF TODAY
For his range of repertory and complete understanding of all the idioms with which he is acquainted, Vladimir Ashkenazy is undoubted king. Mozart, Beethoven, Chopin, Brahms, Scriabin, Prokofiev are all his province and he rules each with his questing mind and incredible hands.

BEST VIOLINIST OF THE PAST
Again Paganini's reputation should win him the accolade but without the aural evidence who is to say he surpassed the musicality of the great Fritz Kreisler? And Kreisler had the advantage of playing all the works written since Paganini's death.

BEST VIOLINIST OF TODAY
This must be a hotly disputed title, there being so many good players about. For fine definition of tone, sweet yet big tone, technical command, the pick of an outstanding bunch must be Itzhak Perlman – who has to play from a chair.

BEST CELLIST OF THE PAST
Pablo Casals, a player of classical strength and emotional drive, succeeded more than anyone in raising the stature of the cello to its present pinnacle.

BEST CELLIST OF TODAY
With a repertory of almost incredible variety, Mstislav Rostropovich is acclaimed wherever and whenever he plays for his marvellously warm tone and total commitment to the music in hand.

BEST COMPOSER/PERFORMER
Benjamin Britten was the epitome of a great playing composer. He will be remembered as much for his major contribution to the repertories of opera, song and instrumental music as for his piano playing and his conducting, which had the unique stature available only to a creative artist in his own right.

BEST ACCOMPANIST
Gerald Moore raised the accompanist's trade from that of humble supporter of singer or instrumentalist to that of high art. He told how he accomplished it in his autobiography, *Am I Too Loud?*

BEST CONDUCTOR OF THE PAST

Wilhelm Furtwängler (1886–1954) must win this accolade by a short head from the even more renowned Toscanini for the wider scope of his repertory, the greater profundity of his interpretations. The breadth and spontaneity of his conducting, the warmth and depth of sound he drew from his orchestra (in the main, the Berlin Philharmonic) and the amazing intensity of his operatic readings have become a legend confirmed by his many recordings. Whether in Mozart, Beethoven, Bruckner, Brahms, Tchaikovsky or Wagner, Furtwängler achieved prodigies in creative interpretation unequalled by contemporaries or successors.

BEST CONDUCTOR OF TODAY

In spite of the considerable and varying claims of such giants of the podium as Karajan, Bernstein, Abbado and Solti, I choose Bernard Haitink, whose consistent fidelity to the composer in hand, and his achievement of precision clarity, never gained at the expense of spontaneity, place him a short head above those who may claim more dynamic personalities. Orchestral players and choral singers unite in their praise of Haitink. His concert repertory is huge, and he has recently demonstrated that he is no less responsive to the needs of opera.

BEST ORCHESTRA

If warmth allied to extreme virtuosity are to be the criteria, as I think they should be, the crown must go to the Berlin Philharmonic, who can and do usually produce a staggeringly refulgent sound. To have heard these players in full cry in Beethoven or Richard Strauss is the experience of a lifetime.

BEST STRING QUARTET

After thirty years in each other's company, the members of the Amadeus have naturally achieved an instinctive rapport and a mature standard of interpretation not equalled by any of their rivals. The breadth of their repertory is also extraordinary.

BEST CONCERT HALL

The most congenial and the most acoustically pleasing concert hall is the Concertgebouw in Amsterdam, a fitting home of the great Concertgebouw Orchestra, at present enjoying a distinguished reputation under its chief, Bernard Haitink.

BEST OPERA HOUSE

For grand opera the choice must be the Royal Opera House, Covent Garden, a building of Victorian elegance at once friendly in atmosphere yet capable of housing lavish productions. For intimate opera, the Cuvilliés Theater, in Munich, a restored rococo gem, deserves the accolade. Here you can re-live the experience of being a spectator at the court of an elegant aristocrat of the past while enjoying the highest musical standards of today.

BEST AUDIENCE
The Dutch, who invariably stand to applaud performances and who have an almost infinite capacity for enjoyment.

BEST RECORD COMPANY
In a highly competitive field standards continually fluctuate, each company vying for the services of the most renowned performers. At present the best is undoubtedly EMI, who are achieving the most convincing and realistic sound both in conventional and the recently initiated digital field. By a short head they have the most distinguished group of artists on their roster but the German firm Deutsche Grammophon is hot on their heels.

BEST ORCHESTRAL RECORD
Performances of Beethoven symphonies on disc are legion so that the continuing ascendency of Otto Klemperer's interpretation of the 'Eroica' Symphony is all the more unexpected, but for its rugged lucidity as a reading, for the superb quality of the orchestral playing (Philharmonia *circa* 1960) and for the clarity of the recorded sound, it has not been equalled, let alone surpassed. Given the greatness of the music itself, this must take the accolade.

BEST RECORD OF AN OPERA
For standing the test of time and for the quality and spontaneity of performance, three sets rank as just about equal: Bohm's HMV set of *Così fan tutte* (not to be confused with his earlier or later sets); Beecham's *La Bohème* with Victoria de los Angeles as Mimi, and Jussi Björling as Rodolfo; either of Hans Knappertsbusch's 'live' Bayreuth sets of *Parsifal*. There is a classic, timeless feeling about all these readings that place them well above their rivals.

BEST CRITIC
The most knowledgeable and entertaining writer is Andrew Porter, late of the *Financial Times*, now working for the *New Yorker*. His judgments have earned him an almost godlike authority among his contemporaries.

BEST MUSICAL ANECDOTE
When Sir Malcolm Sargent visited the Far East, Sir Thomas Beecham commented: 'I see Flash is in Japan'.

BEST COMPOSER OF BALLET SCORES
Undoubtedly Tchaikovsky surpassed everyone past and present in matching music to subject and at the same time wrote music unforgettable in its own right.

BEST CLASSICAL BALLET
Tchaikovsky's *Swan Lake* (choreography Petipa) for its superb score and chances for both refined and brilliant dancing allied to interesting characterization.

BEST TWENTIETH-CENTURY BALLET
Prokofiev's *Romeo and Juliet* (choreography Kenneth Macmillan) for its score, perfectly attuned to the action, for its wonderful evocation of Shakespeare's play, and for the opportunity it gives for varied and characterful scenery.

BEST BALLET DANCER OF THE PAST
By all accounts Pavlova had unique gifts for affecting interpretation of the classics and for delicacy of movement. She also had a star personality.

BEST BALLET DANCER OF TODAY
Over a career lasting more than forty years Dame Margot Fonteyn has established an undisputed supremacy as a stylist and as an interpreter. Her performances of all the major classical roles and of many others created specifically for her by Sir Frederick Ashton have been models of intelligent dancing. We will be lucky to see her like again.

BEST CHOREOGRAPHER OF THE PAST
Michael Fokine, working for the wizard impresario Diaghilev, attained wonders of originality in advancing the possibilities of dance, particularly in the ballets he worked on with Stravinsky, among them *The Firebird*.

BEST CHOREOGRAPHER OF TODAY
The man who more than any other gave British ballet such a pre-eminent place in the ballet firmament is Sir Frederick Ashton. With the support of Ninette de Valois he created virtually a whole repertory for Sadler's Wells (later the Royal) Ballet. His variety of mood and of subject in writing ballets has not been surpassed.

BEST POP GROUP
The quality of their lyrics and the originality of their music ensured that the Beatles were able to match their extraordinary popular success with an artistic stature well beyond that attainable by most of their rivals. Their album *Sergeant Pepper's Lonely Hearts Club Band* (1967) sold a million copies in advance of publication.

BEST POP SINGER
For his success when he was active, and the legend he left behind, Elvis Presley

(1935–77) was undoubtedly the greatest in his field, catching the plaudits of the millions for his rhythmically exciting performances.

Best Composer Of Popular Music In The 1970s
Paul McCartney – for the originality of his songs and their lasting value.

Best Jazz Orchestra
The elegant, distinctive style of Duke Ellington (1899–1974), added to his great popularity, suggest that his was the best jazz band of his or any generation. His genius was creative and influenced all his successors. In spite of his immense success, he maintained his integrity and his loyalty to the jazz heritage.

Best Jazz Singer
The depth of emotion found in the work of Billie Holiday makes her undoubted front runner in this field. She also had an innate sense of style and declaimed the soulful texts of her repertory as if she truly meant them.

Best Brass Band
Black Dyke Mills Band has maintained an unbeatable consistency of sound and adventurousness.

PLAYTIME

◆

Nigel Dempster

BEST GOLF COURSES

The choice of Jack Nicklaus, the world's finest golfer over the last two decades, is St Andrews, Fife, where he has won two British Opens, in 1970 and 1978, closely followed by Muirfield, in East Lothian. The best golf course in America is generally held to be Pebble Beach, Monterey, which is lapped by the Pacific, followed by Augusta National, Augusta, Georgia, home of the Masters Tournament. On the Continent, Sotogrande, Costa del Sol, Spain, is considered the best example of famous golf architect Trent Jones, while scenically, Killarney in County Kerry, once the private course of Viscount Castlerosse, has no peer. In England, the title must be divided between Wentworth, Surrey, and Royal Lytham, St Anne's, Lancashire.

BEST NIGHT CLUBS

Annabel's, Berkeley Square, London, is named after the Marquis of Londonderry's sister, Lady Annabel, who in 1963 when the club opened, was married to Old Etonian Mark Birley, its founder. The cuisine and cellar are still internationally renowned and there is no better manager than Mr Louis who has been there since the opening night. Annabel's is the only night club which has Prince Charles as a member and he is a regular patron. The most popular night club in London for visiting Hollywood stars like Steve McQueen, Ryan O'Neal and Sylvester Stallone, is Tramp, Jermyn Street, which celebrated its tenth anniversary in December 1979.

In Paris the best is Castel's, owned by discerning gourmet Jean Castel, while New York has a new contender in the shape of La Boite to challenge Double's and the city's oldest club, Le Club, which was chosen by John and Caroline Kennedy for their joint birthday party. In Los Angeles, Pip's and On The Rox are the best while Washington night life starts and ends at Pisces.

BEST DISCOTHEQUES

America's best known discotheque, Studio 54, West 54th Street, New York, is in danger of losing its crown to Xenon, housed in a nearby theatre, which is better managed and more exclusive. In London Regine's reigns as a novelty, whereas her clubs in New York and Paris are no longer fashionable. In St Tropez Les Caves du Roi in the Byblos Hotel is the best in the south of France while the King's Club, Palace Hotel, St Moritz, and Greengo, Palace Hotel, Gstaad, are the best après-ski discos in Switzerland. New Jimmy's in Paris is still the best after an almost twenty-year reign; in Italy there is Jackie O in Rome and Number One in Milan and in Australia Pip's in Sydney is a branch of the less good Pip's in L.A. and the best in Melbourne is The Underground.

BEST CARIBBEAN PLAYGROUNDS

The Bahamas, because of their brilliantly clear and clean waters, have become the best Caribbean playground, with Lyford Cay and the Ocean Club, Nassau, leading the field, followed closely by Harbour Island, a thirty-minute flight away, and Eleuthera, a short flight beyond that, the best alternatives. In Barbados, Sandy Lane with its superb hotel (owned by Trust Houses Forte) is the best part of a beautiful island, while Mustique, an hour's flight away, is a 1,400-acre private development boasting among its residents Princess Margaret and the Earl of Lichfield. Political considerations rule out, sadly, Jamaica except for the Round Hill estate, near Montego Bay, and in Haiti there are claims for Habitation Leclerc in Port au Prince. Other former Caribbean havens like Antigua and Martinique have become spoiled by package tours and cruise liners.

BEST WINTER RESORTS – SUN

Mexico has taken over as the country with the best winter resorts and Acapulco, Cuernavaca and Puerto Vallarta have equal claims. In the Pacific, Bora Bora is being developed by film producer Dino de Laurentiis with taste not found in neighbouring Tahiti, and in Fiji the best resort is Pacific Harbour which has Saudi Arabian Adnan Khashoggi as an investor. He also owns the Mount Kenya Safari Club, Nanyuki, which is the best inland resort, while on the Indian Ocean coast the best is the Minarani Club. Under canvas, the best wildlife camp in East Africa is Governor's Camp, Masai Mara, Kenya. Thailand and Singapore are trying to enter the exclusive tourist market for beach resort holidays, but the best in the Far East is the Indonesian island of Bali.

BEST WINTER RESORTS – SNOW

In France the best skiing resorts are Megeve (developed by the Rothschild family), Courcheval and Val D'Isère. Switzerland has Gstaad, now more fashionable than St Moritz, while the best in Austria is St Anton and its neighbour Zurs.

In America Aspen, Colorado, is still the best with Jackson's Hole, Wyoming, considered an equal by many. In Japan Sapporo, home of a Winter Olympics, is the best but overcrowded, and Mount Buller, south of Melbourne, is favoured by Australians. Britain's fledgling winter sports industry is concentrated on the Cairngorms and the best resort is Aviemore, developed by the late Lord Fraser who owned Harrods among his stores empire.

BEST CASINOS

The best casino in Europe is in Baden Baden, Germany, a spa town on the Rhine near Strasbourg and in the Black Forest. The best earner is the casino at Divonne les Bains near the French-Swiss border, which owes its popularity to the fact that there are no casinos in Switzerland. The best in the south of

'We caught him trying to get out.'

France is still the casino in Monte Carlo, while on the Atlantic coast of France, Deauville has a better casino than Biarritz. In Greece the best is Mount Parnes outside Athens, while in London Aspinall's has taken over from The Clermont, ironically started by John Aspinall and sold to the Playboy organization. In America the best is Caesar's Palace, Las Vegas, and the best in the Caribbean is Paradise Island, Nassau, Bahamas.

BEST RACECOURSES

The best racecourse is Flemington, Melbourne, home of the Melbourne Cup, Australia's best race, while the best race meeting is Royal Ascot, Ascot, every June for four days on the racecourse owned by The Queen. The best race is still the Epsom Derby, Epsom, held on the first Wednesday in June – the 1979 running marked the 200th Derby. In France the best urban racecourse is Long-champ in the Bois du Boulogne, where the best race in terms of prize money, the Prix de l'Arc de Triomphe, is run every October; and the best rural race-course is Chantilly where the equivalent of the Derby and Oaks are run.

In America the best race meeting is at Saratoga, New York State, every August, while the best race is the Kentucky Derby at Lexington Downs in May. The best racecourse is Belmont, New York City, on the east coast and Santa Anita, Los Angeles, on the west. In Ireland the best is The Curragh, home of the Irish Sweeps Derby, and the best planned racecourse is the brand new Sha Tin in Hongkong, officially opened in January 1979 at a cost of £65 million. The best racecourse town is Newmarket, the headquarters of British racing, where King Charles II started the vogue for the sport of kings.

BEST FESTIVAL

The best by far is Carnival in Rio de Janeiro, which has been emulated but never bettered, and is still free of the commercialization which has overtaken Mardi Gras in New Orleans. Carnival in the Caribbean is best in Trinidad, although St Vincent, in the Grenadines, is the best small carnival.

BEST GAMBLERS

The world's best poker player is Walter Clyde 'Pug' Pearson, born in Kentucky and now living in Las Vegas, as is the best gambler at tennis, Bobby Riggs, who is based at The Dunes Hotel. The best tennis player to gamble on, how-ever, is Tony Vincent, the USA veterans champion. In backgammon the best gambler is Jean Noel Grinda, a former Davis Cup player in the 1950s and son of a Cannes property millionaire. The best odds-maker is Jimmy the Greek, another Las Vegas resident, who is responsible for fixing the points spread in all American Football games.

BEST PLACES TO MEET MILLIONAIRES

Although millionaires, by definition, can afford to be a peripatetic lot, they tend to congregate in the same places, no doubt for reasons of emotional security. For instance in February it's Sandy Lane, Barbados, or Lyford Cay, Bahamas, the latter being the private development of Canada's richest man, brewer E. P. Taylor, and boasting more than fifty millionaires as owners of villas. Racecourses for the biggest meetings attract the owners of the top race-horses – the winner of the Derby automatically becomes worth £1 million as a stallion and Robert Sangster, who won the 1977 Derby and Prix de l'Arc de Triomphe with different horses, syndicated them for a total value in excess of £10 million.

Millionaires like to leave something for posterity, usually in the shape of an art collection, so are always to be found at the Old Master and Impressionist sales in London, New York, Monte Carlo, organized by Sotheby Parke Bernet and Christie's, or at their jewellery sales in Geneva. Millionaires tend to isolate themselves on private estates, islands, yachts and planes but occasionally they surface in public places like the summer Galas at the Sporting Club, Monte Carlo, and charity functions in the autumn in New York.

British millionaires are to be found tending shop – most stately homes are open to the public and with agricultural land now averaging £2,000 an acre, even a small 1,000-acre estate is worth £2 million. Many are much larger and Earl Grosvenor owns 130,000 acres in England, Wales and Northern Ireland.

Best Beaches

The best beach to see and be seen on in the summer is Tahiti Plage, St Tropez, although around the bay the best private beach is that at the foot of La Madrague, the villa owned by Brigitte Bardot. In the Caribbean, the best beach is on Harbour Island, consisting of three miles of pink sand and bright blue seas. In Jamaica the beach at Negril, totally undeveloped and stretching for seven miles, is the best in that area of the Caribbean. The best publicized but overrun beaches are Copacabana, Rio de Janeiro and Bondi, Sydney, and are best avoided.

Best Marinas

In the south of France the best marinas are Monte Carlo for the Monaco Grand Prix, or Antibes for permanent berthing, while elsewhere in the Mediterranean, Porto Cervo on the Aga Khan's Costa Smeralda development is best for only two months, July and August. In the Caribbean the best marinas are at Lyford Cay, Bahamas; Pointe à Pitre, Guadeloupe; Fort de France, Martinique, and St John's, Antigua. In America, the best is Newport, Rhode Island.

POLITICS

◆

Paul Johnson

BEST ORATOR *Pericles* (*c.* 495–429 BC)
Athenian statesman and populist. He was rich and came from the upper classes but chose, says Plutarch, quoting contemporary sources, 'to solicit the favour of the masses and the poor, rather than the few and wealthy'. A brilliant mob orator, at a time when rhetoric (which means the art of using language to influence others) was the crown of the educational system. He guided Athens during her greatest period of expansion and prosperity, but which culminated in the disastrous Peloponnesian War against Sparta. He was a successful *strategos*, or general, as well as a stern administrator (the Parthenon was built under his direction), but his power lay in his tongue. His manner was haughty, his appearance daunting, his face severe, never smiling even when indulging in wit, his speeches rare – and therefore all the more eagerly awaited.

Runner-up: David Lloyd George (1863–1945) rather than Winston Churchill (1874–1965). Those who heard both agree Lloyd George was better. He was an all-rounder, equally capable of swaying opinion in the open air, in a vast public hall, in the House of Commons and in cabinet, where Churchill often ruined his case by talking too much.

BEST POLITICAL SPEECH
'A speech to the electors of Bristol', by Edmund Burke (1729–97) given in 1774 and vindicating the right of an elected representative to independence of opinion. Politicians probably quote it more often, on both sides of the Atlantic,

than any other speech. But Burke was not usually popular in the Commons: he was known as 'the Dinner Bell' – MPs remembered they were hungry when he got to his feet.

BEST SHORT SPEECH
No argument: Lincoln's Gettysburg Address, given on Thursday, 19 November 1863, when dedicating the war-cemetery. The four contemporary versions (including two drafts in Lincoln's own handwriting) differ slightly but average only 250 words.

BEST MAIDEN SPEECH
During a debate on Free Trade on 12 May 1906, F.E. Smith, later 1st Earl of Birkenhead, rallied the beaten and dispirited Conservatives with his venomous wit. Written, memorized and delivered without notes. After it, the great Irish orator, Tim Healey, sent him a note: 'I am old, and you are young, but you have beaten me at my own game.'

BEST PRIME MINISTER *Sir Robert Peel* (1788–1850)
Son of a Lancashire cotton millionaire. Served in Tory governments as Irish Secretary, when he was known as 'Orange Peel', as Home Secretary, when he invented the London police, known as 'Bobbies' or 'Peelers', briefly as Prime Minister 1834–5, when he invented the election manifesto, and finally as head of a strong Conservative majority government, 1841–6.

Peel carried through a revolution in fiscal, financial, banking and economic policy, culminating in the repeal of the duties on imported corn. This split his party and enabled Disraeli to destroy his government; but it introduced the three most prosperous decades in British history, until the mid-1870s, when massive imports of cheap US food wrecked British agriculture. Peel himself was thrown from his horse in 1850 and died in agony three days later. His followers, known as Peelites, and with Gladstone at their head, eventually joined the Liberals.

BEST PRESIDENT *Franklin Delano Roosevelt* (1882–1945)
US patrician, barrister, State Senator, Assistant-Secretary of the Navy, Democratic candidate for the presidency 1920, Governor of New York and, finally, US President 1932–45. The only American who ever has been, or is likely to be, elected President for four consecutive terms, since retirement after two consecutive terms is now mandatory. Roosevelt's New Deal, inspired by the expansionist principles of the economist John Maynard Keynes (1886–1946), took the United States out of the Great Depression; and Roosevelt, by cunning and stealth, transformed an introspective and isolationist nation into a great world power.

'He's been deposed.'

Best Monarch (Past and Present)

Past: *Henri IV* of France (1553–1620), Protestant-turned-Papist ('Paris is worth a mass'), who ended the religious civil war in France and reconciled the rival factions. He founded the Bourbon monarchy and his work laid the basis of French power and prosperity for the next 200 years. Assassinated by a madman.
Runner-up: *Edward I* of England (1239–1307), statesman, generalissimo, law-giver and administrator, 'hammer of the Scots' and scourge of the Welsh. Both his castles and his statutes have survived the buffetings of seven centuries.

Present: *Queen Elizabeth II* of England (born 1926, succeeded George VI 1952), with her combination of high seriousness, dedication, professional skill and flashes of charm.

Runner-up: *King Hussein* of Jordan who, after succeeding, as a boy, his murdered grandfather, King Abdullah, has miraculously preserved the last throne of the Hashemites through a quarter-century of wars and subversion.

BEST DIPLOMAT *Charles Maurice Talleyrand de Perigord* (1754–1838)
First a Catholic bishop, then a revolutionary, next a Napoleonic imperialist, penultimately a minister of the Bourbon reaction and finally the servant of a bourgeois monarchy. At the Congress of Vienna he skilfully salvaged the wreck of Buonaparte's France, turning his defeated country into a great European power again; and in 1830 he went to London as ambassador and reconciled England to the populist rule of Louis-Philippe. Napoleon, whom he deserted, called him '*merde en bas-de-soie*' (a shit in silk stockings) but he deserved his reputation as the most accomplished negotiator of his age.

BEST INTERNATIONAL FORUM *The International Monetary Fund*
To which is appended the World Bank in Washington. Created in the aftermath of World War II, these joint institutions have acted as a stabilizing factor in the world economy for over thirty years. Their annual meetings are brief and, compared with other international gatherings, comparatively businesslike.

Runner-up: the Food and Agricultural Organization (FAO) of the United Nations, seated in Rome. Has had some major successes in modernizing Third World agriculture, particularly in improving crop-yields.

BEST BOOK ABOUT POLITICS *Leviathan*
Published in 1651, by Thomas Hobbes (1588–1679). Born prematurely when his mother took fright at the coming of the Spanish Armada, Hobbes argued with austere ferocity for the creation of a strong, efficient 'nightwatchman state', as opposed to the chaos created by over-mighty, demagogic parliament. But Hobbes was not, as is often supposed, a totalitarian. He wanted an authoritative central authority 'to keep them all in awe' but otherwise believed that the state should leave individuals to pursue their own interests: 'The freedom of the subject is the silence of the laws.' His arguments for the politics of persuasion, as opposed to the politics of force, were the foundation on which John Locke (1632–1704) built his theory of possessive individualism, which made constitutionally possible the growth of capitalism and representative democracy in both Britain and the United States – to say nothing of the new nations modelled on them.

BEST POLITICAL CAMPAIGN
Hard to beat the whistle-stop, 'Give 'em Hell' campaign which President Harry

S. Truman waged across the United States in 1948. He had reached the White House unelected, as a result of Roosevelt's death in 1945, his administration was riddled with corruption, the Republican tide was running strongly after four successive Democrat victories, and it was universally assumed that Thomas Dewey, the Republican candidate, would win by a landslide: one newspaper even announced it as a fact before the votes were counted. In this last of the old-style, pre-airliner, pre-TV campaigns, Truman reversed the tide and survived to become a tough and decisive President.

BEST CAMPAIGN SLOGAN
President Roosevelt's 1932 message to the voters, insisting that the Great Depression could be ended: 'You have nothing to fear but Fear itself.'
    Runner-up: Henri IV's promise to the French people: 'A chicken in every pot.'

BEST POLITICAL JOKE
Adlai Stevenson, sometime Governor of Illinois and unsuccessful Democrat candidate for President in 1952 and 1956, was an intellectual with a prominent bald head. Accused of being an egghead, he replied, paraphrasing the opening words of the 1848 *Communist Manifesto* of Marx and Engels: 'Eggheads of the world unite – you have nothing to lose but your yokes!'

BEST POLITICAL SYSTEM (PAST AND PRESENT)
Past: In terms of durability, there is nothing to equal the theocratic monarchy of the ancient Egyptian pharaohs. The first dynasty was founded about 3100 BC and god-kings or god-queens ruled Egypt (with three comparatively brief interludes of chaos) until the death of Cleopatra VII Philopator ended the 32nd dynasty in 30 BC. In the first millennium BC, some of these monarchs were Ethiopian, Libyan, Persian or Greek; but the institution remained comparatively popular among the Egyptians right to the end; at any rate, the Egyptian language and culture did not long survive its destruction, and even the Roman rulers of Egypt called themselves pharaohs.
Present: The Helvetic Federation of Switzerland, based on a system of government by cantons (for administrative and ordinary legislative purposes) and referenda (for extraordinary legislative purposes) has united a collection of poor French, German and Italian upland peasants and turned them into the richest nation, *per capita*, on earth. English tourists, who invented mountaineering and winter sports, and who once practically owned the place, can now rarely afford to go there. But the Swiss have paid the price in physical pollution and in a monumental selfishness which led them to boast complacently of their behaviour in World War II: 'We worked for the Germans on weekdays and prayed for the Allies on Sundays.'
    Runner-up: Singapore's Social-Democrat government keeps totalitarian

'*That's a lot more where-it's-at than those old-fashioned delegations with names like "Wisconsin" and "New Jersey".*'

extremists in gaol and trades unions impotent, while preserving economic and political freedom for the rest of the population. Result: this tiny, overcrowded Asian state, with virtually no raw materials, has now reached West European living standards, and it is one of the very few countries in the world which can (usually) be entered without a visa.

BEST POLITICAL NOVEL *The New Machiavelli*
By H. G. Wells (1866–1946), published in 1911. This describes, in considerable detail, the British political scene during the Liberal ascendancy before the 1914–

18 war, and in particular the world of the early Fabians, dominated by Sidney and Beatrice Webb. Part-documentary, part-satire, it presents thinly disguised portraits of some of the progressive luminaries of the age, and Wells was never forgiven for writing it.

Joint runners-up: Gore Vidal's savage picture of US politics in the 1950s, *Washington DC*, and Anthony Trollope's equally fierce panorama of the world of Gladstone and Disraeli, *The Way We Live Now*.

BEST POLITICAL POEM

'Recessional' by Rudyard Kipling (1865–1936), which he published in 1897 as a corrective to the frantic jingoism and imperialism of the age. This sonorous and moving poem, which contains some of the best-remembered phrases in the English language, gives the lie to those of Kipling's critics who accuse him of being the mere trumpeter and fugleman of the British Empire.

Runner-up: 'Horatian Ode upon Cromwell's Return from Ireland' (1650), by the Member of Parliament for Hull, Andrew Marvell (1621–78).

BEST POLITICAL PAMPHLET

No doubt about it – Gladstone's famous scourging of the Turks in *The Bulgarian Horrors and the Question of the East*. Gladstone was in retirement when, in May 1876, Turkish irregular troops put down a revolt against the Sultan by Bulgarian Christians, massacring some 12,000 men, women and children in the process. Disraeli, then Prime Minister, tried to laugh it off, saying 'I take leave to doubt whether torture has been practised on a great scale on oriental people who seldom, I believe, resort to torture, but generally terminate their connection with culprits in a most expeditious manner.' Not amused, indeed furious, Gladstone wrote his tirade, ending: 'Their Zaptiehs and their Mudirs, their Bimbashis and their Yuzbachis, their Kaimakams and their Pashas, one and all, bag and baggage, shall, I hope, clear out from the province they have desolated and profaned.' It was published on 6 September 1876, and in three weeks sold over 200,000 copies.

BEST POLITICAL PLAY

Julius Caesar by William Shakespeare (1564–1616), a racy Elizabethan interpretation of the political skulduggery, murder and infighting which led to the demise of the Roman Republic. But this is political description, rather than comment: Shakespeare usually kept his views to himself, the only real exception being *Troilus and Cressida*, his personal version of the Trojan war, which shows him a conservative proponent of hierarchy and order.

Runner-up: *Strife* by John Galsworthy (1867–1933). Presented in London in 1909, against a background of industrial unrest, this fine play is a fierce attack on extremism and charts the middle ground where Capital and Labour can come together.

BEST POLITICAL MOVIE *The Grapes of Wrath*
John Ford's brilliant realization of John Steinbeck's 1930s best-seller, set in the Great Depression, which depicts the pathos and anger of the forlorn 'Oakies' who fled the dust bowl of Oklahoma to the New Deal work-camps of California. Some of those work-camps still exist, and now house 'Wetbacks' from Mexico.

BEST POLITICAL SCANDAL
For sheer endurance, political importance and labyrinthine complexity, there is no beating the *Dreyfus Case*. Beginning in 1894, when Captain Alfred Dreyfus, a Jew on the French General Staff, was arrested for spying for the Germans, convicted and sent to Devil's Island, it dominated French political, military and ecclesiastical life for more than a decade, shocked the world, inspired Zola's famous philippic, *J'Accuse!*, brought to the forefront the great radical politician Clemenceau, and introduced the term "intelligentsia" into the world's vocabulary. The battle is still being fought around upper-class Paris dinner-tables. As such, it eclipses even Watergate. At the bawdy level, the winner is Britain's 1963 'Profumo Case', revolving around Lord Astor's swimming pool at Thamesside Cliveden, and featuring the Secretary of State for War, the Soviet Naval Attaché, a bent psychiatrist and two talkative 'models'.

BEST POLITICAL HOSTESS
Edith Helen Chaplin, daughter of a Tory Minister of Agriculture, Viscount Chaplin. In 1899 she married Charles Vane-Tempest-Stewart, seventh Marquess of Londonderry. His Lordship was an undistinguished cabinet minister, but Lady Londonderry's grand white-tie parties at palatial Londonderry House in Park Lane dominated political society in the 1920s and 1930s. She is widely credited with seducing Ramsay MacDonald, Britain's first Labour Prime Minister, from his socialist duty, and so precipitating the 1931 National Government and fourteen years of Tory rule.

BEST POLITICAL MEMOIRS
Here the French beat all-comers, in quantity as well as quality. Bracketed first, because it is impossible to choose between these two masterpieces, are *Mémoires d'outre-tombe* by François-Réné, Vicomte de Chateaubriand (1768–1848), which span the Revolution, Napoleonic Wars, Restoration and the bourgeois monarchy of Louis-Philippe, and the equally famous *Mémoires* by Louis de Rouvroy, Duc de Saint-Simon (1675–1755), which illuminate the splendours and miseries of Versailles under the sun-king Louis XIV and his successor. Both are pardonably long and monstrously entertaining.
    Booby-prize: to Julius Caesar (100–44 BC), whose *Gallic Wars* have wearied many generations of schoolchildren.

BEST POLITICAL LETTERS
Horace Walpole, fourth Earl of Orford (1717–97), did not follow his father,

Sir Robert, into the stratosphere of politics. But his letters, over nearly half a century, given an incomparable picture of British public life under George II and George III.

Runner-up: the letters which Thomas Babington Macaulay (1800–59), Whig politician and historian, wrote to his adoring sisters.

BEST POLITICAL BIOGRAPHY

Hard choice, this, since it ranges from Tacitus's life of his father-in-law, *Agricola*, through Francis Bacon's scintilating *Henry VII*, to Martin Gilbert's fifteen-volume and still-far-from-finished treatment of Sir Winston Churchill. But the award must go to Sir John Neale's *Queen Elizabeth I* (1934), for a lucid and penetrating (and admirably economical) study of an immense and tantalizing subject.

Runner-up: *The Letters and Speeches of Oliver Cromwell* by Thomas Carlyle (1795–1881), a granitic and compelling portrait of one British titan by another.

BEST POLITICAL BUILDING

Not Sir Charles Barrie's House of Parliament, *not* the Capitol in Washington DC, *not* Moscow's Kremlin or Peking's Imperial Palace, but the Escorial, the sumptuous palace-monastery built by Philip II of Spain (1527–98) outside his new capital of Madrid, from which to run his vast world empire. It houses the bones of his ancestors and his successors, as well as his own, and its plan follows the pattern of the white-hot gridiron on which St Sebastian was allegedly roasted.

POP CULTURE

Kenneth Robinson

BEST ADVICE BOOKS

Nobody really believes in advice books. They are designed to tell people what they already know. And the best person to do that is Shirley Conran, in her book *Superwoman*. Examples? She gives a tip on how to clean windows, saying that 'first you should draw back the curtains'. This, of course, is very useful if you don't want cleaning fluid all over the cosy chintz. She has other vital things to say. 'If a man presses against you in the train, bus or lift,' says Shirley, 'try to move away from him.' She doesn't explain why, but the flair with which she doesn't ever explain herself is incomparable.

BEST BEAUTY AIDS

'Anything that can be found in a kitchen food-cupboard can be used on the face.' – quote from a women's magazine.

BEST BIBLE STORY-TELLING

The best pop Bible story is not *Jesus Christ Superstar*, which is usually played too loudly, thank heavens, for the shaky theology of its lyrics to be heard. Better, in fact, is another work by the same couple, Tim Rice and Andrew Lloyd Webber, *Joseph and The Amazing Technicolour Dreamcoat*. This looks like being an annual pantomine substitute at London's Westminster Theatre, in addition to its frequent appearances around the world. A series of parodies of song styles makes Pharaoh into a teddy-boy and changes the brothers from country westerners, through rockers to beret-wearers, singing in the manner of Piaf.

Best Building
Your guess is as good as ours, except that we happen to be compiling this list. So how about New York's Guggenheim Museum? It looks like a giant hat that has blown across the sidewalk and got itself jammed between other buildings. Not surprisingly, a fashion designer *has* made a hat looking like Frank Lloyd Wright's spirals. Other buildings, please be copied.

Best Cartoon
Snoopy and company have dominated the gift-shop market for so long, with greetings cards, stuffed toys and all kinds of gimmicks, that it is easy to forget the whole business started with the strip cartoons which are still published all over the world. Some of the funniest cartoons are in the religious books, like the *Gospel of Peanuts*, and these have helped to give the inventor, Charles Schulz, a tremendous reputation for integrity. It doesn't bear thinking about, all that money mixed up with all that piety, but anyway the cartoons are still top of the culture scene in their own category.

Best Comedian
Ken Dodd is *the* pop culture comedian. He aims, with his material, at the groundlings. But with his steady build-up of laughs, he intrigues anyone who watches him only to marvel at his timing, his wonderful collisions of words – and how it is all done.

Best Commercial-Dodger
The advertising companies say there are class trends in current television commercials and that this is very significant of something or other. It is true that Campari has had fun with a girl sounding like Twiggy and talking to a top-drawer escort. And somebody or other's credit card had a stuffily snobbish advertisement. But it is not the commercials themselves that qualify for a pop-culture nomination, but the means of avoiding them. The latest automatically controlled video machine can be left beside your set, recording for a whole evening. The next day you can watch a replay of programmes with all the commercials edited out, and the gaps filled in.

Best Diary
There are, in fact, *two* coveted diaries. The *Debretts' Peerage Diary*, which reminds you about the line of succession to the throne, and the *Sex Maniac's Diary*, which reminds you about things you had probably hoped to forget. The publishers of the first can be tracked down in the London telephone directory. The publishers of the second live in a Mayfair basement with a parrot.

Best Eatery
McDonald's is more than a restaurant, it is an experience. However big the

queue, you hardly have time to adjust your free paper hat before you are drinking the thickest milk-shake ever made – almost unspillable but, miraculously, drinkable. The cold thud as this drink hits a hot hamburger inside you is a curiously pleasing sensation. It is reminiscent of the normal process of eating, but much more interesting. In the best-equipped restaurants, you can also have the experience of sitting on high chairs which slope forwards. This is said to discourage customers from staying too long. Concentration is needed if you are not to crash to the ground, taking with you one of the indoor plants that are a trademark of the place.

Best Entertainment Centre

It's worth going to the National Theatre, beside the Thames, not to see a play, but to have a meal or coffee in one of the buffets.

This incredible building was designed, by Denys Lasdun, so that from the promenades or the buffet seats, at all levels, you can see and hear what is going on elsewhere. There is always free entertainment in the foyer – jazz, chamber music or something between the two. And there is always a free art exhibition to not quite look at. This is the way the arts *should* be enjoyed, with only a tiny part of one's attention.

Best Exhibition Hangover

The best reminder of a recent international exhibition is the poor old Atomium, in its park at Brussels, with its overtones of H. G. Wells's *Things To Come*. It is now a sad and bleak reminder of the superb 1958 exhibition. The happiest gimmick left to us after an exhibition is, of course, the Eiffel Tower. And the most useful is the Royal Festival Hall, in London, a reminder of the 1951 Festival of Britain. The hall was designed in the late 1940s by architects of the London County Council. It is already a period piece of cosily-fussy and quaintly-elegant interior design, a lot of it trying to be as functional as architects of the time longed for buildings to be. The holes under the upturned seats were supposed to absorb as much sound as a seated person. It has since been discovered that they don't. The sense of occasion in the building is all that it should be. The food is not meant to be funny.

Best Furniture

Knock-down furniture is becoming a world-wide favourite. So say the *purveyors* of knock-down furniture. A British manufacturer of the stuff has said that 'a man likes to buy a chair on a Saturday afternoon, slip it into a box, drive it home, assemble it and then sit on it to watch the televised football match'. If you have never met anybody like this, it means nothing. Once everybody is doing something it is no longer pop culture. Pop does *not*, for goodness sake, mean popular.

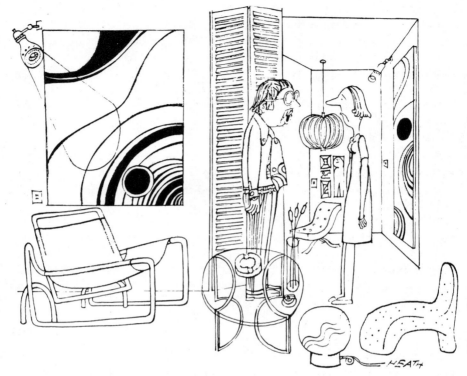

'I'm not quite sure how to put this darling, but ever since we've had the house modernised, you don't fit in any more.'

BEST HAIR FASHION

A current hair-style is known as 'Star Trek'. This is achieved by crimping and by the not very subtle use of pipe cleaners. And that is quite enough about that.

BEST FEMALE PERSONALITY

There has never been anybody quite like Britain's Barbara Cartland. Not only has she written 250 romantic novels, in which heroines' eyes tend to fall to the floor as frequently as suitors' knees, but she has offered all manner of help to would-be ardent lovers, including large daily helpings of vitamins and honey. Her book about love and lovers in great paintings is a miracle of audacity and egotism. There is no painting she does not see in relation to her own life. Her description of Venus being dressed by her acolytes is, she says, very much her own story all over again. Delicious! And so is her unlikely recording, with the

London Philharmonic Orchestra, of famous love songs. She has a little voice but a lot of nerve. And she is nearly seventy!

BEST HERO

Superman has been given fresh life as a modern folk hero, thanks to the film about him. The posters were right when they said we would believe a man could fly. Glenn Ford, who played the part of Superman's foster-father, spoke for all of us when he first saw his child and said, 'Well, if that ain't all get out'. And it certainly was. And how glad parents everywhere must have been that Superman turned out to be such a clean-living romance-dodging person, with nothing on his mind but the saving of the good and the punishing of the bad. He is the only character in film history to have kissed the grubby face of a dead girl. But as he promptly reversed the clocks, brought her back to life and never saw her again, all was well.

BEST HOME ENTERTAINMENT

The video machine, which will bring you instant hire-purchased replays of television programmes, is becoming the up-market version of holiday slides. The strange thing about recorded television is that it looks much better than the original. You feel a kind of do-it-yourself pride in programmes. 'Yes,' you will say, 'we recorded this fragment of Al Jolson more by chance than anything. No, sorry, that's not it – that's President Carter. We'll just wind back a little. Ah no, that's Miss World. We kept her interview for Nicholas because of his recent trouble – No, *that* in fact is how to make trees for your model railway. But look, before you go, how about another piece of cake and the Pope?'

BEST FESTIVAL

There is not much pop culture at the annual festivals. Except at Edinburgh, when the concerts and art shows are mercifully interrupted by the dreadful drums and bagpipes at the nightly tattoo. The audience watches from a stand strapped over the edge of the castle rock. Habitués stand beneath this every night, watching the audience's feet stamping insensitively to the sound of the so-called music. Will the whole thing collapse? This, though unofficial, is the great pop-cultural hope at the festival.

BEST GUIDED TOUR

A visit to the Tower of London is not what you would expect. The Yeomen of the Guard have turned into comedians. Every detail of the death of the little princes, or the stretching of Guy Fawkes on the rack, is given a music-hall twist. The whole thing is shockingly funny and the facts stay in the mind. Like Ann Boleyn's execution being delayed, so she had to walk round the block.

BEST HUB OF THE EMPIRE

Piccadilly Circus is a sort of hiccup in the traffic flow. Although it is not *really* the centre of anything, it is good for a smile or two as a centre for pop culture that seems largely irrelevant to the place. Tourists who want to take something home of dear old London will find home-movie films with not very Cockney themes, like 'Laurel and Hardy at Sea', 'The Harlem Globe Trotters Do It Again' and 'Mankind Lands on the Moon'. There is also something called Piccadilly's fourteenth-century inn, where Chinese waiters serve Italian dishes beside a plastic image of Sir Winston Churchill. And you can hear Churchill in a multi-slide show called 'The London Experience'. This is an hour of dazzling pictures, sound and smoke, in which the audience sometimes looks as if it is on fire – during simulations of the Blitz and the Great Fire of London. Incidentally, the Churchill voice is too good to be true. 'We tried using the real thing,' said the management, 'but it didn't sound right, so we got an actor to do it instead.'

Best Indoor Game
Pop culture does not mean cheap culture. The best game of the past year or so is the £750 chess-set, based on a medieval version, with chess-men imprinted on wine glasses. The set is sold with a crate of vintage wine, and each player must take a large gulp every times he makes a move. The game can go on for several days, and the board is made of glass, so it can be seen just as easily from underneath. A close runner-up for best game is the £50 draught board, with see-through pieces marked as 'His' and 'Hers'. Experienced players say this *does* something for the game. None of them will say quite what.

Best Industrial Design
London's Design Centre is a good attempt to popularize consumer goods of good design. Thousands of pictures and products are on display. *Design* magazine and other publications record the accidental humour of designers trying to express themselves in words. Bidets are said to be 'sculptural' (ouch!); cutlery 'fits into the palm of the hand' (surprise, surprise!), and a spoon is 'designed to enter the mouth comfortably'. The Centre is a good place for window-shopping, a few laughs and then a quick escape to the dear old vulgar world outside.

Best Invitation
The New York Hilton is surely the only hotel in the world that advertises 'Cocktails and hand-holding from 4 pm to midnight'. Observers have not *actually* noticed this phenomenon taking place, but it seemed to qualify for a mention here, purely on the strength of the invitation.

Best Kitsch And Sink
It is all there, from kitsch to kitchen sinks, at the Ideal Home Exhibition – the annual treat for British housewives at Earls Court. Everything that isn't anything happens here, and royalty always has the first look. Didn't the Duke

of Edinburgh find himself reported in the papers for sniffing at the turkey croquettes? Wasn't the Queen Mother heard to say it was 'a real treat'? Exhibits include burglar-scarers that keep changing the lights all over the house through the night, as well as switching on record-players and television sets. There are do-it-yourself hints ('Why not hang an old milk-crate from the ceiling for storing underwear?'). And there is a strong international representation, including a Finnish sauna bath made in Italy and marketed in Hampshire. Every year the organizers hang out the words spoken at the exhibition by King George V. 'Here', he said, 'are the foundations of national glory.' Mind the heated lavatory seats on your way out.

Best Male Personality

Liberace remains top of the pop-culture scene in the entertainment business. He makes you want to ask not *how* he does it, by *why* he does it. He cannot need the money. And surely he knows, as a musician, that he ought not to do what he *does* do to Chopin and Gershwin. He is loved quite hysterically by his audiences, and only if you see him in person – and not on television – can you understand why. His clothes, his cars, his pianos and his swimming pools, which he loves showing to audiences on a cinema screen, put him beyond envy. That is part of his secret. The rest is his love for *being* loved and his uninhibitedly childish behaviour, which appeals to the child in nearly everybody.

Best Misguided Tour

You can take London's Jubilee walk all by yourself. If you start in Leicester Square and follow the markings on the ground, you will skirt Trafalgar Square, St James's Park and Westminster Abbey, and finish with an appalling riverside walk north of the Thames, ending up at Tower Bridge, where a magnificent sign warns you 'Do Not Loiter On the Bascule'. The walk is recommended only because you are not bawled at by a guide, and because it was thought suitable, though heaven knows why, as a Jubilee tribute to the Queen.

Best Mobile

These were once terribly one-up decorations to hang in the living-room. They were usually imported from Scandinavia, or made by grown-ups who had been watching children's television. Today's mobiles leap frantically up and down on springs, frightening cats, babies and fathers. The best is a bird called Woodstock, from the Peanuts cartoons. It squeaks with all the realism of a battery-driven bird.

Best Museum

Only one of London's museums tries to cater for lovers of pop culture. Roy Strong, at the Victoria and Albert Museum, is always hoping to capture the

'Man, I really got the Blues,
there's a waiting list for that new Rolls.'

fleeting present. Not only does he preserve modern furniture in his basement, treating the machine-made product with as much care as an antique, but he puts on exhibitions about the way we live now. Fortunately we do *not* live like this, and never have done. But it is always entertaining to watch a museum, with priceless treasures of past centuries, trying to look po-faced about, say, a house with no door on the bathroom, a teapot with a swan on the lid and a chair made from car exhausts.

BEST NOSTALGIA ENTERTAINMENT

There's a lot of it about. The most potent example is at the City of Varieties, in Leeds, where audiences dress in appropriate clothes for the atmosphere of an Edwardian music hall. There is a waiting list for eight years for this free BBC show. It would be easier to join the Players Theatre Club in London, which is rather more subtle. All the music-hall material here is of pre-1914 vintage. This is almost too early for anyone to feel nostalgic about. So it is an interesting – and less weepy-making – popular entertainment.

BEST PARODIST

Neil Innes, a remarkable young man who invented the Rutles, based on the Beatles, for BBC Television, has acquired a following for never being himself. His Rutles were almost an improvement on the Beatles. Quite often his parodies make the bad worse and the good better. It is worth seeking him out, on television, stage or records, for his Bob Nylon, a wonderful send–up of a folk singer who cannot really play his guitar or write good lyrics, but is confident, with his seedy panache, that he can save the world with his songs.

BEST PHOTOGRAPHY

The most OK thing in the world of picture-making started in America and is now known as 'Concerned Photography'. This involves taking pictures of people having a street accident; lying in a gutter, preferably with a guitar; or falling out of a hospital bed. This last example, which is quite a classic, makes you wonder how long the photographer *waited* for the patient to fall out of bed. He surely couldn't have . . . ? Qualities required by a 'Concerned' photographer are a depressive imagination, or just plain daftness. Examples can range from pictures of a block of Chicago flats, where a murder has just taken place, to an elephant losing its dignity – a subject made popular by New York's Jill Freedman.

BEST RADIO QUIZ

The great thing about a radio quiz is that the audience feels it is learning something while somebody else is made to look silly. One of the most successful is *Just A Minute*, in which the team have to speak for sixty seconds, on a given subject, without hesitation, repetition or deviation. The questions often elicit some *Reader's Digest*-type information. But beware the charlatans on the air. One man on this programme spoke about Roman culture and *invented* such characteristics as the Palace of Homilies, the Federated Gondola Carvers and the Mantelli Brothers.

BEST RADIO RECEIVER

From Hong Kong comes a radio made to look like a hamburger. This is ideal for listening to pop music in public places. No one knows where the appalling noise is coming from, and if anyone gets suspicious you can always take a bite out of your plastic bun.

BEST SATURDAY-NIGHT FEVERISHNESS

This can be learned, on most nights of the week, at the Dance Centre, in London's Covent Garden – a handy spot for tired business men. Large mixed teams are made to perform, in dismal rooms lined with grey breeze-block walls. These people look like the rehearsal teams in any Hollywood musical about amateur theatricals. Most kinds of modern dancing are taught. 'Be funky', says an advertisement, 'in six lessons'.

BEST SOUVENIR

The Danes have a souvenir that is both cultural and popular. It is popular because it is cheap, and it is cheap because it is back to front. It is, in fact, a model – made by a lot of firms, with slight variations in materials – of the famous mermaid sitting on her rock. The makers all show her facing the wrong way. By doing so they avoid paying royalties on the sculptor's original. To find more about this pop culture, you should pop along to the cultural attaché.

Best T-shirt

The latest catalogues show that the *double-entendres* on T-shirts are rapidly becoming less subtle. The best of the newcomers is a sort of double act. For HER there is the message 'I'm Sexy' and for HIM 'I'm *With* Sexy'. This is a clever piece of women's libbery. Without the girl beside him the poor man looks quite ridiculous. But even this would be better – and certainly safer – than going around with the shirt that says, indiscriminately, 'I'm with an idiot'.

Best Telephone

The Post Office's Mickey Mouse telephone. This large, coloured model of the Disney character who has outlived his animated cartoons is just the thing for those who think it is just the thing.

Best Television Programme

The best pop-culture television is BBC's *Read All About It*, where a pretence is made that the books under discussion are, in fact, worth discussion. Guests are either too belligerent or too kind. Nobody ever says anything memorable and the whole thing is a collectors' piece for its superbly-entertaining futility.

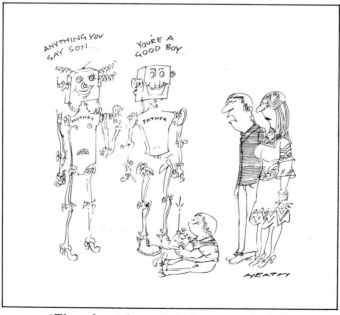

'These electronic toys are getting out of hand.'

Best Useless Object

It is not only a *British* custom – the making and selling of useless consumer goods – but the more our inflation inflates itself, the more the British buy what they like instead of what they need. So say the people who make or sell such products. The best – partly because her work has been given the seal of approval by the Design Centre – is Sylvia Lybydenski, whose team of women slaves daily over the making of stuffed hand-sewn replicas of television sets, type-writers, telephones and even imitation food – including plates of eggs and bacon and giant cups of coffee. Each of these items squeaks when you squeeze it. The costs seem high, but who can determine the value of something nobody really needs?

Best University

The only pop-culture university is the Open University. Even if you are not registered you can share some of the lectures on BBC radio or television. And if that doesn't make you laugh where you shouldn't, then you *deserve* to register – and to suffer like all the others.

Best Vending Machines

Gone are the days when you got only a packet of cigarettes or a bar of chocolate from a vending machine. Today it can be a hot dollop of mashed potato, an umbrella or a bunch of bananas. The umbrella machine can also be adapted to sell golf balls. There are even places where you can leap out at night, after supper, and buy an ice-cold daffodil or two from a refrigerated machine. Or a bucket of ice, suggests a firm in Nottingham. Not to mention zip-fasteners, scent and knitting wool. And hot chips.

Where do you find them? You have to look. The makers say that in some cases they have overestimated needs. Maybe by the time you read this we shall be back to only cigarettes and chocolates.

SPORTS

Ian Wooldridge

BEST SHOT
Disdaining such plebeian targets as cardboard bulls-eyes or clay pigeons, *Frederick Oliver Robinson, second Marquess of Rippon*, who, over the space of 71 years from 1852, murdered 556,813 head of game with relentless accuracy. Victims ranged in target area from snipe to rhinoceros. Credited with phenomenal speed shooting, including 28 pheasant in 60 seconds, 575 grouse in a day and 8,732 partridge in a season.

BEST RUGBY UNION PLAYER
Acknowledged by Charles, Prince of Wales, as 'better known than I am', Welsh scrum-half *Gareth Edwards.*

BEST BOXER
Long friendships, family bonds broken by interminable arguments over respective merits of Muhammad Ali, Joe Louis, Jack Dempsey, Rocky Marciano: all to no purpose since greatest weight-for-punch fighter ever was British flyweight *Jimmy Wilde* who emerged from 700-bout fairground booth-boxing apprenticeship against men twice his size to win the world title in 1916, score 98 knock-out victories, establish a sequence of 88 successive fights without defeat and still live to the age of 77.

BEST WEIGHTLIFTER
Unsubstantiated claims that Greek show-off Milo of Crotona carried a one-

'George prefers to make his own judgement.'

ton ox almost 200 yards *c*. 540 BC ignored in favour of grotesque Soviet super-heavyweight Olympic champion *Vasili Alexeev*.

BEST GOLFER

Understandable sentiment for Bobby Jones, majestic, dignified master of hickory shafts, will cloud the argument but few realists will contest Lee Trevino's assessment of fellow-American professional *Jack Nicklaus* as, by several fairways, the greatest golfer ever born.

BEST RACING GREYHOUND

Now permanently stuffed in Britain's Natural History Museum, Irish-born *Mick the Miller*, winner of nineteen successive races and two consecutive Greyhound Derbies.

BEST SOCCER PLAYER

Pele, born Edson Arantes do Nascimento, Brazil, 1940, to confound surprisingly modest physique and tower above all other footballers, living or dead.

BEST INTERNATIONAL SOCCER TEAM

Free-running, brilliantly-improvising *Brazil* who won consecutive World Cups in Stockholm, 1958, and Santiago, 1962, with eight players constant to both occasions.

BEST CLUB SOCCER TEAM

Liverpool's claim, despite excellent, consistent performances in the 1970s, does not survive even cursory comparison with Spain's *Real Madrid* team of the late 1950s and early 1960s. Playing arrogantly in all-white, inspired in alternate bursts by the Latin virtuosity of Alfredo di Stefano and European overdrive of Ferenc Puskas, their soccer was frequently an uninterrupted ninety-minute cadenza that lifted the sport dangerously close to the realm of fine art.

BEST SNOOKER PLAYER

Brilliantined *Joe Davis*, England, with 687 century breaks in public performance.

BEST SPORTING NICKNAME

'Phanto', conferred by team colleagues on obdurate Australian opening Test batsman *Bill Lawry* after innings of strokeless immobility at The Oval, London, had been described by British sportswriter as work of corpse with pads on.

BEST LONG-JUMPER

Unlikely to be dethroned over the next half century, America's *Bob Beamon*, whose prodigious 29 ft $2\frac{1}{2}$ in leap at 1968 Mexico Olympics smashed the previous record by $21\frac{1}{2}$ in, caused apoplexy among measuring officials and despair among rivals condemned to growing old as second best.

BEST SPORTS ROMEO

In a highly competitive field, probably *Joe Namath*, swarthy New York Jets quarter-back, who claimed to have passed better than the time of day with more than 1,000 ladies during a playing career prematurely ended by a crippling knee injury.

BEST ICE-HOCKEY PLAYER

Indisputably *Bobby Hull*, Canadian-born scorer of 1,012 goals with 988 assists during his twenty-two-year career with Chicago Black Hawks and Winnipeg Jets.

BEST MALE SWIMMER

Probably Johnny Weissmuller while escaping crocodiles, poisoned darts or Christian missionaries in countless Tarzan films, but, in the absence of electrically-timed evidence, *Mark Spitz*, monosyllabic American seven gold medals winner at 1972 Munich Olympic Games.

BEST FEMALE SWIMMER

Probably stunning East German blonde *Kornelia Ender* but the verdict is in abeyance until her country's equivocal attitude to use of drugs in sport is investigated.

BEST SPORTS FAN
Now farming in New Zealand, formerly Indian Army, *Lt-Col E.D. 'Eddie' Timms*, who carried copies of Wisden for nightly reading throughout World War II and, while in charge of the construction section of Siam Railroad, insisted his local coolies were instructed in the rudiments of cricket before work every morning to absorb the essential characteristics of team spirit and fair play.

BEST WOMAN GYMNAST
Words like Korbut and Comaneci fall freely from the lips of recent converts, but, once seen, Czechoslovakia's mature, incomparable *Vera Caslavska* never forgotten.

BEST RACING TIPSTER
Arthur Salter, erstwhile Robin Goodfellow of the London *Daily Mail* who 'went through card' three successive days to forecast an unparalleled eighteen-horse winning sequence.

BEST GRAND PRIX RACING DRIVER
Emotional arguments are heightened by posthumous loyalties to many superb drivers, but arguably an honourable draw between *Alberto Ascari*, rescued from drowning when locked brakes hurled him into Monaco harbour only for him to die shortly afterwards at Monza, and *Jackie Stewart*, emotionless, precise, perfectionist Scotsman who walked away from his brilliant career declaring, 'Never once, while driving competitively, have I seen the sight of my own blood.'

BEST MARBLES PLAYER
Len Smith, team member of Britain's Toucan Terribles.

BEST FENCER
Grievously misrepresented by Errol Flynn leaping around on medieval refectory tables and Burt Lancaster lopping the sword-arms off unannounced dago visitors on sundry quarterdecks, fencing's reputation was hugely restored by Frenchman *Christian d'Oriola* who won four world titles with foil 1947–54 and took Olympic titles 1952 and 1956.

BEST CRICKET BATSMAN
Eschewing classical style and wearing size five boots, now the most prized exhibit in Melbourne Cricket Museum, *Sir Donald George Bradman*, ruthless

'You know you're being very foolish?
Tomorrow you'll have tennis elbow.'

antipodean executioner of all styles of bowling who, on average, scored a century once in every three innings. He amassed 29 centuries averaging 99.94 in 80 Test innings for the country north of New Zealand.

BEST CRICKET BOWLER
With ape-long arms, immense hostility and masterly control of swing and break at above medium pace on shirt-front pitches, *Sydney Barnes*, who dominated the last days of true Golden Age of Cricket. In a comparatively brief England career between 1901 and 1914 he took 189 wickets at 16.43 runs apiece in 27 Test Matches. In his final professional season in League cricket, then aged 61, he took 86 wickets at 11 runs each.

BEST CRICKET ALL-ROUNDER
Contemptuous of all records and statistics, *Sir Garfield St Aubrun Sobers*, just 'Gary' to his mates, left-handed Barbadian genius whose electrifying stroke play, fast bowling, orthodox and wrist-spin bowling and acrobatic fielding made him an incomparably versatile cricketer whose every appearance on big

occasions was a command performance. Ironically he preferred punting on horses and playing golf.

Best Cricket Captain
Powerful arguments to be made for Sir D.G. Bradman (see above), diminutive colonial who drove cricketers like General Patton drove GIs, and Richie Benaud, Australian, whose strategic insight and gambler's flair were often mistaken by fallen opponents as inexhaustible luck. But ultimately it must be *Douglas Robert Jardine*, austere Scottish-born snobbish Wykhamist who regarded all journalists and all Australians as rotters and led England to spectacular Ashes victory in Australia, 1932–3, by advocating the most brutal 'bodyline' fast bowling assault on batsmen ever seen. The same Don Bradman, who had to face it, was asked at the time of Jardine's death, twenty-five years later, to contribute a comment for the obituary notice. He replied: 'No comment.'

Best Sports Inventor
Bernard J.T. Bosanquet, father of former British ITN television newscaster Reginald Bosanquet, who in an idle moment hurling tennis balls about on Oxford University billiards table unearthed the secret of contra-spin. Applying his discovery to cricket, he produced the googly: an off-break delivered with a leg-break wrist-action with which he promptly took six Australian wickets for fifty-one in a Test Match in Sydney. In Australia a googly is still known as 'bosie'.

Best Matador
Elegant, icily formal and mortally wounded in Linares ring, August 1947, Manuel Rodriguez y Sanchez, otherwise known as *Manolete*.

Best Jockey
Though heresy to American proponents of Willie Shoemaker, and despite the accelerating challenge by child prodigy Steve Cauthen, also United States, Newmarket's *Lester Piggott*, whose inherent skill and affinity with winning bloodstock is matched only by his ability to collect speeding convictions as result of motoring.

Best Sports Event To Play In
Eton Field Game, evolved in 1860 for pupils of limited intelligence, minuscule sporting aptitude, or both. Only played at Eton, thus preserving the proud college record of 130 years without a single defeat.

Best Stadium
Subjectively, when seen at vespers on a warm May evening, Worcestershire County Cricket ground in the heart of Elgar's England, where indifferent spec-

tator facilities are overwhelmingly compensated for by the glorious pastoral setting dominated by the cathedral. Objectively, the massive, ugly, functional but breathtaking *Maracana Stadium*, Rio de Janeiro, where crowds of 200,000 have been worshipping successive Brazilian football teams since 1950. A Latin masterpiece in cantilever engineering, the volume of concrete used in its construction would have erected two Empire State Buildings. Luxurious panelled, carpeted dressing-rooms the size of a provincial ballroom provide individual thermal baths and oxygen-therapy units for every player.

Best Royal Sportsperson

Despite stern challenge from King William I of England, who was allegedly able to leap directly on to his charger while fully clothed in armour, and ex-King Constantine of Greece, competent Olympic yachtsman, arguably *Princess Anne, Mrs Mark Phillips*, fearless horsewoman, whose selection for the 1976 British Olympic equestrian team owed nothing to her fashionable London SW1 address.

Best Gambling Game

Two-up, intellectual and therefore illegal Australian contest of chance, mostly privately promoted behind sheep-shearing barns or Sydney Opera House, requiring contestants to distinguish whether two spun coins come down heads or tails.

Best Male Chess Player

Erratic, reclusive, unknowingly rude, eccentric American IQ titan *Bobby Fischer*, who is so good that he doesn't bother to play for the world title any longer.

Best Female Chess Player

Gorgeous Tblisi, Soviet Union, housewife *Nona Gaprindashvili*, who came from 35,000-member, 1,000-simultaneous-board local chess club to annex, rather than merely win, world title.

Best Table Tennis Player

Early teenage graduate of Peking's Children's Palace after Chairman Mao had decreed the game free from imperialist depravity, *Tse-Tung Chuang*, men's world singles champion 1961–3–5.

Best Billiards Player

Australian *Walter Lindrum* who, aged fifty-four, raced to a century break in 27·5 seconds.

Best Polo Player

Handicap 10 Argentinian captain *Juan Carlos Harriott*.

BEST TEAM MANAGER

Talking 180-words-per-minute Runyonese in a manner which would make England's Brian Clough look like the epitome of modesty, inveterate advocate that nice guys finish last, *Charles Dillon 'Casey' Stengel*. Indifferent baseball player who later outrageously managed New York Yankees to ten American League Championships and seven World Championships in twelve years.

BEST BASKETBALL PLAYER

Relatively modestly constructed at mere 7 ft $1\frac{1}{2}$ in, America's *Kareem Abdul-Jabbar*, known before the black revolution in US sport as Lew Alcindor.

BEST LAWN BOWLS PLAYER

Long-standing British supremacy maintained when dignified Percy Baker was superseded by *David Bryant* who skippered England fours aged twenty-five and still mid-career at almost fifty, has already won more championship titles than any rival.

BEST CROWD

Statistically the ten million who annually watch the Tour de France cycling marathon but behaviourally almost any *British speedway crowd* where strong

'How am I doing?'

all-family influence, fair-play quotient and mutual respect among rival fans are outstanding in an era of marked world-wide decline in crowd conduct.

BEST ICE FIGURE-SKATER
While latterly a dubious contributor to modern culture as the originator of TV Superstars gimmick, *Dick Button*, who dominated the field 1948–52 with eighteen world, Olympic, North American, United States or European titles.

BEST SHOW-JUMPER
On incontestable evidence of consistency and uncanny mastery of difficult horses, *David Broome*, Great Britain.

BEST RECOVERY FROM SPORTS INJURY
Austrian racing motorist *Nikki Lauda*, driving in Monza Grand Prix forty-one days after receiving the Last Rites following horrendous burns sustained before being dragged from his blazing Ferrari at the Nurburgring.

BEST ALL-ROUND SPORTSWOMAN
Babe Zaharias, born Mildred Didrikson, smashed the world javelin record at sixteen, won the world 80-metre hurdles record and equalled the world high jump record at eighteen, won two Olympic gold medals for the United States and then, bored, took up golf, winning US and British amateur championships and US professional title three times before losing a heroic fight against cancer, aged forty-two.

BEST WOMAN ATHLETE
Emerging undistraught from the Nazi occupation of the Netherlands, *Francina 'Fanny' Blankers-Koen*, ebullient star of 1948 London Olympics, winner of nine gold medals in major championships for sprints, hurdles, jumps and pentathlon.

BEST MARATHON RUNNER
Paralysed in a car crash, dead at forty-one, Ethiopian *Abebe Bikila*, former bodyguard to Emperor Haile Selassie, who confounded pundits by winning the 1960 Olympic marathon in Rome bare-footed and repeating the triumph, shod, at the Tokyo Olympics 1964.

BEST SPRINTER
One of eight children of an Alabama cotton picker, *James Cleveland 'Jesse' Owens*, very black athlete who slightly dented Hitler's Aryan master-race theories at the 1936 Nazi Olympics in Berlin by winning four gold medals in 100 metres, 200 metres, long jump and sprint relay. The previous year, in the United States he enjoyed the greatest afternoon's work in athletics history

by equalling world 100 yards record, breaking world long-jump record, world 220 yards record and world 220 yards hurdles record in the space of forty-five minutes. 'Quite a day,' he confessed with rare lack of modesty, 'particularly as I had a back injury at the time.'

BEST MIDDLE-DISTANCE RUNNER
While this title is probably at the mercy of Britain's Steve Ovett and Sebastian Coe, and despite powerful lobbies for Finn Paavo Nurmi, arguably *Lasse Viren*, gaunt, emotionless Finnish master of the Munich Olympics 1972 and the Montreal Olympics 1976. Charged with 'blood doping', the extraction then replacement of oxygen-charged blood immediately before the race, Viren stared down accusers and retired to train north of the Arctic Circle.

BEST OLYMPIAN
Massively publicized Al Oerter, American discus thrower from the 1956 Melbourne Olympics onwards, deserves international ovation. But there was also Denmark's *Ivan Osiier*, who fenced in the Olympic Games of 1908, 1912, 1920, 1924, 1928, 1932 and 1948 and only missed the 1936 Olympics in Berlin because he regarded A. Hitler as a jolly rotten sport.

BEST OLYMPICS
The *XVIIth in Rome*, 1960, celebrated in a classical setting and a warm atmosphere of international goodwill and probably the last before drug-taking became a prominent factor in determining results.

BEST SPORTS SCIENTIST
Professor Arnold Beckett, London-based dedicated campaigner for the elimination of drug abuse in sports.

BEST SINGING-SPORTSMAN
Despite promising recording of 'Big Bad John' by Welsh soccer international John Charles, probably *Paul Robeson*, All-American footballer 1918.

BEST STEEPLECHASER
Contemporary national idolatry for almost-human Arkle and Red Rum is unlikely to sway cognoscenti from *Golden Miller*, winner of the Cheltenham Gold Cup for five successive years, 1932–6, and Grand National victor, 1934, in then record time.

BEST POKER PLAYER
John Hardie 'Johnny' Moss, who in three years in Las Vegas, 1951–4, won £4 million during sessions up to forty hours long and despite strictures from his wife Virgie-Ann, a strictly anti-gambling Baptist.

BEST BULL-RUNNER AT ANNUAL PAMPLONA ENCIERRO, SPAIN
Fermin Echeverria, thrice-gored local café proprietor.

BEST DOWNHILL SKIER
Close finish between French piste-artist Jean-Claude Killy and Austrian farmer's boy Franz Klammer decisively settled by intervention of crazy Jap *Yuichiro Miura* who flung himself down almost two miles of the upper reaches of Mount Everest at speeds in excess of 93 mph.

BEST SPORTS COMMENTATOR
Churchillian-toned master of the short, graphic phrase surrounded by long silence, Britain's *Henry Longhurst* elevated golf commentary to verbal literature and enthralled America where verbosity, hyperbole and disastrous syntax were eroding English language like a bat out of hell philology-wise.

BEST MALE TENNIS PLAYER
While awaiting the enthronement of Sweden's Bjorn Borg, the title remains with Australian *Rod Laver*, the thin-lipped monosyllabic perfectionist who is to Nastase (to ram the point home) what Sir Alec Guinness is to Bruce Forsyth.

BEST FEMALE TENNIS PLAYER
Distressingly early death by cancer virtually ensures her canonization in sport but *Maureen Connolly's* reputation confounds such cynicism. The hyphen between crinolined ladies perpetuating baseline rallies with fly-swat-shaped rackets and today's muscular Amazons hitting overhead smashes like lumberjacks, America's Little Mo remains No 1 with anyone who ever saw her play.

BEST SPORTS ADMINISTRATOR
Irish peer and sometime war correspondent and film producer *Lord Michael Killanin*, whose 1972 election as President of the International Olympic Committee injected urgently needed pragmatism to a movement about to suffer cardiac arrest.

BEST SPORTS MATRIARCH
Amir Bee, three of whose sons, Hanif Mohammad, Mushtaq Mohammad and Wazir Mohammad played Test cricket with distinction for Pakistan and a fourth, Raees Mohammad, was once twelfth man.

BEST DURATION SWIMMER
Tired of dodging oil-leaking supratankers in English Channel, London newspaper reporter *Kevin Murphy* who flogged through treacherous currents to circumnavigate 55 miles round the Isle of Wight in 26 hours 51 minutes.

BEST SQUASH PLAYER
Male chauvinists may vote for Pakistan's Hashim Khan but others would name Australian *Heather McKay* as the woman who showed the other half how to win consistently.

BEST CYCLIST
The outrage of Italian and Belgian supporters for Fausto Coppi and Eddy Merckx respectively must be risked by the selection of Frenchman *Jacques Anquetil*, five times Tour de France winner, four times successively 1961–4.

BEST WATER POLO PLAYER
Winner of five Olympic medals 1952–60, ambidextrous Hungarian *Dezso Gyarmati*.

BEST SPORTS LAWSUIT
Seven-day 1891 Society-rocking action, *Gordon-Cumming v. Wilson and Others*, before Lord Chief Justice Lord Coleridge, in which outraged inveterate snob Sir William Gordon-Cumming, soldier and land-owner, unsuccessfully sued for slander after being accused of cheating at baccarat in a game at which Bertie, Prince of Wales, later King Edward VII, was banker.

BEST SPORTING ELECTRICIAN
Ex-Major Boris Onischenko, former Soviet Master of Sport, who wired up a 'bell push' device in the grip of his épée to score spurious electrically-recorded 'hits' during the modern pentathlon fencing at the 1976 Montreal Olympics. Unmasked by British opponent Jim Fox, Onischenko was last heard of driving a taxi around his native Kiev.

BEST SPORTS SHOCK
1–0 soccer victory by *United States* part-timers over 250–1 England favourites in World Cup match, Belo-Horizonte, Brazil, 1950.

BEST SPORTS SPECTACLE
Spartakiada, sexennial 100,000-participant display to the glory of Czechoslovakian physical culture, largely to the music of Smetana, in Prague arena, which is six times larger than London's Wembley Stadium.

BEST SPORTS CAPITALIST
Turning professional after three Olympic gold medals and ten successive world championship titles, 1927–36, shrewd Norwegian honey blonde ice figure-skater *Sonja Henie*, who reportedly amassed £17 million from skating roles in ten films and countless ice-revue spectaculars before dying from leukaemia aged fifty-seven.

Best Rugby League Player
Fast, courageous, massively stylish, chosen aged twenty for his first international tour after only half a season in top-grade game, Australian centre *Reg Gasnier*.

Best Golf Course
Tough pin-placings, glorious floral setting, immaculate upkeep and world-wide television exposure of us Masters tournament suggest Augusta National, Georgia, usa, but purists name *Troon*, murderous, weather-beaten links mecca on Scotland's Ayrshire coast.

Best Indoor Arena
Until Sydney Opera House is converted into an indoor cycling arena, and despite the strong claim by Rome's Palazzo dello Sport where former Cassius Clay won an Olympic boxing medal, undoubtedly the gold-domed, wood-panelled *Budokan*, High temple of Japanese martial arts, Tokyo.

Best Sports Endurance Test
1,100-mile *Iditarod Trail*, 15–28-day sled-dog race in temperatures lowering to 80°F below, across wild-animal-ruled Anchorage-Yukon-Nome area of Alaska.

Best Wrestler
Unbeaten in brief, ferocious 186-fight career, Japanese featherweight *Osamu Watanabe*.

Best Sports Short Story
26,531-word man *v.* marlin fight *The Old Man and The Sea* by Ernest Hemingway.

Best Sports Reference Book
Unparalleled in accuracy, sound editorial opinion and dedication to subject since its first edition in 1864, *Wisden Cricketers' Almanack*.

Best Water Skier
Despite 38-buoy slalom performance by Italian Robby Zucci, now Britain's *Mike Hazelwood*.

Best Sporting Retreat
Valley of Peace Cricket Ground, near Christchurch, New Zealand, founded in 1926, since when no woman has been permitted to enter its gates. Asked what would happen if the Queen of England dropped by, an official said: 'We would most certainly stop playing, go to the gate and speak to her.'

THEATRE

Sheridan Morley

The theatre is not, in my experience, quite like anything else, which perhaps explains why this section may not precisely resemble those surrounding it in the book. A best film, or indeed a best book, remains the best however often you put it up on the screen or take it down from the shelf: *Citizen Kane* is looking no worse now than it did in 1941. Plays aren't like that. They depend totally on performance, on the night you happened to encounter them for the first time. I have seen perfectly terrible *Hamlets* and I have seen appalling plays made marvellous by a single actor, even a single production idea.

For those reasons, I have thought it best here not to go on the evidence of my eyes and ears alone: what follows is therefore divided into two halves. The first half deals with the theatre prior to 1960, which was the year in which at the age of eighteen I began going to the theatre regularly (i.e. more than twice a week) and to realize that I wanted more than anything else to be a drama critic. For this half, the pre-1960s, I have made up a series of lists which reflect, decade by decade, what I believe to be the majority opinion of those (critics and audiences alike) who were around at the time and who are therefore the only reliable guide to what was best.

In the second half of this section, dealing with the years since 1960, you will find a wholly personal selection of what I believe to have been the theatrical best. It is, to say the least, an arguable selection, but then nobody ever said a critic had to be right: they only said he had to be sure of what he liked and, perhaps more important, of what he didn't like.

Pre-1900

Best playwright in English language: William Shakespeare (1564–1616).
Best playwright in any language: William Shakespeare (1564–1616).
Best tragedy: *Hamlet* (Shakespeare, 1601).
Best comedy: *The School for Scandal* (Sheridan, 1777).
Best thriller: *The Changeling* (Middleton and Rowley, 1622).
Best history: *Henry V* (Shakespeare, 1598).
Best actor: Henry Irving (1838–1905, first stage knighthood 1895).
Best actress: Sarah Siddons (1755–1831).
Best musical: *The Beggar's Opera* (Gay, 1728).
Best child actor: Master Betty (1791–1874).
Best French comedy: *Tartuffe* (Molière, 1664).
Best French tragedy: *Phèdre* (Racine, 1677).
Best solo performers: Charles Dickens; Oscar Wilde.
Best theatrical company: Comédie Française (founded 1680).
Best clown: Joey Grimaldi (1778–1837).
Best Greek comedy: *The Birds* (Aristophanes, 414 BC).
Best English comedy: *The Importance of being Earnest* (Wilde, 1895).
Best English tragedy: *Tamburlaine* (Marlowe, 1587).
Best Greek tragedy: *Antigone* (Sophocles, 442 BC).
Best curtain line: 'Dead, and never called me Mother' (Maria Marten, 1827).
Best Richard III: Edmund Kean (1787–1833).
Best Italian comedy: *The Servant of Two Masters* (Goldoni, 1745).
Best Russian comedy: *The Government Inspector* (Gogol, 1836).
Best Macbeth: David Garrick (1717–70).
Best Shakespearian heroine: Ellen Terry (1847–1928).
Best epic: *Peer Gynt* (Ibsen, 1867).

1900–1910

Best actor: Herbert Beerbohm Tree (1853–1917).
Best actress: Sarah Bernhardt (1845–1923).
Best playwright: George Bernard Shaw (1856–1950).
Best comedy: *The Cherry Orchard* (Chekhov, 1904).
Best tragedy: *The Dance of Death* (Strindberg, 1901).
Best children's play: *Peter Pan* (Barrie, 1904).
Best theatrical company: Abbey, Dublin (founded 1904).
Best poetic drama: *The Playboy of the Western World* (Synge, 1907).
Best light comedian: Gerald du Maurier (1873–1934).
Best musical: *The Arcadians* (1909).
Best designer: Edward Gordon Craig (1872–1966).
Best curtain line: 'To die will be an awfully big adventure' (Peter Pan, 1904).
Best theatre: Royal Court in Shaw-Barker seasons, 1904–7.
Best English play: *His House in Order* (Pinero, 1906).

Best critics: Max Beerbohm, George Bernard Shaw.
Best English comedy: *The Admirable Crichton* (Barrie, 1902).
Best drawing-room comedy: *Smith* (Maugham, 1909).
Best star vehicle: *Major Barbara* (Shaw, 1905).
Best problem play: *The Silver Box* (Galsworthy, 1906).

1910–1920
Best poetic dramatist: Stephen Phillips (1864–1915).
Best musical: *Chu Chin Chow* (1916).
Best actor-manager: George Alexander (1859–1918).
Best repertory theatres: Liverpool (founded 1911); Old Vic (rep started 1914).
Best northern comedy: *Hobson's Choice* (Brighouse, 1916).
Best European play: *Six Characters in Search of an Author* (Pirandello, 1918).
Best American musical: *The Bing Boys on Broadway* (1918).
Best American Actress: Maude Adams
Best British drama: *Heartbreak House* (Shaw, 1919).
Best northern drama: *Hindle Wakes* (1912).
Best fantasy: *Dear Brutus* (Barrie, 1917).
Best Anglo-American comedy: *Our Betters* (Maugham, 1915).
Best epic: *The Dynasts* (Thomas Hardy-Granville Barker, 1914).
Best actress: Sybil Thorndike (1882–1976).
Best rustic comedy: *The Farmer's Wife* (Phillpotts, 1916).
Best curtain line: 'Damn Mrs Pearce; damn the coffee; damn you; and damn my own folly in having lavished hard-earned knowledge and the treasure of my regard and intimacy on a heartless guttersnipe' (Higgins, *Pygmalion*, Act III; Shaw, 1912).

1920–1930
Best operetta: *Bitter-Sweet* (Coward, 1929).
Best fantasies: *Outward Bound* (Vane, 1923); *The Apple Cart* (Shaw, 1929).
Best play: *St Joan* (Shaw, 1924).
Best English dramas: *The Vortex* (Coward, 1924); *The Skin Game* (Galsworthy, 1920).
Best Irish play: *Juno and the Paycock* (O'Casey, 1925).
Best domestic comedy: *Hay Fever* (Coward, 1925).
Best romantic dramas: *The Constant Nymph* (Kennedy/Dean, 1926); *The Last of Mrs Cheyney* (Lonsdale, 1925).
Best farce: *Thark* (Travers, 1927).
Best school play: *Young Woodley* (Van Druten, 1928).
Best war play: *Journey's End* (Sherriff, 1929).
Best French comedy: *Amphitryon 38* (Giraudoux, 1929).
Best musical: *Lilac Time* (1922).
Best American play: *The Emperor Jones* (O'Neill, 1921).
Best American musical: *Lady Be Good* (Gershwin, 1926).

Best curtain line: 'O God that madest this beautiful earth, when will it be ready to receive Thy saints? How long, O Lord, how long?' (Epilogue, *St Joan*; Shaw, 1924).

Best thriller: *Rope* (Hamilton, 1929).

Best actor: Henry Ainley (1879–1945).

Best actress: Edith Evans (1888–1976).

Best comic dramatists: Frederick Lonsdale; Noël Coward.

Best musical dramatists: Ivor Novello; Noël Coward.

Best young actress: Meggie Albanesi (1899–1923).

Best American actor: John Barrymore (1882–1942).

Best revue stars: Jack Buchanan; Jessie Matthews.

Best impresario: Charles B. Cochran.

Best concert-party: The Co-Optimists.

Best sisters: The Dolly Sisters; Zena and Phyllis Dare.

Best repertory theatre: Oxford (J.B. Fagan).

Best comedians: Sonnie Hale; Leslie Henson; Jack Hulbert.

Best thriller writer: Edgar Wallace (1876–1932).

Best Broadway Shakespearian: John Barrymore (*Richard III*,1920)

Best Follies: Ziegfeld's

Best Brother and Sister Act: Fred and Adèle Astaire

Best College Musical: *Good News* (Da Sylva, Brown, Henderson, 1927)

Best Longest Hit: *Strange Interlude* (Eugene O'Neill, 1928, five hours)

1930–1940

Best actor: John Gielgud.

Best actress: Peggy Ashcroft.

Best comedies: *Private Lives* (Coward, 1930); *French Without Tears* (Rattigan, 1936).

Best American drama: *Mourning Becomes Electra* (O'Neill, 1931).

Best Scottish play: *The Anatomist* (Bridie, 1931).

Best epic: *Cavalcade* (Coward, 1931).

Best theatre: Shakespeare Memorial (opened 1932).

Best fantasy: *Tobias and the Angel* (Bridie, 1932).

Best history: *Richard of Bordeaux* (Daviot, 1933).

Best poetic drama: *Murder in the Cathedral* (Eliot, 1935).

Best thriller: *Night Must Fall* (Williams, 1935).

Best musical: *Glamorous Night* (Novello, 1935).

Best American comedies: *Idiot's Delight* (Sherwood, 1936); *Man Who Came To Dinner* (Kaufman/Hart, 1939).

Best time play: *Time and the Conways* (Priestley, 1937).

Best regional plays: *The Corn is Green* (Williams, 1938); *Our Town* (Wilder, 1938).

Best French comedy: *Les Parents Terribles* (Cocteau, 1938).

Best French drama: *Voyageur sans Bagages* (Anouilh, 1938).
Best Irish company: Dublin Gate (Edwards/MacLiammòir, founded 1928).
Best one-act plays: *Tonight at 8.30* (Coward, 1936).
Best grande dame: Marie Tempest (1864–1942).
Best American musical: *Porgy and Bess* (Gershwin, 1935).
Best curtain line: 'How Robert would have laughed' (Daviot, *Richard of Bordeaux*).
Best family play: *Dear Octopus* (Smith, 1938).
Best repertory theatre: Birmingham (founded 1913).

1940–1950
Best actor: Laurence Olivier.
Best actress: Pamela Brown.
Best European play: *Mother Courage* (Brecht, 1941).
Best fantasy: *Blithe Spirit* (Coward, 1941).
Best war play: *Flare Path* (Rattigan, 1942).
Best Broadway musical: *Oklahoma!* (Rodgers-Hammerstein, 1943).
Best Broadway play: *The Glass Menagerie* (Williams, 1944).

'*As an actor he was a great success in the early sixties, but he didn't seem to move with the times.*'

Best French play: *Huis Clos* (Sartre, 1944).
Best English drama: *The Winslow Boy* (Rattigan, 1946).
Best epic: *The Iceman Cometh* (O'Neill, 1946).
Best curtain line: 'I have always depended upon the kindness of strangers' (Blanche du Bois, *A Streetcar Named Desire*; Williams, 1947).
Best European comedy: *Ring Round the Moon* (Anouilh/Fry, 1947).
Best English comedy: *The Chiltern Hundreds* (Home, 1947).
Best poetic drama: *The Lady's Not For Burning* (Fry, 1948).
Best play: *Death of a Salesman* (Miller, 1949).
Best thriller: *An Inspector Calls* (Priestley, 1945).
Best Scottish comedy: *Mr Bolfry* (Bridie, 1943).

1950–1960
Best actor: Paul Scofield.
Best actress: Dorothy Tutin.
Best European comedy: *The Love of Four Colonels* (Ustinov, 1951).
Best poetic drama: *Saint's Day* (Whiting, 1951).
Best Broadway musicals: *My Fair Lady* (Lerner-Loewe, 1956); *West Side Story* (Bernstein-Sondheim-Laurents, 1956).
Best thriller: *The Mousetrap* (Christie, 1952).
Best American play: *The Crucible* (Miller, 1953).
Best English comedy: *Penny For A Song* (Whiting, 1951).
Best English drama: *Look Back in Anger* (Osborne, 1956).
Best curtain line: 'You've been a good audience. Very good. A very good audience. Let me know where you're working tomorrow night – and I'll come and see you' (Osborne, *The Entertainer*, 1957).
Best domestic comedy: *The Chalk Garden* (Bagnold, 1954).
Best European drama: *I Am A Camera* (Van Druten, 1954).
Best English musicals: *The Boy Friend* (Wilson, 1954); Salad Days (Slade, 1954).
Best European drama: *Waiting For Godot* (Beckett, 1955).
Best Australian play: *Summer of the Seventeenth Doll* (Lawler, 1955).
Best French comedy: *Waltz of the Toreadors* (Anouilh, 1956).
Best theatre company: English Stage Co., Royal Court (founded 1956).
Best Irish play: *The Hostage* (Behan, 1959).
Best English playwrights: Pinter, Wesker, Osborne, Bolt, Delaney.
Best star vehicle: *A Day By The Sea* (Hunter, 1953).
Best one-act play: *Separate Tables* (Rattigan, 1954).
Best director: Joan Littlewood.
Best solo show: Emlyn Williams as Charles Dickens.

Since 1960
BEST PLAY *Forty Years On* (*Alan Bennett, 1969*)
The only play (apart from Hare's *Plenty*) in the past two decades that has had

the courage, and the good humour, to tackle England's immediate past. Within the context of a school play Bennett managed to deal with Chamberlain, Munich, the Abdication, World War II and various other historical accidents before arriving, in the curtain lines, at the best definition of our present predicament I have yet heard: 'To let: a valuable site at the crossroads of the world. At present on offer to European clients. Outlying portions of the estate already disposed of to sitting tenants. Of some historical and period interest. Some alterations and improvements necessary.'

BEST WORD PLAY *Rosencrantz and Guildenstern Are Dead (Tom Stoppard, 1966)*
The first and still the most impressive of Stoppard's gallops through the English dictionary, this one was based on *Hamlet* as seen through the oblique and often eccentric view of its two least important characters, traces of whom could still be found in Stoppard's writing as late as *Travesties* (1974).

BEST ENGLISH MUSICAL *Oliver!(Lionel Bart, 1960)*
This has the dubious distinction of being not only the best (*Evita* is discounted on the grounds that though its composers and cast were British, its director and choreographer were Americans) but also the only post-war British musical which could be (and was) sent to Broadway with pride rather than deep embarrassment. Dickens had a good deal to do with its success (though subsequent Dickensian musicals have proved rather less triumphant) but the real stars were Sean Kenny's sets and the superb central performance of Ron Moody as Fagin.

BEST OLD-STYLE BROADWAY MUSICAL *Hello, Dolly!* (*Stewart-Herman, 1964)*
This achieved 2,844 Broadway performances by following all the old laws of that particular jungle. Based on an already tried and tested non-musical success (in this case Thornton Wilder's *The Matchmaker*), it came complete with an exclamation-mark in the title, a simple singable score and one truly great star-turn in Carol Channing. The moment when she first appeared at the top of what I now seem to recall as a red velvet staircase, to be told by a collection of singing waiters that it was great to have her back where she belonged (mysteriously, since the plot indicated that she had never actually been there before), will live forever in my memory as the peak of old-style Broadway achievement. By the time she got to the bottom of that staircase, not only the waiters but a hitherto unexciting and unexcited Monday-night audience were on their feet, and rightly. It had almost nothing to do with a great show, which *Hello, Dolly*! visibly wasn't; but it had everything to do with a deep and instinctive understanding of what the New York theatre was all about.

BEST NEW-STYLE BROADWAY MUSICAL *Company* (*Sondheim, 1970)*
To Stephen Sondheim, almost alone, goes the credit for pulling the Broadway

musical into the second half of the twentieth century (*Dolly* could have been, and for all I know was, written in about 1930). You don't come out of a Sondheim show humming the sets or the costumes or the first-half finale: you come out humming the Divorce Act. He is the master poet and lyricist of a disenchanted, high-rise, urban culture, the nearest the theatre has ever got to a *New Yorker* cartoon. *Company* (based on a series of one-act plays by George Furth) had no hit song, no happy ending, no message of good cheer for the world at large. Rather was it a bitter, cynical and deeply unsentimental look at the state of matrimony in New York ('Marriage may be where it's been, but it's not where it's at') which resolutely refused to tug any heart-strings. It had all the warmth of an electric carving knife, and all the cosy charm of a crossword puzzle. Technically it was as flawless as the Pan Am skyscraper in Manhattan: a brisk, glittering show which might have been assembled by computer and was in its own way as brilliant a dissection of marital bliss as Albee's *Virginia Woolf*.

BEST DOUBLE-ACT *John Gielgud and Ralph Richardson*
First in David Storey's *Home* (1970) and then in Harold Pinter's *No Man's Land* (1975), they established that not only are they, barring Olivier, the two greatest actors in the land but that they are privy to an eerie partnership stretching far back and beyond whatever any playwright asks of them. There is no greater exponent of mannered eccentricity than Sir Ralph, no more moving actor alive today than Sir John: twice knightly they are dynamite.

BEST COMPANY *The Royal Shakespeare*
Founded in 1960 by Peter Hall and sustained in his image by Trevor Nunn.

BEST THRILLER *Sleuth* (Anthony Shaffer, 1970)
The only one that's truly managed to get us away from Agatha Christie, and therefore now as often imitated as the Dame herself.

BEST SOLO SHOW *Alec McCowen's recital of St Mark's Gospel*
Not a reading but a performance in the best Emlyn Williams-MacLiammoir tradition, and the evening that put McCowen once and for all up there with the very best.

BEST SHAKESPEARIAN *Alan Howard*
Whose *Coriolanus* was the height of RSC achievement in the 1970s.

BEST BRITISH MUSICAL COMEDY *Privates on Parade* (*Peter Nichols, 1976*)
A camp, in all senses of the word, account of army entertainers in the 1940s, made all the more memorable by Denis Quilley's stunning drag impersonations of Dietrich, Carmen Miranda and Vera Lynn.

BEST REVUE *Beyond the Fringe (1960)*
Creator of a line in university humour that ran through to television's *Not the Nine o'clock News* in the late 1970s; but on stage it proved an impossible act to follow, which is why revue is now no more.

BEST ACTRESS *Maggie Smith* •
Who, rivalled only by Glenda Jackson, has managed to move transatlantically throughout the 1960s and 1970s from high comedy to high tragedy and back without showing the stretch-marks.

BEST LAUGHS *Alan Ayckbourn (notably in The Norman Conquest and Bedroom Farce)*
Who, were it not for the sustained and splendid nonagenarian presence of our greatest living comic dramatist, Ben Travers, would have already inherited that title.

BEST EPIC *The Royal Hunt of the Sun (Peter Shaffer, 1964)*
The nearest the National Theatre ever got to Hollywood, though interestingly when Hollywood tried to film this everyday story of Inca folk it was a disaster.

BEST UNINTENTIONAL LAUGH-LINE
'These Crusades are spreading like wildfire'–spoken by an extra in *Troubadour*, a 1978 medieval musical financed by the Japanese and arguably their worst mistake since Pearl Harbour.

BEST CURTAIN CALLS
Marlene Dietrich, whom I saw collecting at a matinee one wet Saturday afternoon in 1972 a standing ovation and enough bouquets to run her own branch of Interflora. There she stood on the stage of the Queens Theatre, an old and defiant German lady with a slight limp, swathed in acres of white fur, coolly receiving applause, sifting and apparently checking it for volume and duration, receiving it as a sovereign right with no element of mock surprise or humility in her manner. Hers was an object lesson in stardom, an icily unsentimental and unforgettable performance by the woman who remains the greatest feat of theatrical engineering since they invented the revolving stage. To evoke nostalgia and then transcend it was the best of her many conjuring tricks and I shall tell my children and my grandchildren that I saw Dietrich work. They may not care, but I still do.

BEST CURTAIN LINE
'There will be days and days and days like this'–spoken by Kate Nelligan at the end of her stunning performance in David Hare's *Plenty* at the National, a reverse chronicle of post-war Britain which established beyond all reasonable doubt that there weren't going to be any more days like that whatsoever.

Best Concert Show *Side By Side By Sondheim*
This was not just because I was occasionally allowed to appear in it. It took an English team led by Ned Sherrin, David Kernan, Julia McKenzie and Millicent Martin to prove even to Americans the genius of Sondheim as a lyricist, and no other compilation songbook evening, not even *Cowardy Custard*, managed to teach us quite so much about the character of its creator.

Best Musical About A Bicycle Repair Shop In Northern Ireland *Spokesong*

Best Definition Of The Broadway Ethic *A Chorus Line*.

Best Evocations Of The Semi-Detachment That Lies At The Heart Of British Intellectual Life *Simon Gray (Butley, Otherwise Engaged, Close of Play)*

Best Performance By A Young Actor Playing An Old Man *John Wood as Henry Carr in Travesties*

Best Performance By An Old Actor Playing A Mole *Richard Goolden in Toad of Toad Hall*

Best Performance By A Middle-Aged Actor Playing A Middle-Aged Australian Woman *Barry Humphries in A Night With Dame Edna*

Best Of The Joan Littlewood Musicals At Stratford East *Oh, What A Lovely War!*

Best Example Of A Great Actor Going Over The Top *Laurence Olivier in Othello*

Best Example Of A Great Actor Going Wrong *John Gielgud in Othello*

Best Example Of A Static Play Made Quicksilver By A Director *John Dexter's production of Equus by Peter Shaffer*

Best All-Star Midnight Matinee *The Noël Coward seventieth birthday tribute at the Phoenix Theatre, 16 December 1969*

Best Drag Act Not Counting Barry Humphries *George Devine in John Osborne's A Patriot For Me*

TRAVEL

Alan Whicker

BEST WAY TO GO *Concorde*

It's not so much Mach 2 or the absence of jet lag, or the way they splash Dom Perignon '70 around like Ordinaire; it's the way they treat you *on the ground* – as though a chummy house-party had gathered to fly to New York. There's a holiday atmosphere, rather as it was thirty years ago when lumbering Argonauts took three deafening days to reach Tokyo, with the same passengers and crew all the way; before reaching Calcutta, romances were blooming ... Concorde's special check-in, smoked salmon and champagne in its departure lounge, free calls to friends abroad before take-off – it's the way first-class travel ought to be.

BEST LUGGAGE *T. Anthony, New York*

Quietly distinguished but not such an instant target that baggage-handlers or professionals will sweep it off the carousel and leave you their old hold-all. Luggage should be easily identifiable, but not as promising as Vuiton, Cartier or Gucci; they proclaim your affluence and demand attention from villains.

BEST TRAVEL ACCESSORY

Small powerful radio to pick up the incomparable BBC World Service, without which jet-lagged nights in distant hotel rooms are long, and days uninformed.

BEST TRAVELLING COMPANION

Someone of the opposite sex who also does the packing.

*'Of course, this wasn't an island paradise
until the white man introduced alcohol.'*

BEST UNACCEPTABLE TRAVEL HINT *Moderation*
When flying eat little and drink no alcohol. This saves your digestion and the after-effects of too many drinks at 30,000 feet, where each glass packs a treble-punch; but oh the *tedium* of being sensible for hours ... I have yet to achieve this.

BEST BORINGLY ACCEPTABLE TRAVEL HINTS
Loose clothes with slippers and cardigans for night-flights; battery razor and toothbrush in case of delay; paperbacks in case of inadequate magazine supply; local currency for porters and taxi upon arrival; carefully cultivated ability to fly into a deep calm....

BEST HOTELS
Hotel Utah, Salt Lake City: massively comfortable old pile owned by the Church of Latter Day Saints and run with that high degree of friendliness,

honesty and efficiency which characterizes Mormons. Good view of their Temple, where marriages are sealed for eternity. No liquor served in restaurants, though some arrangement can be made with room-service.

The Berkeley, London: well-run country house in the heart of London, a delicious omelette Arnold Bennett pleasantly and swiftly served on Wedgwood in your room, where the decor will be tasteful and charming, with every comfort to hand.

Hotel Sacher, Vienna: red-plush museum full of silver-haired Herr Obers who care; next to the Opera House.

BEST AIRCRAFT

If you're travelling first class, it has to be the *Boeing 747*, simply because you're up-front with nothing ahead but the sharp-end and the sky; you can also wander upstairs to that lounge they never know what to do with. On the other wide-bodies you sit and look towards lavatories and kitchens in front of you, with their night-time traffic. Narrow bodies are too constraining now, except on short flights when any jet will do, though the 737 is preferred.

BEST CITIES

Venice: the most glorious man-made setting, preferably in the autumn when most of the tourists have gone and the sunsets have returned. The Piazza San Marco reverts to its role as an elegant medieval club where you sit over your negroni and nod to the other members.

Vienna: the nostalgic city with a streak of gentle hopelessness, where Freud discovered sex. Viennese have also mastered the art of civilized drinking: the Heurige wine, light and slightly sour, has been sold by the country wine-houses since the days of the Roman Legionnaires. It should be drunk in some Grinzing garden, accompanied by cold cuts and sausages and a tearful violin. . . . Baroque Vienna knows that an illusion which makes you happy is better than a reality which makes you sad.

Florence: not only lovely but exactly the right size for a city; containable. The pretty girl you glimpse in Via Tornabuoni will surely be in Lelands tomorrow.

BEST MAPS *Michelin*

Though even with these excellent 1 cm–to–2 km paper maps, your destination will always be on the edge of the next number.

BEST AIRLINE

World-wide – Air New Zealand: even condescending American women travel writers admit it is the best cabin-service in the world, and aircraft maintenance is also impeccable. After a month filming around New Zealand I came away fearing I'd never feel secure on any other airline.

Europe-based – Swissair: the correct combination of efficiency, style and friendliness. In general the worst airline, half-empty, is liable to feel more comfortable than the best airline, packed. British Airways, long a favourite, can do excellently on intercontinental flights but is sadly let down by domestic services using an inadequate number of obsolescent aircraft. It's a jolt to return from the domestic jets of developing nations like Malaysia, India, Paraguay ... to be stuffed into a tired old Viscount which paid for itself twenty years ago, serving routes on which BA announce they lose money – though they sometimes have no seats available for the next *week*. The 300 miles by propeller from Jersey to Manchester take as long as the 900 mile jet-flight to Rome, cost rather more than charter to New York – and you'll not be offered as much as a dry biscuit. Close your eyes and think of Concorde.

Best Sunshine *In mid-Pacific*
Where from the sun-deck of a liner the world's most unsullied ultra-violet gets to you before you've had time to finish your beef tea. With proper care you get a fast Florida tan without those boring days amid acres of greasy flesh turning endlessly on their spits, as at Miami Beach.

Best Sunset *Waikiki*
From a bedroom in one of the ocean-front fringe of hotels – known as The Vertical Beach – at this garish resort you can lie in bed and watch the even more garish Pacific sky ablaze with improbable colours. The Venetian skies in October display a softer, less savage brush.

Best Airline Dish
If the food's too pre-cooked and re-heated, ask for dolcelatte or gorgonzola, with a pear; a most delicious taste combination – no biscuits or bread necessary. If unavailable, settle for blue cheese and an apple. Alternative enjoyed on a British Airways DC10 to Los Angeles: hot scones, strawberry jam and Devonshire cream; seven miles up, simple dishes are the best.

Best Sights
Lake Atitlán and Chichicastenango, Guatemala, for the lake's calm beauty, and the dramatic intensity of Indians burning incense up on the steps of their Catholic Church – worshipping both the Virgin and their idols.
Rio de Janeiro, Brazil, for the grandeur of the harbour, with which only Hong Kong and possibly Sydney can compare.
Lake Palace at Udaipur, Rajasthan, a place of magic amid the harsh scrubland of Rajasthan.
Taj Mahal, Agra, the only world's wonder which exceeds its reputation.

Best Outlook
From the balcony of your room in the upside-down Hotel Tiara 'A' outside

Papeete, Tahiti. It's a wholly outward-looking place; look inward, and you'll notice the service is awful.

Best River Trip *Down the Rhine*
for twelve hours, from Bonn to Mainz
This ever-active highway snakes between vine-covered slopes, past the Lorelei Rock and gaunt, towering castles, as you sit in a glass-domed saloon and watch Wagner's world go by. The white ships of the KD German Rhine line feed you splendidly, even berth you adequately if you choose the five-day Rotterdam–Basle cruise, tying-up each night within some interesting city.

Best Adventure-Voyage *Prinsendam*
Two weeks around Indonesia; out of Singapore to Penang, around Sumatra to Nias and Krakatoa, down Java to Bali. Only 9,000 tons but with six decks; Holland America's food good if you stick to steaks, Indonesian stewards cheerful; cabins small but the sight of Pasadena Blue Rinses meeting the Stone Age men on the equatorial isle of Nias worth the whole two weeks. Also bull races on Madura, and the animists' trance dance in Surabaya where the man believing himself to be a horse munches grass and then (the link is obscure) finishes by eating electric light bulbs with many a snap, crackle and pop.

Best Travel Precaution
Upon arrival anywhere make sure your escape-route is planned. Before leaving the airport, collect every relevant airline schedule, so you can give flight numbers and departure times over the telephone when booking-out. Never leave this to anyone else, like hotel porters or local travel agents.... The last time I delegated, I was booked to an airport that did not exist. You must know exactly how you can get away, and when.

Best Gentlemen's Changing Rooms *Willingdon Sports Club, Bombay*
Where retainers trained in the gracious days of the Raj will instinctively stoop to put on a chap's trousers, sensing when a chap's not used to performing such tedious chores for himself. Pleasantly antiquated exercise-machines on which you can plod along quietly, without having to mingle with those who perambulate conventionally along the ground; usual failed-boarding-school food available.

Best Valet Service
Connaught Hotel, London, W1.

Best Children's Holiday *Disney World* in Florida
An improvement upon the Californian Disneyland. To both one goes reluctantly – and stays to be enchanted. Disney crowd control is illuminating and

fearfully effective; they should be running the world, when it would be a far better, cleaner, happier and rather sickly-sweet place.

Best Cruiseship *Cunard's QE2*
Though displaying a tendency to boiler-fatigue, she has an overwhelming choice of amenities and activities which enable you to escape shipboard bores and get lost among 1,400 other passengers. Even after a month in this floating Waldorf Astoria, you're still getting lost, still noticing the elegant brunette who's suddenly appeared.... Cabin stewards are bucolic, companionable, concerned, cossetting. Your cabin must entitle you to eat in the excellent Queen's Grill; the other three restaurants are good but unmemorable, though you can order from your wildest dreams and always have caviar. On my first cruise from Hong Kong across the Pacific and through the Panama Canal to Port Everglades I took a pile of books as protection against the weeks of boredom; not one was opened.

Best Travellers Cheques *Dollars*, still
I once wandered the Province of Quebec, sterling cheques in hand, beseeching scornful Canadian cashiers who did not wish to know about the Mother Country, thanks.

Best Credit Card
Always the *other* one.

Best Island For Visiting *Bali*
The ornament of tropical Asia, most magical of Indonesia's 13,000 islands. This never-never-land is one huge botanical garden pervaded by a sort of enchantment. Every Balinese is an artist and all life's a ceremony – there's a collective obligation to make things beautiful. Since my first visit ten years ago, Bali has seen a tourist invasion, but apart from a few roadside traps selling tourist schmuck and a florid rush of stores around the Ubud artists' village, remains a delight. I once bought a few Balinese naive village paintings for $10 each and later, at Nieman Marcus in Houston, saw inferior examples floodlit and offered at $1,000 and up.

Best Island For Living *Jersey*
Tranquil isle of pines and pink granite, with some beauty and charm, happily free from natural or man-made disaster, anarchy or riot. Even in these brusque days its public servants are invariably pleasant: postmen wait while you finish your letter; septic tanks are politely and euphemistically emptied by, wait for it, the Resources Recovery Board; even Traffic Wardens are friendly and helpful – and that's *impossible*. The island enjoys the stability of an honest and competent Judiciary, Government and Police, London newspapers at breakfast,

British television, tax at a tolerable twenty per cent – and a ten-minute flight to Brittany, for lunch.

BEST WINDOW-SHOPPING
Via Condotti, Rome; Worth Avenue, Palm Beach; Faubourg St Honoré, Paris; Fifth Avenue, New York.

BEST JAUNT *The vineyards* around Epernay during the vendage
A local monk called Dom Perignon first put the pop into champagne, and today's wine makers still know how to entertain guests magnificently. Superlative food and wine at the Château de Saran, formerly the summer home of the Moët branch of the family. This largest champagne company has nineteen miles of cellars, where thirty-two million bottles lie in wait for the fortunate.

BEST GUIDE BOOKS
Fodor's: detailed, entertaining, splendidly informative, though hotel ratings can be too bland; it rarely warns. The unspeakable Lallgarh Palace in Bikaner is merely misspelled and offered as 'red sandstone and Italian marble, all rooms with bath, golf and squash nearby' without suggesting the grubby fly-infested nightmare, the murky platefuls awaiting the unsuspecting.
Michelin: basic information, valued opinion; in no way entertaining – though its hieroglyphics keep you on your toes.
APA Productions, Singapore: Guides to Bali, Java, Singapore and Malaysia; beautifully produced, excellent pictures, thoughtful opinion.

BEST TRAVEL BOOKS
James Cameron: on India.
Kate Simon: on anywhere.

BEST HIDEAWAY *Norfolk Island*
Tiny piece of Switzerland floating in the South Pacific between Australia and New Zealand, where the descendants of the Bounty mutineers were sent when they left Pitcairn. Only three miles by five, its seas vivid blue and mountainous, grass a lush deep green, famous pines the perfect silhouette. Norfolk, once a penal colony, was becoming a tax haven until Canberra stepped in. The Qantas DC4 (only a grass strip) takes up to five hours to cover the 1,000 miles from Sydney, but when you arrive it's worth every minute. Shorter Air New Zealand F27 flights from Auckland. Norfolk folk, many named Christian after their ancestor Fletcher, or Quintal, McCoy, Adams, Nobbs ... speak 'Norfolk' with the West-Country burr of their mutinous forbears combined with the soft speech of those most welcoming Tahitian maidens. It's an island where nothing bites and nothing stings and they feed the pigs on passion fruit.

'For God's sake make up your mind, Nina –
where do you want to go?'

BEST SPECTACLE *Carnival in Rio* – the samba city
The Greatest Show on Earth starts around ten o'clock on Saturday night and
goes on, throbbing and vibrating without pause, until Ash Wednesday. All ordinary activity stops: Rio closes down – then opens up. A circus for the masses,
put on by the masses themselves, an annual super-colossal production sprawl-
ing across its incomparable city-stage. In the world's biggest binge thousands
live out their fantasies, so it's also a time of violence: the murder rate increases
dramatically and lovers solve the eternal triangle by knocking off one of its
corners, or collect for the cost of their costumes at the point of a gun. If you
weary of the excitements of the streets, there are the costume balls, where 6,000
writhing Cariocas blend into a deafening, pulsating mass of Hieronymus Bosch.

BEST MASOCHISTIC SPECTACLE *Thaipusam*
Awesome Hindu Festival and annual act of repentance on the isle of Penang,
Malaysia. Penitents mortify themselves, pierce their cheeks with six-foot spears
and their tongues with skewers, then trudge for miles through stunning heat
dragging decorated kavadis, trolleys attached by hooks to the skin of their backs.
They feel no pain 'because their minds are on God'. Despite such fierce and
determined self-abuse, I saw not one speck of blood.

Best Souvenirs
Western Samoa: hand-painted wooden combs for removing lice.
New Hebrides: bride-money necklaces; amass sufficient of these tiny shells and you can make a down-payment on a wife.
Quito, Equador: shrunken heads.

Best Useful Souvenirs
Kerala, India: lace from the convents of Cochin and Trivandrum. Unlike every other Indian salesman, the Sisters don't bargain. However, they do offer a discount you get nowhere else: they promise to pray for you....
Penang, Malaysia: safari suits, hand-painted Batik kaftans.
Bombay, India: lizard-skin handbags, travel wallets, shoes made to measure in the Taj Mahal Hotel arcade.
Asuncion, Paraguay: embroidered evening shirts.
Hong Kong: pure crêpe de Chine from CAC, the Communist China shops; surly service, but value for money. Hand-embroidered linen sheets from Mandarin Arcade shops.

Best Buys For Bookworms *Bootleg books*
Pirated outside the copyright laws in Taipei, Taiwan, at a fraction of their cover price. Encyclopedias, manuals like How to Fly a 747 or any tomes you've yearned for are well worth lugging home.

Best Place To Get Into High Society *Palm Beach*, if you happen to be male and available
On this well-manicured Florida sandbar there are £2 million-homes with only one bedroom; matrons – most of them 'thirty-nine and holding' – easily outnumber acceptable escorts, but are dauntless in their determination to go on partying till they drop. (It would not help your acceptability, however, to make a television programme about the place....)

Best Airports
Schiphol, Amsterdam: modern, friendly, efficient, uncrowded – 8·4 million passengers in 1977 against Heathrow's 20·6 million, Gatwick's 5·8 million.
Cointrin, Geneva: only ten minutes from the city centre; medium-size, underground walkway to departure lounges in mid-tarmac – a calm airport.

Best Girls' Outing
The Greenhouse at Arlington, between Dallas and Fort Worth, where Presidents' wives, film stars and formidable Texan matrons plan to grow young and beautiful, at a price. Once a week they're allowed out on a shopping expedition to the parent company's Nieman Marcus department store in Dallas. Big black

Cadillacs line up and the rejuvenated blue-rinses dash out, giggling like school-girls escaping at half-term, each feeling like a new man.

BEST ROADS *United States*
For sheer national consistency; good everywhere, and used by the world's best drivers who move steadily, don't switch lanes and are rarely anxious to prove their masculinity. Italian autostrade have patches of inspired engineering, a joy wiped out by skilled but murderous driving.

BEST PUBLIC ESCAPE-HATCH? *New Hebrides*
A British-French condominium offering instant financial advantages with certain delayed physical disadvantages. On the isle of Aneityium I found the only white man, who had been living among 40,000 Polynesians for twenty-one years, was a Kiwi with the endearing name of Artie Kraft. His neighbour had just fallen out of a mango tree and impaled himself most profoundly upon a lemon tree; Artie, the local squire, had to sew his stomach and guts back in again, working on instructions over a radio link from the doctor of Tanna, the next island. Every stitch in time made 75 per cent – even 60 per cent – seem less impossible.

BEST PRIVATE ESCAPE-HATCH WITHOUT LEMON TREES *Brecqhou*
The rocky islet off Sark, which Mr Leonard Matchan bought in the sixties for £40,000. Sole resident, he now pays no tax at all while living contentedly less than 200 miles – or an hour in his chopper – from London and Paris.

BEST TRAVEL FOR WHEELCHAIR CASES
The QE2 has special cabins designed for those confined to wheelchairs; with many passenger lifts and sloping companion ways, the handicapped are considered and not excluded from activities.

BEST PLACE TO GET KNIGHTED *The Hutt River Province*
In Western Australia some eight hours' drive north from Perth, Leonard and Shirley Casley turned their twenty-nine-square-mile farm into an independent Principality on 21 April 1970. After seceding from Australia, Prince Leonard and Princess Shirl have created a number of earls and noblemen for their work on behalf of the province. He made me a Roving Ambassador; I have a most convincing diplomatic passport which I plan to test when entering some country in which I could stand going to jail. . . .

BEST TAXIS *Australia*
Not because Aussie drivers are experts at anything but because in their land of equality, where you prove you're not stuck up by sitting in front, not only

do you not need to tip the driver ... but on occasion he will even tip *you*, by letting you off the odd few cents.

BEST TRAINS
Japanese streamlined expresses between Tokyo and Osaka which stop and start with such stunning punctuality that if your knowledge of Japanese place-names is a wee bit rusty, you can be swept on another fifty miles without as much as an Oriental 'Ah So'. Japanese men, with their tendency to undress in front of you, do not make the best travelling companions.

BEST SCENIC TRAIN RIDE
Through the Rockies from Calgary to Vancouver. Enormously broad trains snake slowly backwards and forwards, climbing through the mountains in such a way that from your lounge chair up in the scenic dome, you see the tail of your own train passing you at a lower level – in the opposite direction! It's weird. Finding profits came more easily from freight, the railway wanted to stop this passenger service but the government insisted, so now sulky trains set off at most discouraging hours, chosen deliberately to pass through most of the magnificent scenery in the darkness ... but there's still enough daylight left to make the ticket worthwhile.

BEST HOTEL MASSAGE *New Otani, Tokyo*
Japanese massage is nationally good, but this enormous hotel runs an admirable organization of magic-fingered girls somewhere in its nether region. They have numbers so, as soon as they begin to know their way around you, a call and a 'Come up No 67' has results guaranteed to send you to sleep before she glides out.

BEST MAN-MADE SCINTILLATION *The Strip at Las Vegas*
After dark – a brilliant Dante's Inferno appealing to much that's bad in the human race: avarice, something for nothing, greed ... with a sideline titillation of sex and booze provided for the high-rollers. Having said that, the sight of those brilliant Bacchanalian casinos with their galaxy of entertainment, the frenzy of the vast gaming floors, the menace of two-way mirrors and all those motionless dark-jowled pallid men in dinner-jackets with dead faces but restless eyes ... make it the most stimulating place in the West to spend a few days. Any longer, you go mad.

BEST UNDERGROUND *Vienna*
So modern the automated trains gliding around at speed beneath the ancient city do not need drivers. However, it was feared the sight of a driverless train pulling up automatically at each station would frighten passengers – so they put a uniformed man in that empty cab as an ornament, just to sit and look

reassuring. Canadian metros in Montreal and Toronto are also clean, quiet and comfortable.

BEST COACHES *Greyhound and Trailways*
Their enormous six-wheelers barrelling along freeways across the United States have to be the fastest, most functional road transport in the world.

BEST TRAVELLER'S STIMULANT, IF YOU CAN GET IT DOWN
In Taipei, capital of Taiwan, certain Chinese pharmacists dispense snake snacks and snake wines which they guarantee will cure what ails you. The noxious liquid, stored for three years in bottles containing dead snakes, is said to increase sexual potency, end fatigue, help sufferers from liver, gall bladder and kidney trouble. I can affirm that anyone strong enough to swallow it *has* to be fit and well.

BEST VOODOO EXPEDITION *Voodoo colony of Oyo Tungi*
A Yoruba village surprisingly enough on the Georgia-South Carolina border near Beaufort, where a group of American negroes practise the dark arts, apparently to some effect. Health Inspectors, Sheriffs, County officials who at first wanted them to leave all seemed to suffer heart attacks, or a change of attitude. Outsiders can have someone cursed to death for around $500 – cheaper than a hit-man and, as the Chief told me, more discreet. Unlike other aboriginal curses, the victim does not need to know the curse has been placed but merely, he explained, dies unobtrusively – perhaps under a truck.... Up the road Ed McTeer, who was Sheriff of Beaufort County for thirty-seven years, will remove spells for nothing. He doesn't complain of the Voodoo cultists: 'It isn't good for one doctor to criticize another'.

BEST CAR *Bentley Continental* Mulliner Park Ward SIII 1964–65
The line of this superb motor has never been bettered; must be the two-door, for the four-door loses grace and style. The elegant radiator is less assertive, more acceptable today than the Rolls. For preference, a telephone in the centre armrest and a Webasto roof with deflector, giving convertible motoring without the gale. Disadvantages: early corrosion behind rear-wheel arches, to be set against performance, comfort, engineering, daily enjoyment – and capital appreciation unique in the motoring world.

WOMEN'S FASHION

◆

Ann Ryan

BEST RULE OF DRESS
That clothes must be appropriate.

BEST-AVOIDED FASHION
That of the too-recent past.

BEST FASHION INFLUENCE OF THE 1970s *Yves Saint Laurent*
In 1966 he predicted the demise of the so-called fashion edicts – screaming newspaper headlines: 'Paris Abolishes the Bust', 'Paris Puts Women in the Sack', and so on, following the twice-yearly launch of the Paris couture collections. 'Now that women have liberated themselves from our dictatorship and the corset of other people's ideas,' he said a few years later, 'they themselves become infinitely more important than the clothes they wear.'

His first job at the age of seventeen was with Dior and at twenty-one, on the death of Christian Dior in 1959, the multi-million-franc empire which was the House of Dior, was left in his hands. In 1962 he opened his own business and has never looked back. He is lauded and copied by the world's fashion industry, constantly evolving new lines which have repercussions round the globe. One of his wisest remarks was 'Women should be terrified of mere elegance as of the grave, for it is the death of fashion.'

He regularly produces irreverent themes – see-through blouses, tarty satin shorts and mini-dresses for disco devotees – alongside his more serious creations, and he was not afraid of shocking the world when he posed wearing nothing but his spectacles in a photograph used to advertise his range of men's toiletries.

BEST-PAID MODEL
Make-up-less, gap-toothed, tousle-haired 'Model Girl Next Door' *Lauren Hutton*, the highest paid model in history – two hundred thousand dollars a year in the early 1970s in America for personifying Charles Revlon's Ultima beauty products. Not in spite of, but because of, her gap-teeth and her banana nose she is one of the beauties of our time.

BEST FURRIER *Italy's Fendi*
Using off-beat furs which do not offend the conservationists, the fur clothing is produced with a totally contemporary spirit, turning fur coats into garments as everyday, casual and comfortable as a knitted cardigan.

BEST FASHION INFLUENCE OF THE 1950s *Cristobal Balenciaga*
One of the few great couturiers of this century. He was a legendary figure. Brooding and withdrawn, he presided like a mystical deity over his Paris couture house and was revered by customers and staff alike. He took on young André Courrèges as an assistant in 1951 and the impression he made on him was profound. In the ten years Courrèges remained with him Balenciaga taught him everything, not only about couture but about life. 'Those ten years were very hard, but that didn't worry me,' Courrèges said of his time with Balenciaga. 'Balenciaga was very exacting, very hard to please. Everything had to be done for him very quickly and very well.' When Courrèges finally decided to leave and set up his own business he put in his place a young man called Emanuel Ungaro. Years afterwards Ungaro said, 'When I saw Balenciaga for the first time it was a discovery. Something so important for my life and my mind. Balenciaga is an extraordinary person. He has a very strong dimension. He is generous and so clever and so human. I worked very, very hard there, but I was happy to work with him. He bears you, carries you shoulder-high . . . he urges you to express yourself . . . contact with him is of a mystical quality.'

BEST-HEEDED SAYING ABOUT BEAUTY
'Beauty is altogether in the eye of the beholder.' – Lew Wallace (1827–1905).

BEST OBSERVATION ABOUT BEAUTY
'There is no excellent beauty that hath not some strangeness in the proportions.' – William Edmonstone Oune Aytoun (1813–65).

BEST INFLUENCE OF THE 1940s *Christian Dior, with his New Look in 1947*
It was all in the air already, women aspiring to be beautiful and feminine again,

men longing to see their companions other than their uniformed equals. There was a general urge for softness, tenderness and beauty. A man as sensitive as Christian Dior felt this urge perhaps more deeply than anyone else: the time was ripe to turn away from the makeshift fashions with their flashy overtones and Christian Dior wished, above all, to present a well-mannered fashion and to render women beautiful once more. The scene was set, waiting for someone to raise the curtain. Christian Dior, shy and reserved, who hated personal publicity, was the one to raise it, when he fathered a revolutionary silhouette christened 'The New Look'. It banished war-time drabness and reinstated Paris as the creative centre of fashion. Hailed by the great majority as a masterpiece, his collection was panned by some, among them Mrs Bessie Braddock with, 'The longer skirt – the ridiculous whim of the people ... people who worry about longer skirts might do something more useful with their time.' And 'This New Look business is just completely silly,' from Mrs Mabel Ridealgh, MP.

BEST OBSERVATION ABOUT STYLE

Style is the dress of thought; a modest dress,
Neat, but not gaudy, will true critics please.
– The Rev. Samuel Wellesley (1662–1735).

BEST HAIR

Girls living in the Italian Alps have the finest heads of hair in the world. It's in such good condition that it is bought by hair experts in research laboratories who use it for testing products such as shampoos and conditioners. The Italian girls' secret is simple. They wash their hair in soft mountain water using ordinary soap. They never colour, bleach or perm it. They wear it very long, possibly plaited and tied in a handkerchief, protecting it from the sun and wind.

BEST ROYAL STYLE-SETTER *Queen Elizabeth the Queen Mother*

With a good old-fashioned Scottish upbringing, she had conservative tastes and a love of daring finery when she became Queen in 1937. Dressed by Norman Hartnell, she wore velvet or furred suits, jewellery, flowers in the morning, a picture hat and a long, full dress for receptions. And a crinoline for evening – full-skirted and décolletée in the Victorian off-the-shoulder manner, and often in her favourite colour, powder blue. Her clothes fitted her personality like a glove and were brilliantly suited to her way of life. On tour they were tremendously admired in France, America and Canada. In 1937 and 1938 every designer had fallen for the fairy-tale glamour of the sentimental crinoline.

BEST FASHION MAGAZINE *Vogue*

'Fashion investments were redefined in *Vogue* in 1974 in a profile of an imaginary woman, the new fashion collector; she spends more money on her clothes than most women, but when they are searching around for something new,

'*Quite right – we met in London;*
I always buy British clothes.'

she is already perfectly dressed. When their clothes are beginning to look wrong, hers are right. So in the end, she probably spends no more than they. An investment is really something that continues to give pleasure long after the novelty is over, and that means beautiful cloth, faultless cutting and making, and great discernment on the part of the designer and buyer. One of *Vogue*'s chief functions today is to provide all that is necessary to give a reader this discerning eye. As one well-dressed woman with very little money told a newspaper the other day: "I always buy *Vogue*, that's my main extravagance."' – from *In Vogue, Six Decades of Fashion*, by Georgina Howell.

BEST FASHION NEWSPAPER *America's Women's Wear Daily*
Published daily by Fairchild Publications Inc. in New York, it has a world-

wide circulation within the fashion trade and anyone involved in fashion, gossip, what the Beautiful People are wearing. Nicknamed 'The Bible of Seventh Avenue', it brings to the immense fashion industry of America and to the fashion industries of just about every other English-speaking country advance news – its forte is keeping a jump ahead of everybody else – of fashion trends, colours, fabrics and accessories in all the leading fashion-producing countries. No-one connected with fashion can afford to be without it.

BEST FASHION ARTIST *Kenneth Paul Block*
He is the star artist of *Women's Wear Daily*, working with tremendous style and formidable talent even under the most pressured circumstances of a daily newspaper, such as covering the Paris couture and ready-to-wear openings. At such time he is called upon to churn out pages of drawings, sometimes of actual garments but often interpretations of the vaguest sketches or information from designers or reporters hot on the scent of a scoop in advance of the actual shows. It is these scoops which keep the paper ahead of the rest. Block also draws the fashion advertisements for the New York store, Lord and Taylor.

BEST FASHION MODEL *Britain's Twiggy* (*Lesley Hornby*)
With her extraordinarily beautiful face, which could look at one moment impish and at the next ethereally angelic, her thin, angular body and long legs, she was the perfect clothes-horse for the Biba era in the late 1960s and early 1970s in London. On her, the fantastic mixture of grown-up glamour and little-girl dolly fashions of that exotic emporium which young people adored looked absolutely right. She had a quick wit, a loud laugh and great charm. From modelling she progressed to tap dancing, singing and acting.

BEST FASHION PHOTOGRAPHER *America's Richard Avedon*
'Fashion has become something that is almost entirely visual – that is, photographic. As fashion becomes pure appearance, it finds its perfect summing up in photographs. What people understand of fashion is now mostly set by photographic images. More and more fashion *is* fashion photography.' – Susan Sontag, author of *On Photography*.
   The final accolade for Avedon: an exhibition entitled 'Avedon: photographs 1947 to 1977' was staged at the Metropolitan Museum of Art in New York in 1978.

BEST TRUISM ABOUT STYLE
'*Le style est l'homme même.*' (Style is the man himself.) – Georges Louis Leclerc de Buffon (1707–85).

BEST-SHAPED NOSE
'*Le nez de Cléopatre, s'il eût été plus court, toute la face de la terre aurait changé.*'

(Had Cleopatra's nose been shorter, the whole history of the world would have been different.) – Blaise.Pascal (1623–62).

Best Beauty Salons *Elizabeth Arden*
They give a top-to-toe beauty service with hairdressing and pedicures and everything between, including slimming treatments. Their standard is universal all over the world, so when in doubt go through the red door.

Best Health Resort *Incosol, Marbella*
Conceived as a luxury health resort incorporating a fully equipped medical clinic, it is also a five-star hotel. The sixth and seventh floors of the ultra-modern building are reserved for guests having medical treatment so that the rest are spared the possibility of encountering a trolley-pushing nurse in the corridors. Those who go purely for the peace and tranquillity, taking in the sporting facilities such as golf, tennis and riding, with perhaps a sauna and massage at the end of the day, can make hogs of themselves in the normal restaurant without being aware of those undergoing diets and stricter regimes.

Enormous salons lead into billiard, ping-pong and card rooms, shops, hairdressing and beauty salons. A large indoor swimming pool connects under a bridge with an outdoor one, both of them heated, so it is possible to swim all the year round. Those on a diet can choose their lunch from a dietetically prepared buffet beside the pool. Incosol bakes its own calorie-free bread, serves low-calorie cocktails and even those allowed only 500 calories a day have quite an exciting time choosing from various fish and meat salads which have been expertly concocted to stretch the precious calorie allowance as far and as tastily as possible. In the clinic are saunas, massage rooms, ozone treatments, underwater massage, water jets, steam cabinets, gymnasiums and so on.

Best Inexpensive Beauty Tip
After scooping out the flesh from an avocado, rub the inside of the skin on your face. The oil does a good softening job on your skin.

Best Beauty Tip *Keep fit*
Eat less and exercise more. Drink plenty of water as this cleanses the system and keeps the skin clear. Tap water is fine if you can stand the taste. If not, drink mineral water which is even better. The good ones are slightly diuretic and the mineral contents contribute to your well-being.

Best Make-Up Advice
Get it from Joan Price's Face Place salons in London. They are unique in that you can try out the best beauty products that are available world-wide before making an investment. At other beauty salons only their own products are avail-

able for you to try. At Joan Price's you can play around with all sorts of different brands and colours, while expert advice is at hand.

BEST SKIN-CARE PRODUCTS *Moisturizers*
Use them regularly and you'll have a better skin for longer.

BEST MAKE-UP
A set of pencils for use on lips, eyes and cheeks plus mascara and lip gloss. These are all you need because you have, of course, a good skin as you've been looking after it, haven't you?

BEST PERFUME
One that gives pleasure both to you and to everybody around you. It's a case of finding what suits your skin-type as pigmentation, acidity and so on play a part.

BEST-IGNORED ADVICE ABOUT PERFUME
'It's good for blondes' or 'Best on brunettes.' Hair colouring has nothing to do with the success of perfume. It is entirely a question of what type of skin you have.

BEST UNDERWEAR INVENTION *The bra*
The garment which was called up towards the end of the First World War to reinforce the camisole was at first named bust-bodice. Soon it was re-named brassière, an odd choice, since in France it is known as *soutiens-gorge*. Brassière is now shortened to bra.

BEST BRA DESIGNER *America's Rudi Gernreich*
In 1965 he invented the No-Bra Bra. Alison Adburgham recounted its London debut in *The Guardian*: 'It shot to success in America and he has now designed a complete range of Next-to-Nothings: the No-Sides-Bra, the No-Back-Bra. A representative of Exquisite Form, the corsetry company manufacturing his designs, explained that while they were cantilevered for comfortable support, "Even a heavily-endowed girl can wear these bras, they will handle a 38-inch bust," and demonstrated the supports, the stresses, the 200 per cent stretch in all directions, doing up and undoing the zip which controlled the plunge of a corselette described as "An Incredibly Lithe Non-In-One".'

BEST OFF-THE-CUFF DESCRIPTION OF A GARMENT
When a visitor from the Third World went into a London store to buy a bra for his wife, he didn't know what to ask for so requested 'knickers for uppers'. (True story.)

Best Fashion Influence Of The 1960s *Mary Quant*

She put the mini-skirt on the map, broke all the fashion rules and epitomized Swinging London and the Youth Revolution. She was backed up by the Beatles, early pop music, the first discotheques and the new permissive way of life. In 1966 she was created an Officer of the Order of the British Empire, elected a Fellow of the Society of Industrial Arts in the following year, and made a Royal Designer for Industry by the Royal Society of Arts in 1969.

Jean Muir, another star in the fashion firmament, voiced the consensus when she said, 'Mary epitomized whatever Swinging London and the Youth Revolution were about. When history is written, that is what she'll stand for. Boy, what an impact she had!'

Best Hairdresser Of The 1960s *Vidal Sassoon*

He introduced a sharp, angular cut in keeping with the short skirts, the Youth Revolution and Swinging London, doing away with tight perms and back-combing. He spread the gospel of good cutting and his empire proliferated. The angular cuts were fine for framing youthful faces, less attractive when the faces were ravaged. From his stable emerged many winners in the hairdressing stakes who later set up their own businesses all over the world.

Best Decade For British Fashion *The 1960s*

For the first time in history, the limelight was wrested from Paris to focus on London as the centre of all that was exciting in fashion. British fashion, spear-headed by Mary Quant and a battalion of young designers who gained courage from her success with off-beat, often outrageous creations, was part of a new lifestyle which was to oust old conventions and bring in a new permissive age with youth at the helm that was envied and emulated by young people in other countries.

Best Comment On Rainwear

> John Had
> Great Big
> Waterproof
> Boots On;
> And A
> Great Big
> Waterproof
> Hat;
> John Had A
> Great Big
> Waterproof
> Mackintosh.
> And That
> (Said John)
> Is That. – A.A. Milne (1882–1956).

BEST SPACE-AGE COUTURIER *André Courrèges*
Trained by Balenciaga, it took him a while, after setting up his own business, to break away from old-style couture and put across his own signature. He managed it in his spring 1964 collection, a jolt into the present and the future, and for several years after that he was the most news-worthy designer in Paris. He used tall, bronzed model girls who jumped about athletically in beautifully-made coats and dressed in starkly sculptured uncluttered shapes. The trousers they wore were immaculate and everything was accessorized with flat white ankle boots and short white gloves. The fabrics were futuristic – vinyl and sheer plastic combined with gabardine – and the result extremely sexy. He regarded bras as ridiculous Victorian relics, but at that time to go bra-less was daring indeed. His clothes were designed to make bras obsolete anyway. Dresses were cut to reveal the natural curve of the breasts at the sides and were bare-backed to show off a tanned torso. Midriffs were bared and so was the curve of the *derrière* below trousers cut to dip low in the back. Fashion writers were jammed thigh to thigh on cubes of vinyl at his openings, passing out regularly as the oxygen ran out in his small, low-ceilinged salon. As someone remarked at one of his jam-packed Press shows: 'All he needs to do now is turn on the gas!'

BEST ATTRIBUTES FOR FASHION WRITERS
Robust health and stamina.

BEST FASHION FOR COMFORT *Trousers*
Beach pyjamas were the first manifestation of trousers or 'slacks' for women. In 1926, film stars and model girls began to be photographed in 'Lounging Pyjamas' and 'Smoking Suits'. These were very similar to beach pyjamas. They had the same very full legs and were made of patterned silk or cotton. Women first began to wear long flannel trousers for tennis in 1927. Since then women have worn trousers for comfort and practicality but they were banned from smart settings such as the Royal Enclosure at Ascot and from expensive restaurants until the edict began to crumble in 1972 when women would take off their trousers in the powder room and go into lunch in their shirts which, being the length of the skirts of the day, were acceptable.

BEST-DEPLORED FASHION
Anything made from the skins of rare animals.

BEST PRODUCER OF ACCESSORIES *Gucci*
Started by Guggio Gucci in Florence in 1905 producing saddles and magnificent leather travel sets custom-made for kings and maharajahs (hence the bit and bridle motifs on many Gucci products), today there are fifteen Gucci shops scattered world-wide and umpteen Gucci departments in top stores. The firm makes status symbol shoes, handbags, luggage, belts and all manner of leather

goods flashing the GG monogram (standing for the initials of the founder) which denotes membership of the good life. As well as leather goods, Gucci sells furs and ready-to-wear for men and women and has added tablecloths, lamps, clocks, jewellery and various other household items to its repertoire.

BEST ACCESSORY *The handbag*

Every woman has one and every man wishes he had one. Before their invention, women used to carry their bits and pieces in their pockets or strung from a chatelaine around their waists.

'In 1887 "A Swelless of the Period" carried dangling from her silver belt a scent bottle, whistle, silver flask and cup, dressing-comb, mirror with locket, elegant purse, small telescope, glove loop, pedometer, chased silver revolver, cartridge case, and an egg-shaped box containing powder and puff.' – from : *A Punch History of Manners and Modes* by Alison Adburgham.

BEST SUIT MAKER *Gabrielle ('Coco') Chanel*

Born about 1886, give or take a year or two (no-one was ever quite sure of her age), she died in 1971. Her eye for proportion – how high above the wrist-bone should the sleeve end, how long a jacket should be in relation to the skirt, and how wide in the same context – were things she knew by instinct. Her sense of colour was impeccable, wonderful blends of colours woven into what the French called 'tweeds', but which were as much like British tweeds as rice pudding is to a soufflé. Pure silks and softest jersey used in combination with the tweeds, all unique to Chanel, added up to a way of dressing which was very feminine and gave out an aura of expensiveness difficult to define. Cecil Beaton called it 'looking expensively poor'. Many tried to copy the suits but no-one quite managed it.

BEST-DRESSED WOMEN

Those who can 'do their own thing' with flair and style. Today there are no fashion dictators. While the Press gives reports and illustrations of what the fashion designers are doing, it is up to each and every woman to make the best of her shape, age, lifestyle and bank balance within the very flexible boundaries of the latest trends. No longer is it chic to follow fashion slavishly. It is much more admired to put the latest looks together in your own individual way, mixing colours, fabrics and accessories.

BEST FASHION FOR THE BEACH

Total nudity if the bodies are young and beautiful. If not, some degree of covering is much more appealing.

BEST SWIMWEAR *French*

They have been making it longer than anyone and have, after all, the best beaches on which to show it off. They have perfected the technique of making bikinis that is about as complicated an engineering feat as a suspension bridge.

Best-Loved Fashion Of The British Popular Press *The bikini*
It first appeared on the beaches of France in the late 1920s and men have ogled and fantasized about it ever since. Editors firmly believe that photographs of girls wearing bikinis (and lately monokinis) sell newspapers.

Best Staying-Power In Hairdressing
Miss Iris M. Rennell, of St Helier, Jersey, dressed women's hair non-stop for seventy-seven hours at her Aphrodite salon in 1970.

Best Substitute For Bath Oil
Baby oil added to the bath water. And it's cheaper.

Best Definition Of Luxury
The thing that is in shortest supply.

Best Lingerie *British*
About six star designers, each specializing in some way or another – one has made pure silk her signature, another broderie anglaise, and so on – are world-beaters when it comes to the creation of beautiful lingerie.

They score too in being able to manufacture their flattering, seductive and feminine ideas where designers in other countries, who are able to mass manufacture good lingerie, fall short when it comes to design.

Best Fashion For Seduction *The Seventh Veil*
A single flimsy layer of sheer fabric is much sexier than total nudity.

Best Jeweller *Cartier*
The House of Cartier has been lighting the courts and salons of the world with jewels of a legendary magnificence since 1840. While the precious stones in their fabled settings cost many thousands of pounds, there are more accessible pieces in Cartier today such as gold cuff links, gold swizzlesticks and gold collar stiffeners, and the doorman treats you as graciously if you turn up on foot as if you arrive in a Rolls.

Best Skiwear *Killy Clothing*
Designed by former ski champion Jean-Claude Killy, the styling is superb and the garments beautifully made. It is obvious that they are designed by a skier as they are functional as well as looking dynamic.

BEST USA READY-TO-WEAR

Headed by Calvin Klein, Ralph Lauren and Perry Ellis, a new wave of world-beating sportswear and daywear gathers pace at the start of the 1980s. It epitomizes the relaxed, slouchy chic currently so fashionable, never restricting, but revealing the body in subtly sexy yet sporty ways. These designers, and several more on the same wavelength, complement the high fashion ready-to-wear of household names such as Geoffrey Beene, Galanos, Halston and others, whose throw-away *luxe* and blatant opulence adorn the Beautiful People at benefit balls and aboard gold-plated yachts.

BEST USA FASHION VALUE FOR MONEY

For sheer size and scope, mail order businesses in the United States leave the rest of the world standing. Fashion figures prominently in the giant chunks of glossy, tempting literature which drop daily through millions of mail boxes from Colorado to the Caribbean, and it's not only the play-safe-suit-everyone classics that are featured. The latest, most tuned-in lines are available as well, often reaching the customer – via a speedy delivery service – before they hit the racks of her nearest fashion store. The saving of transport costs, time, energy and frequently of money as well (for the fashion items can cost less this way than in a retail store), makes this a most economical method of shopping. An added plus, not always found in other parts of the world, is the guarantee by most US mail order firms of a full refund for any reason at all.

YOUNG WORLD

◆

Benny Green

BEST SCHOOLS

Today the 'best' schools, in the sense of the most exclusive and most expensive, remain, as always, the English public schools, so called because they are intensely private. As a group they are symbolized by Eton and Harrow, which retain their high reputation in spite of the fact that so many prominent British Cabinet Ministers attended them. On a more mundane level, the English Grammar Schools maintained an elevated standard until their dismantling as part of a grand design to improve British education to the point where nobody could read or write; there is also the long tradition of academic efficiency of the Scottish educational system to consider. But taking the more worldly view, that is, the view of a child obliged to attend school on pain of legal punishments, the best schools today remain what they always were – the ones where acts of truancy are a practical possibility. In a sense there are no good schools, only good teachers and good pupils, which means that the prize for this section depends on the accident of staffing, vocation and other nebulosities.

BEST UNIVERSITIES

Although there are universities all over the world which dispute the seniority of Oxford and Cambridge, it remains doubtful if any of them may justifiably claim to be more comfortable than either of those two venerable conspiracies. Among those usurpers with the strongest claims are Columbia University, New York, whose proud boast it is to have supplied the toothless lion for the MGM trade-mark; also Trinity College, Dublin, which expelled Oliver Goldsmith for having had the effrontery to show he was sexually normal; also West Point Military Academy, which established its reputation once and for all as a perceptive judge of talent by deciding that James McNeill Whistler did not have enough brains to be a general. Of the two great English universities, it is Oxford which takes the palm, for its nurturing of the Reverend Spooner ('You have hissed my mystery lectures'). The only other university which remotely approaches this sort of eminence is Edinburgh, which in 1879 bestowed a doctorate on W.G. Grace.

BEST TOYS

As every child knows, the best toys are those which belong to other children, but it should be recorded that so far as durability is concerned, Tonka Toys achieve the remarkable feat of living up to their publicity. Advertising campaigns showing lorries unable to dent a Tonka toy are perfectly genuine, a fact which causes considerable anguish to parents who nurture a secret desire to smash the toy in question into small pieces. It should also be said that Tonka models of trucks and tractors are remarkably accurate facsimiles of the real thing, which is of course the most serious argument against them. Using the criteria of imaginative design and the use of pleasing materials, Galt Toys in wood show the most ingenuity, their train tracks and small dolls deserving special mention.

BEST BOARD GAMES

Most modern board games are mere variations on the ancient institutions of Lotto and Chinese Chequers, but Monopoly has succeeded in becoming an institution by retaining its popularity into a second generation, even though the property values deployed in the game have been rendered quaint by the inexorable processes of inflation. This quaintness, which lends an air of nostalgia to the game which its inventors could scarcely have envisaged, surely endows Monopoly with its renewed popularity, whereas its old stablemate, Totopoly, which is nothing more than Monopoly with horses, has suffered a comparative eclipse. Of rival games, Cluedo may be said to be the most maddeningly inscrutable, and Campaign the one whose book of rules is the most intellectually demanding. Of genuinely modern games, the best is Simon, a computer which plays a succession of musical sounds whose sequence the player has to memorize and repeat. Pop stars are advised to keep well away from Simon, for reasons which ought to be obvious.

BEST MUSEUMS IN USA

National Air and Space Museum, Smithsonian Institution, Washington: among the sensational attractions to be found here are a piece of Moon rock, every flying machine from biplane to rocket, also a simulation of First World War battle conditions, from sandbags to shell-fire; in fact nothing else at the Smithsonian can match the Air and Space Section with the possible exception of Irving Berlin's piano, which, as it changes key by means of a handle, is far more technologically ingenious than any mere flying machine. In the Guggenheim Museum the seeker after inspiration will find all the holy cows of modernism, from Moore to Miro, Ernst to Cézanne and back again, which takes just under an hour, unless you miss your connection. The *Children's Museum, Staten Island,* will educate the tots in the function of the human body, especially that model of the intestines stretched out to its full length of 25 feet. There are also ways provided of making you change colour and changing your perspective from midget to giant, also a brilliant exposition of the nature of light. There are also facilities for putting your head in a tunnel. Everyone to his own thing. Despite its world fame as a centre of art scholarship, the Metropolitan Museum of Art really is a centre of art scholarship. It comprises 40 sections, ranging from Islamic Art to Arms and Armour, and from The Temple of Dendur to Closed to the Public. Facilities for wheelchairs and photographers. Anyone may sketch, and there are frequent recorded tours of exhibits.

BEST HISTORICAL MONUMENT
The Tower of London, because a stroll within its precincts successfully conveys the dimensions of a certain period of history. The presence of attendants wearing Beefeater uniforms, and also of the ravens whose symbolic importance to the survival of the Tower is legendary, add to the illusion that life is one long comic opera by Gilbert and Sullivan. There are also executioners' axes, some chopping blocks and a few dungeons to convince the modern child that things fortunately are not what they used to be.

BEST PUPPETS
The Muppets, which are so ingeniously conceived that they are even able to surmount the handicap of being hamstrung by the intrusion of dreadful real-life performers even more inanimate than the puppets. The Muppets have attained their eminence by reversing showbiz trends and reviving the forgotten glories of Vaudeville, an institution which revels in the deliberately bad joke and in the semi-comic traumas of back-stage confusion. Kermit, the amphibian Master of Ceremonies, is one of the very few anthropomorphic characters to come remotely near the eminence of Mickey Mouse, which raises the issue of...

BEST CARTOON CHARACTER
Celebrations for Mickey Mouse's fiftieth birthday, added to the sticker revolution, have done much to restore the Mouse to his former eminence in the Disney stable, but Goofy remains the most comical of the Disney menagerie. Of usurpers, Tom and Jerry have TV to thank for their sustained popularity,

'Gerald, think of the children.'

especially among imbecilic sociologists who make periodic pronouncements that so much violence makes maniacs of us all. Of contemporaries of Tom and Jerry, Bugs Bunny has some claim to seniority, but the years have not been kind to his dated carroty epigrams. By far the most unexpected cartoon film triumph has been that of the Pink Panther, because this success has been achieved by virtue of a return to the conventions of the Silent Screen, where the plot was embellished by music instead of dialogue. The surreal events of the Pink Panther's life are doubly meritorious because of the musical accompaniment, one of the very few examples of genuine as distinct from bogus musical skills triumphing in the moronic 1970s.

BEST WAXWORKS

Most waxwork models in most waxwork exhibitions have both the texture and the outward appearance of a hundredweight of chopped liver an hour after the end of a bar mitzvah celebration, but there are intermittent periods when the Madame Tussaud's Exhibition attains heights not normally looked for in waxworks. These periods occur when special set-piece exhibitions are mounted which utilize sight and sound as well as dummies. The most memorable example of this, and probably the finest waxwork achievement in history, was the Madame Tussaud's reconstruction of the Battle of Trafalgar, which conveyed the horror as well as the picturesque elements of the battle.

Best Comedian
The rash of ancient movies on TV has transformed this section from a topical to an all-time category, which means that if the best comedian is the one who makes children laugh the most, then Charlie Chaplin wins by several horse-laughs. Some of the very early Chaplin one-and-two reelers seem unfunny today, their arthritic movement an impediment to laughter. Even so, Chaplin wears infinitely better than any other screen comics with the honourable exception of Laurel and Hardy, who undoubtedly benefit in the posterity stakes from the improved technology of movie-making in the 1930s. The partnership's acts of manic self-destruction and their heroic dedication to the proposition that there is very little the modern male can do for himself, certainly qualify them for inclusion in the pantheon of timeless comedy; it would seem that among their more Olympian achievements are the delivery of the grand piano up a flight of precipitous steps, the giant ice-cube which melts away before reaching its destination, and the transmutation of Laurel into a monkey after swallowing the pill which encourages a reversion to earlier evolutionary forms.

Best Amusement Park
At the risk of seeming unimaginative, the choice must be in favour of Florida's Walt Disney World, which has eclipsed even its family rival Disneyland in California, both in physical scope and artistic imagination. The World site, covering over 2,500 acres, is an impressive example of what mankind can achieve when really determined not to grow up; but in so lavishly praising the technological refinements which have made Walt Disney World a viable proposition, it should not be forgotten that much of what is to be found in this World is more of a reconstruction job than a genuinely creative one. The centrepiece of the World, Cinderella's Castle, owes little in origin to the Disney Studios, and ironically some of the most successful attempts in Florida to render what was once thought to be irrevocably two-dimensional into something three-dimensional concern educational rather than purely entertainment artefacts, especially Liberty Square, a remarkably successful attempt to convey the hushed aura of an American colonial town.

Best Children's Books
In this, the most contentious area of all, there has been very little movement in the last thirty years, the world continuing to be divided into the enlightened who rate Lewis Carroll's *Alice* books highest of all, and the clodhoppers who reject them as old-fashioned failures. The *Alice* books retain their popularity, in spite of a succession of dreadful attempts to transpose them on to either the large or the small screen, and now rate among the very few genuinely Vic-

torian publications which appeal to the young reader. E. Nesbit's best books, especially *The Treasure Seekers* and *Five Children and It* continue to enjoy vast new audiences through the agency of paperback editions, and her *The Railway Children* was the beneficiary a few years back of a movie version which kept faith with the original spirit of the story. Among contemporaries of Nesbit, Kenneth Grahame continues to tower over all rivals, and *The Wind in the Willows* retains its claim as the best children's book of the twentieth century.

Another stayer has been the Winnie the Pooh saga, although how much this is due to genuine juvenile rapture and how much to relentless and at time dubious marketing tactics is difficult to say. Because in recent years children's literature has achieved the accolade of being recognized as a separate entity, standards have tended to be very high, ranging from the wordless idylls of Paddy Pork for children who can't read but can follow a story, to the sophisticated legends of Leon Garfield which are pushing into areas of advanced adolescence bordering on full adult readership status. In a field so rich in virtues, it is probably gratuitous to nominate specific books, but Eve Garnett's *Family at One-End Street*, George Selden's *The Cricket in Times Square*, and Hugh Lofting's *Dr Dolittle* books, whose vocabulary and psychology are pleasurably ambitious, demand mention. Among neglected and underrated children's books, there is the case of Lawrance Smith's *The Deeds of Doyly McPurr*, an anthropomorphic romance of infectious humour and unusual originality.

The most dramatic development among children's books in recent years has not been the writing of new ones but the annexing of old ones. Many popular classics which were once considered to be loosely adult in appeal are now found on the children's library shelves. These include the Jane Austen novels, Anthony Hope's *The Prisoner of Zenda*, several of Dumas' and Dickens' novels and even one or two by George Eliot. In the light of this development, it obviously becomes impossible to decide exactly what a child's book is, let alone which is the best.